Screen Time in the Mean Time

A Parenting Guide to Get Kids and Teens Internet Safe

DR. TRACY BENNETT

For Dad who taught me unconditional love

For Mom who taught me courage and tenacity

For Carly, Jillian, and Kylan,

who taught me everything that truly matters

TABLE OF CONTENTS

INTRODUCTION

In modern times, child screen use has had a greater impact on the American family than anything since the abolition of child labor in 1938. Parenting has become a full-time preoccupation. Kids don't labor for parents, parents labor for kids. Because of what we perceive as society's high expectations of parents, raising healthy, happy kids has become overwhelming. We are expected to faithfully care for and entertain our children most of our waking hours without complaint. Although parents are waiting later to have kids and having fewer kids per family, with both parents working and the disappearance of extended family help, we have fewer supportive resources than ever before.

Even with little support, we have been accused of "helicopter parenting" to keep our kids safe and successful. We too often expect our kids to earn 4.0 GPAs, awards in robotics, and trophies in sports. Cs aren't "average" anymore, now they're a mark of parents not helping enough with homework. Our fear that we aren't doing enough trickles down to our kids in the form of encouraging lectures and, too often, scathing shame and disappointment. We know this is too much pressure. So in between the "enriching" activities we work so hard to provide, we allow them leisure time…more leisure time than any children in history.

Parents are no longer willing to order their kids to go play outside until the streetlights come on. It's too scary knowing what we do about child predators, bullying, sex, and drugs. To keep kids safe, we shelter them inside our houses to save them from the world's perils. Instead of running amok like we did with hordes of neighborhood kids creating spontaneous, street-smart missions, they watch screens. And while they're on their screens, we're also on ours. Screen time gives us much needed breaks and provides what we hope is enriching content and a primer in digital literacy. But the troubling behaviors our kids demonstrate while compulsively viewing videos, social media, and video games eerily resemble signs of addiction. And we are the dealers, providing screens too often while they're too young. We are hooked too. We feel guilty, but it's often the best we can do. Screen technology has transformed childhood and parenting.

As a clinical psychologist who has worked with families for more than twenty-five years, I believe the state of families is not actually as dire as this scenario suggests. With the education that information technology affords us, modern-day parents are generally informed, empathetic, and strategic. As a result, kids are as capable and emotionally sophisticated as ever before. But inappropriate screen content and too much screen time is rapidly becoming an epidemic problem. Families need more support to achieve optimum balance, without the shame and the blame.

Screen Time in the Mean Time offers that support. Because we can all use a go-to quick parenting guide at our fingertips, I've begun Chapters One through Four with what-to-dos to keep our kids screen safe, followed by the developmental reasons why the particular strategies fit. For the reader who prefers to skim past deeper explanations and brain facts, they may find the sections with what-to-do parenting strategies to be just right. While other readers who want to know why these strategies work will appreciate the more technical developmental applications. Chapters Five through Eight cover the complex and often surprising risks and benefits of screen use. Parents appreciate learning about the interesting facets of screen use and are often eager to share the knowledge with friends and family. We all want to be our children's go-to person when they are hurting or in trouble. With the relationship-building strategies in Chapter Nine, you can learn to form a stronger, more positive connection and get important conversations started. Chapter Ten offers the innovative, effective parenting strategies I teach in my practice every day. As our kids get more mature and educated by the Internet, we must be increasingly informed and innovative in our parenting. Finally, Chapter Eleven pulls it all together and offers answers to real life parent questions. *Screen Time in the Mean Time* will equip you with the tools you need to get your kids screen safe while rebooting your powerful parent-child connection. It's time to let go of the guilt.

CHAPTER 1: SCREENS HELP BABYSIT: AGES NEWBORN TO TWO

Becky is a 32-year-old married mother of three who came to my office because she feels depressed, overwhelmed, and unmotivated. She's been married for nine years and considers her marriage to her husband John to be "OK but not great." She complains that after work and kids all day, neither of them have the energy to do much but binge watch Netflix. She and John haven't had sex in several weeks, and she can't remember the last time it was truly satisfying. She admits to having a lot of resentment, because she feels John escapes family responsibility by playing video games and secretly watching online pornography. John is resentful that Becky has gained weight and doesn't exercise. They've even quit making plans with friends, because they're too busy with kids' homework, soccer, and dance responsibilities. Becky worries that the highlight of their day is evening cocktail hour, when John drifts off to play video games and she goes on Facebook.

Overall, Becky feels overtasked with the responsibilities of her three kids, ages fifteen months, four years, and eight years. She complains that her kids fight too much, and she too often caves and give them screens to get some peace. She feels guilty and ashamed about the screen time and is dismayed to say that even the baby sometimes prefers screen time over mommy-daughter playtime. The baby isn't walking yet, and Becky worries that her speech is delayed. She reached out to her church group for help, but ultimately felt like more of a failure when a few in the group insisted she wasn't being strict enough. This experience made her feel even more like a social outcast and a failure as a mom, driving her back onto Facebook for reassurance. She worries that every member of the family is a slave to their screens and the loss of connection makes her feel sad, anxious, and ashamed.

How Much Are We Using Screens?

We have all witnessed America's transformation from books and bicycles to screen-driven learning in the last twenty years. Anxiety and mood disorders among kids and teens have skyrocketed, and I believe overall child resilience has also declined. In response, I've altered my approach to psychotherapy and developed innovative parenting strategies to address screen issues. Parents "winging it" with screen use is too risky. Although kids insist they are experts in the digital realm, and parents are too often willing to look the other way, access to an unfiltered, unmonitored Internet portal without a fun, informed, and nurturing parent-child alliance will have real consequence sooner or later even in the healthiest of families.

Let's face it, almost all-American children from every socioeconomic group use mobile devices, most often starting before they can even walk. Parents spend an average of more than nine hours a day on screens, and kids spend more than ten and a half hours a day, more time than kids spend with parents or in school.[1] Parents rely on screens to keep kids busy so they can get things done. A 2015 survey showed that parents give children screens when they are doing house chores (70%), at bedtime (29%), and to keep them calm (65%).[2] By the age of three, most children are using the screens independently and one-third engage in media multitasking.[3] Furthermore, more and more schools are adopting technology-savvy curriculums and providing hand-held tablets to offer all children equal access to advanced learning tools. There's no going back now, screen media has transformed childhood; it's here to stay.

With Google's advent as recent as 1998, parents are digital immigrants rather than digital natives.[4] It is no surprise that digital age parents feel overwhelmed and under-supported. Most of us agree that the cyber world is a Wild West show, under-regulated and rapidly changing. In a 2016 survey by Northwestern University, 50% of parents of tweens and teens reported they were concerned that the use of social media hurt their kids' physical activity, 56% worried their kids may become screen addicted, 43% worried their kids spent too much time online, and 34% thought screens negatively impacted face-to-face communication. However, an overwhelming 94% also reported that they believe technology positively supports education, increases kids' exposure to other cultures (77%), allows opportunity for the expression of personal opinions and beliefs (75%), supports creativity (79%), and allows their children to find and interact with others who have similar interests (69%). Forty-four percent even believe that social media helps their children's relationships with friends.[5]

Fortunately, with all the information about screen risk that has been covered in popular media, parents are starting to ask for help and seek solutions. In a 2017 survey, parents ranked Internet safety as their fifth biggest child health concern (with bullying/cyberbullying number one and not enough exercise number two).[6] The problem is that researchers and educators are scrambling to keep up with change just as parents are. Psychologists are discovering through research evidence and clinical observation that screen use is, in fact, changing the structure and functioning of the brain. By spending a lot of time outsourcing abilities like memory, speed, calculation, entertainment, and communication, we are increasingly becoming cyborgs. Not only are these changes rapidly affecting *how* we manage our virtual lives, but they are transforming our nonvirtual lives as well.

Should Babies Be Allowed Screen Time?

Despite recent recommendations from the American Academy of Pediatrics (AAP) to discourage media use for children younger than two years old, little ones are spending on average one hour a day in front of screens, with daily use consistently increasing.[7][8] Forty percent of infants are watching television as young as three months old, with 90% watching by twenty-four months.[9] Marketers are clearly aware that overtasked parents of infants and toddlers want entertaining and educational media for their toddlers and are hungry for a break. Apps in the toddler and preschool category account for 72% of the top paid apps.[10] Research about interactive screen media is new and remains controversial. Parents of young kids want to know if screen use causes risk to young kids. Is the effect neutral or is there benefit?

One weekend on a recent getaway with my husband, we saw a group of young mothers enjoying an afternoon glass of wine while their toddlers sat strapped into strollers gazing at tablets. What initially struck me was how these women could afford the sleepy effects of day drinking with babies so young. My toddlers drained every ounce of energy I had by the afternoon. As much as I would have loved it, day drinking would have rendered me useless for mothering. Upon reflection, I perhaps should have been more concerned with the fact that the strapped-in babies were passively staring at screens instead of crawling on the grass between delighted mommies.

Don't get me wrong, I'm not judging. If a tablet or smartphone had been available during that stage of my parenting, I am certain I would have occasionally escaped with it too. But I would have felt guilty and craved guidelines about *how much* was okay and *why*. Credible authorities like the AAP recommend no to little screen time for infants and toddlers, but the why is a harder question to answer with interactive screen research still in its infancy.

As a university lecturer, I'm compelled to recommend, "No screen time AT ALL until at least age two." Two-dimensional screen time in the place of frequent synchronized communication between parent and child may lead to delays in cognitive, motor, language, and social-emotional development.[11] Furthermore, the educational merit of programs targeted to infants and toddlers remain unproven.[12]

As a mother, I'm compelled to say, "Pffft. Technology is not the enemy. YOU try to keep a little one stimulated every second of the day and tell me a break here and there isn't warranted." Perhaps the occasional ten-minute session for wee ones when mom and dad are desperate to eat more than three consecutive bites at a restaurant isn't a big deal. Lighten up and incorporate limited screen time when necessary to an already enriching day."

Finally, as a psychologist I suggest moderation, because too much screen time negatively affects development. New research presented at the 2017 Pediatric Academic Societies Meeting found that, based on a 2011–2015 study of 894 subjects aged six months to two years, screen use may pose significant risk of speech delay. At the eighteen-month checkup, 20% of the children in the study had daily average handheld device use of twenty-eight minutes. For each thirty-minute increase in screen use, researchers found a 49% increased risk of expressive speech delay.[13] Although more studies must be conducted to further support this finding, this provides alarming evidence of risk. In October 2016, the American Academy of Pediatrics announced the new recommendation that children under eighteen months old should have minimal screen use other than video chatting. For children eighteen months to twenty-four months, they should only be allowed high quality, age-appropriate programming like Sesame Street.[14] What should parents look out for?

Replacement Cost

Too much screen activity replaces nurturing caregiver-child play and may lead to developmental delay. Consider for a moment the profound impact screen viewing can have on the explosively developing infant brain knowing that too little balanced enrichment affects synaptic growth. Different activities lead to different types of cognitive engagement.[15] Furthermore, child psychologists have conclusively demonstrated that multi-modal learning (visual, auditory, and kinesthetic) is best for rich and meaningful stimulation across multiple brain regions. For example, pretend play requires intonation, facial expression, gesture, and language, which provide the core developmental functions necessary for social skill development. Hours of eye gazing, emotional synchronizing, and verbal and nonverbal encouragement is an intricate dance that builds mutual attachment and teaches the child about the responsiveness and safety of the world. Face-to-face and skin-to-skin contact is necessary for the development of emotional soothing and regulation. Even interactive screen time, like video chatting, is a cheap substitute to snuggles and face-to-face play.

Not only must babies and toddlers stay off screen devices to have learning opportunities, but so must overtasked parents. A lack of responsiveness by caregivers to an attention-bidding baby may cause confusion, distress, and potentially lead to *learned helplessness*, which is the loss of motivation due to too many failure trials. It leads one to wonder if too much passive screen viewing may lead to attachment problems like those proven with nonreactive, depressed mothers. A child must be reinforced for interactive behaviors, not ignored because the audience is a distracted parent or an actor on a screen. We certainly don't want an infant to stop trying to elicit interaction because of too many failed attempts at securing caregiver response.

Overstimulation Risk

Not only is screen time an issue for parents to consider, so is screen content. Entertainment content with violence or quickly changing and flashing images and audio content may be over stimulating to the immature neurological framework of young children. Chronic, overstimulating cognitive load can be dysregulating and lead to unwanted brain, body, and behavioral changes like developmental delay, impaired attention and executive function, hyperactivity, distress and tantrums, disinterest in learning, eye and neck strain, and decreased ability.[161718]

Moreover, it has been hypothesized that prolonged exposure to rapid image changes during critical periods of brain development may precondition the mind to expect high levels of stimulation.[19] This preconditioning may cause children to become more quickly disinterested in other types of learning activities, ultimately interfering with skill mastery.

Personality change as the result of too much cognitive load due to frenetic screen activity viewing may also be a concern. In a study by Christakis and colleagues (2004), laboratory mice that were exposed to light flashes and sounds similar to child television programming for six hours per day for forty-two days were later found to be more hyperactive and engage in excessive risk-taking when compared to mice that did not have light and sound exposure.[20] Further, in a 2007 study involving newborn to three-year-old children, it was found that viewing violent or non-violent entertainment television was significantly associated with attention problems, whereas viewing educational television was not.[21] The type of chosen screen content matters.

Engagement Potential

Young children do not process and respond to screen content as adults do. However, under certain conditions they can engage with and learn from videos, particularly if instructed by characters or actors they relate to. Furthermore, passive is not the same as interactive viewing. Touch-screen and virtual reality technologies provide more child-led, creative engagement. Just as children attach to people in their nonvirtual life, they also attach to characters from a screen. Relationships that children form with television or video characters have been called *parasocial relationships*. It has been demonstrated that children as young as two years old already recognize branded characters and associate them with products.[22] Furthermore, factors such as trusting and identifying with the character, feeling safe with and attached to the character, and thinking the character is real are factors that optimize engagement and learning potential.[23]

Not only do kids attach to screen characters, they can also learn from them. For example, in a "seek and find" study by Lauricella and colleagues (2010), it was demonstrated that children aged thirty to thirty-six months learned better when viewing puppets hiding in a video scene that allowed keyboard engagement (pushing the spacebar to make the puppets appear) or when viewing a live scene versus passively viewing a video.[24] Also, in earlier Georgetown studies it was demonstrated that twenty-four month olds struggled to learn from seek and find videos unless they had an on-screen character to guide the task. In other words, kids learn best from live rather than video demonstrations (commonly called the *video deficit*), and character and interactive engagement results in better learning. Because children form emotional attachment to screen characters, it is worthwhile for parents to take extra care assessing the appropriate influence of video and television content for toddlers.

Finally, there are many factors and screen options that turn little minds "on" to learning rather than "off." For example, the interactive capacities of the electronic tablet offer sophisticated features that increase engagement and customize progressive content. The satisfying "I did it" feeling toddlers earn from tablet use impacts dopamine in the reward pathway of the brain, triggering desire to play. However, too much reward may lead to the problematic compulsive use patterns seen in older children and adults.[25] Another issue of debate is if screen learning is a benefit or distraction from other types of learning. For example, young children may be more distracted away from the storyline by the wow factor of e-book screen features rather than benefited.[26]

Open-ended formats that allow the child to explore and feel a sense of control at their own pace are likely better for skill development than passive screen viewing or predetermined story formats. We must be watchful that kids are engaging with screen materials in a way that demonstrates true engagement rather than mindless distraction. Playing games with your kids and discussing what they've learned is an excellent way to ensure they get educational benefit with a payoff that transfers into their nonvirtual life. Research must continue as more immersive, augmented reality features are being developed.

GetKidsInternetSafe Screen Guidelines for Ages Newborn to Two

No screen time before one year of age.

From one to two years old, limit screen exposure to brief intervals with the most age-appropriate, calm, and interactive content. No more than three episodes of thirty minutes a day of screen use for toddlers.

Nothing replaces the benefits of sensible parenting. Our brains do not work like computers. Our memories aren't sequences of X's and O's, and our hardware is not replaceable. We are born with brains that are primed to learn. We are specially wired to make social connections. When we learn, multiple areas of our brains activate, making each brain and each experience unique only to us. Parents are best equipped to evaluate and respond to a young child's fluctuating attention and nuanced motivational states with soothing joy and warmth. By providing a variety of learning activities throughout the day rather than relying on the screen to babysit, you are optimizing healthy brain development. Just because the baby reaches for it, does not mean it is in her best interest to have it.

To keep a baby's brain engaged, they need dynamic, enriching, balanced interaction. To develop motor coordination, they need lots of opportunity for movement and interaction with three-dimensional objects. For socioemotional development, they need caregivers who look in their eyes and narrate the constant happenings of the world for progressive bi-directional adaptation of language and gesture. Engaged caregivers gently lead children to an increasingly complex understanding of temporal and causal aspects of a situation, including self-reflection and *metacognition* (thinking about thinking). When children's requests for interaction is consistently met, they learns to trust the world enough to keep asking questions and practicing new and challenging skills. Caregivers must be eager to reward attempts at learning rather than punish them with neglect. Child learning is primarily a social experience, not an academic one.[27] Simply put, screens do not provide the responsive enrichment that a loving caregiver does.

Parents must be available to respond to attention-bidding babies. If you are feeling guilty about attending too much to your screens instead of your child, trust your gut and adjust. Infancy flies by and critical learning windows close. You will miss it when it's gone, and your child may too in the form of developmental delay.

A crash course about child brain development and critical learning windows will help you best apply common sense to determine when screen use may enhance development or be detrimental in terms of content choice, level of stimulation, and time engaged in use.

Developmental Psychology Crash Course:
Children Ages Newborn to Two

Brain imaging and recording technology have improved dramatically within the last decade, offering newly sophisticated, detailed evidence of brain changes throughout the developmental process. However, there are limitations to the type of experiments researchers can conduct due to the complexities of sedating children. Scientists used to believe that we are born with all of the brain cells, called *neurons*, we would ever have. Now we know that, in the right circumstances, new neurons can grow in a process called *postnatal neurogenesis*.

Throughout development, the brain undergoes a constant *remodeling process*, simultaneously undergoing dramatic progressive change (neuronal growth), regressive change (neuronal elimination, also called *pruning*), and repair. Over time, our brains become increasingly constrained and compartmentalized in function. This gradual pruning and tuning results in highly specialized and effective brain pathways as we age.[28]

For simplicity's sake, let's consider the mind a collection of mental modules, or specific mental faculties, tuned to specific types of environmental input. To grow optimally, each module must be consistently stimulated to progressively develop. Therefore, *nature* (the child's inherited brain hardware) develops in relation to *nurture* (experience of the environment).

To make things more complicated, our hardware affects what kinds of stimulation we seek out, and our environmental enrichment affects how our brains develop. Developmental psychologists call this *nature via nurture* and stress that enrichment during critical learning windows is essential for optimal brain development. The better the match between children's capacities and the demands placed on them, the better the learning. However, if the mismatch is too big, stress and dysfunction may result.

If loving parents expertly ratchet up difficulty level at a customized rate that best fits their child, the outcome is excellent learning. If one does not experience intellectual enrichment during the window when the brain is receptive to that specific influence, it can result in developmental delay. Here are simple, easy-to-understand brain development facts to illustrate how important it is to provide enrichment throughout the lifespan, including lots of parent-child interaction with screen play and in real life (IRL).

Brain Development

Within the first few years of life, an infant's brain triples in size, with new neural pathways growing at a rate of 7,000 to 10,000 new connections. The explosion of brain growth during infancy is bigger than ever seen again during the lifespan. It's not the brain cells that grow in an infant brain. We are born with our lifetime supply of neurons. It's the spaces between neurons, called *synapses*, which grow in number because of stimulation. We are born with about 2,500 synapses; by age three we have 15,000!

Along with the increased number and variety of synapses that grow during infancy, myelination also occurs at a rapid pace.[29] *Myelination* is the process of sheathing axons (brain cells) with white matter to insulate them and allow them to conduct the electrical impulses that create "thinking." A nutrient-rich diet, lots of room to roll, crawl, and walk, and restorative sleep are also critically important for healthy structural brain development.

In regard to the sequence of brain structure maturation, remodeling appears to go from older to newer brain structures. We call that "from the bottom up." Deeper structures like the brain stem, which controls functions necessary for life like breathing and heart rate, build first while the cerebral cortex, involved in higher-order thinking, fine tunes later. As higher brain structures develop, we see newborn (*neonatal*) reflexes disappear, while others develop into more complex strings of behavior.[30]

In the first two weeks of life, babies develop healthy respiration, circulation from the umbilical cord to the lungs, body temperature regulation, and feeding and elimination processes. From three weeks to twelve months, babies acquire social smiling and emotional regulation, as well as motor skills like visual scanning, manipulation like reaching and grasping (hand skills), self-feeding with solid food, and locomotion (crawling and walking). They are also beginning to establish a sleep pattern and maintain a sleep–wake cycle, and explore sound production in preparation for speech.

Cognitive and Motor Development

Play can be unstructured, structured, passive, or interactive. During the sensorimotor stage of development (birth to two years old), children must physically manipulate objects in a complex environment while simultaneously receiving instruction and stimulation from loving caregivers for healthy cognitive and motor development. With the child's biological blueprint for learning already in place, environmental enrichment allows the baby to transition from reflexive to purposeful goal-directed behavior. Parents show the baby *how* and *what* to think, slowly building the complexity of teaching with a delighted dance between baby and parent. It's not just parents interacting with babies that prompt response; babies also elicits response from parents by acting adorably while verbally and nonverbally communicating. With *bidirectional interaction*, influence goes both ways.

Research demonstrates that children learn better in collaboration with others rather than alone. For example, children are more likely to engage in symbolic play if playing with somebody else rather than alone. The more sophisticated the child's tutor in advancing the complexity of the play, the quicker the child's skills advance. Working with another person increases the child's motivation to learn, requires the child to articulate ideas, allows the child to build upon another's increasingly complex cognitive strategies, and teaches the child how to understand the beliefs and feelings of others (building empathy). There is significant discussion in the psychological community about whether excessive screen use is impairing children's abilities to learn and practice empathy, an essential skill for communication and relationship building.

To develop gross motor skills, babies and toddlers need free-play opportunities to roll, scoot, crawl, walk, and run. They also must manipulate and orally explore three-dimensional objects, like throwing balls and feeding themselves, to develop fine motor skills with good coordination and physical dexterity.

Language Development

For young children to develop all aspects of language, they must have frequent conversational engagement with caregivers. Newborns show preference for mom's voice over any others. Research shows that parents tend to create a supportive learning environment, starting with *parentese* (also called *child-directed speech*), which is initially short, simple, high-pitched, and repetitive sentences that gets baby's attention and affects his mood and behavior. The parent then gradually speaks with longer and more complex sentences that are grammatically correct and introduced just ahead of the child's increasing abilities. Children of parents who frequently expand, recast, and otherwise extend their children's speech acquire complex speech more quickly.

During the first year, a baby's burgeoning familiarity with the phonological (sound) aspects of language is laying the foundation for language development. At two to three months, infants can distinguish consonant sounds. By seven months, they have learned the first rule of social language (*pragmatics*) to not interrupt and wait for their turn to talk. By eight to ten months, babies use gestures and facial expressions to communicate and eventually pair with words and then sentences. Babies are active rather than passive learners and, therefore, thrive with bidirectional, responsive, interactive stimulation.

Social-Emotional Development

The strategies parents employ during interaction with their baby has a profound impact on the baby's emotional development and self-regulation. The better the "fit" between parent and child, the more secure the *attachment* and the better the child learns to regulate emotion. Babies develop various emotions in their first two years of life, all of which are highly influenced by how parents react. Young children gradually shift from relying on caregivers for emotional regulation to self-regulation.

Before six months old, babies stimulate attachment with eye contact, cooing, crying, smiling, clutching, and touching. By six months old, infants have learned some self- and other-regulation by turning away or seeking objects to suck. Infant boys are more likely to elicit soothing from caregivers than infant girls. At twelve months, infants rock, chew on objects, suck on or caress *transitional objects* (special toys or blankets), or move away to soothe distressing emotion. By eighteen to twenty-four months, toddlers assertively request action from caregivers, distract themselves, and actively suppress anger and sadness.

Not only are toddlers responsive to others in the nonvirtual world, they are also affected by what they see on screens. However, their abilities to understand content viewed on screens changes with age. For example, Mumme and colleagues report that ten-month olds lack the ability to interpret emotional content from television, however twelve-month olds will avoid and react negatively to an object that elicited a fearful reaction of an adult on television.[31]

A critical contributor to healthy attachment is the bidirectional, synchronized routines that parents and infants establish over the first few months of the baby's life. Even babies as young as two months show distress by a parent's lack of emotional responsiveness. With the coordinated, consistent dance between parent and child, babies learn how to trust the world and build self-regulation. Babies use animated social and verbal expressions, like smiling and crying, to communicate as well as to respond to caregiver expressions and verbalizations. This skill is called *social referencing*. The more practiced the dance routine between caregiver and baby, the better they get at interpreting each other's signals and making necessary adjustments, eventually blooming into a mutually satisfying and strong reciprocal attachment.

Attachment occurs in four phases. From birth to two months, babies move from undiscriminating social responsiveness to orienting to all humans. At four to five months old, infants discriminate social responsiveness, meaning they recognize familiar people and becomes anxious with strangers. By seven months, they actively seek contact with familiar people. Finally, by three years old parent and child have a goal-directed partnership. Toddlers have learned to predict the behaviors of primary caregivers and adjust their behavior to maintain physical closeness.[32]

There are four primary attachment patterns that result from child factors, caregiver factors, and the "fit" between child and caregiver. The more secure the attachment, the better the child is at complex and creative problem solving and symbolic play, demonstrates more positive emotions, and is judged by others as more attractive.

Secure attachment is characterized by a child who consistently and effectively seeks comfort from their caregiver.

Anxious-resistant insecure attachment is characterized by habitual clinging and crying to elicit comfort from the caregiver. This style often results from inconsistent caregiving due to depression or other impairing caregiver characteristics (e.g., history of abuse, unhappy marriage, poverty-stricken, overwhelmed, and substance abuse).

Anxious-avoidant insecure attachment is characterized by a child who habitually avoids or ignores the caregiver. This style typically results from a rigid, self-centered caregiver who is often impatient, unresponsive, and has negative feelings about the infant or from overzealous parents who provide too much intrusive stimulation.

Disorganized/disoriented attachment is characterized by a sequence of erratic responses from the child, like freezing, crying, or running away from the caregiver. This style often results when the child has experienced neglect or abuse.

During toddlerhood, children are learning to develop *autonomy versus shame and doubt*. They primarily *parallel play* with peers (alongside one another rather than with each other) progressing into more complex interactive socialization. With play, toddlers explore personal boundaries and are starting to develop a conscience. Healthy toddlers explore with an eye on their caregiver and actively test limits. By three years old, most kids are ready for preschool and love to learn in a group setting with same-age peers.

CHAPTER 2: THE BROWSING TECHNOLOGY NATIVE: AGES THREE TO SIX

Mr. and Mrs. Smith brought in their five-year-old kindergartener, Mikey, with complaints of chronic nightmares, fear of being alone in a room, clinging and crying when anticipating his parents going out without him, extreme fear of the dark, "bad guys," and monsters, temper tantrums, defiance, and school refusal. Although they reported that Mikey has always been a demanding little guy, most of these symptoms cropped up a few weeks after Christmas when he returned to school. They are unaware of any triggering events and are worried about Mikey's sleep deprivation from coming into their room multiple times each night and making every excuse to avoid going to sleep.

After an extensive intake with the family, it was discovered that Mikey's unfiltered browsing on his tablet may have resulted in trauma from viewing violent videos. His unchecked time watching and playing mature-rated video games are also major contributors to his anxiety, tantrums, and defiance. When asked directly, Mikey stated that he accidentally came across violent pornography online but didn't know what it was and chose not to tell anybody. He is afraid it is his fault that the content appeared. He feels guilt, shock, and confusion about what he watched and said his bad dreams sometimes involved naked people, violence, and weapons. Mr. and Mrs. Smith were surprised to hear that Mikey watching his teenage brother play first-person-shooter video games and his own gaming activities may be over-stimulating to his immature nervous system. This is evident because his extreme and prolonged tantrums occur when he was asked to get off his screens. Mr. and Mrs. Smith punished him, thinking he was being entitled, demanding, and manipulative when, in fact, he was actually over-stimulated from long hours of gaming.

GetKidsInternetSafe Screen Guidelines for Ages Three to Six

No more than one hour/day of screen time on weekdays and two hours/day on weekends.

Preschool- through first-grade-kids need a lot of pretend, three-dimensional, and active play for healthy development. Depending on maturity and use factors, some kids do well with limited screen time; whereas others do not. If your child can meet his or her responsibilities and maintain healthy friend and family relationships, one or two hours of screen time per day may be a reasonable guideline. However, for busy kids or kids who show pre-addiction signs, parents may want to block screen time completely during the school week, or even all of the time, until the child demonstrates better screen management skills.

Educational programming and software are a go.

Psychology research demonstrates that educational software can be beneficial with children this age. Content balance is critically important to optimize benefit.

Hold off on gaming systems, smartphones, or social media.

It's easy for little ones to get dependent on mobile technology due to undeveloped nervous systems. Limited use of tablets with only email, video conferencing, and edutainment activities makes sense, but hold off on gaming systems or smartphones until later. Let your kids have the opportunity to get used to school and group socialization before allowing screen activities that are embedded with content persuasively designed to shape compulsive use patterns, like social media and immersive video games.

GKIS Home Staging

Preschool is a great time for children to start developing technology skills, digital literacy, and digital citizenship. To launch a healthy relationship with screens, kids need warm, encouraging guidance from their parents. Parents who set standards and praise without being overly critical have well-adjusted kids. Theorists call this *authoritative parenting,* and evidence demonstrates it is better than *permissive* (uninvolved) or *authoritarian* (overly controlling) parenting styles.

Authoritative parents are proactive rather than reactive. They set the stage for success rather than chasing destructive child behaviors. Children from authoritative home environments not only achieve more in school, but they also demonstrate a stronger willingness to seek out and master challenges for personal satisfaction. Here are some staging tips for parents, starting with getting yourself ready for best GetKidsInternetSafe parenting practices.

Prepare to be a Credible Authority

Explore your opinions about technology and fine-tune your technology skills and use patterns before your children use the browser. Are you a *digital native* or a *digital immigrant?* If you're a native, this step of staging may be effortless. But if you're digital immigrant or even a *tech resistant,* then you may need to actively explore your feelings about technology so you don't pass erroneous views about screen risks on to your child. Your opinions will become more informed as you explore the web and browse key words that you think your kids may use. This will help you become acquainted with the digital landscape your child will be wandering into. You may notice that even the most seemingly innocent words can lead one to dark places on the web. For instance, a dad once told me that he was horrified to see such sexualized images when he entered the word "pigtails" in his computer browser while looking for hairstyles with his daughter. Knowledge about what's online is the first step to successful staging.

Also, recognize that by posting your children's pictures on social media, you are creating their *digital footprint* that may be permanent on the World Wide Web. Consider what you think is appropriate to post and with what privacy settings, particularly given your children's inability to provide informed consent. Baby pictures are one thing, but as your children mature so do their digital footprints. I personally choose to post with strict privacy settings on personal social media profiles, tend not to include images of my children's faces on public profile and cover photos or public forums like GetKidsInternetSafe (GKIS), and refuse permission on school district consent forms for child images on school social media and marketing materials. I was even reminded the other day that something as simple as an ultrasound picture today might reveal private, currently undetectable medical information tomorrow. Determine your comfort level.

Consider how technology will interact with your children's abilities, strengths, vulnerabilities, and moods. Don't risk them stumbling around online to "find their way" or staying on so long they develop addictive use patterns. Parents often think kids seek what they need, as if they are pre-programmed to know. With an immature ability to reason, kids need their parents' active guidance online as well as offline. Preliminary research demonstrates that screen use stimulates the brain in similar patterns that other types of drug and behavioral addictions do.[3334] In my practice, I have found that certain kids are vulnerable to screen addiction, particularly those who are peer neglected or peer rejected and those with traits of introversion and cognitive rigidity (e.g. looping or getting "stuck" on thoughts or perspectives) like anxiety, depression, AD/HD, and autism.

Do your research BEFORE you purchase devices or software rather than impulsively succumbing to pester power. Appropriately rated educational programming and software has been found to be beneficial for preschool-age children. However, there is a wide range of quality apps labeled "educational" that are not outcome tested. I recommend the use of educational apps and software at this age, but determine educational merit before allowing use. Start with co-engagement, and do not allow your child screen access without strict filters and monitors.

When assessing quality of educational screen content, consider if the characters are warm and engaging. Is there a prosocial message? Is pace appropriate for processing and learning? Is it devoid of distressing content like violence or sexuality? Also, be cautious of unverifiable claims, especially by marketers promoting a product. Does the product have manipulative neuromarketing techniques that incentivize your child to BUY MORE? If so, don't allow it. Consider initial and upgrade costs, as well as safety and durability issues prior to making a purchase. Also, don't give your child buyer's access. I had a first-grader client who charged up $500 in game gems on his tablet before his mom discovered the charge. His mom convinced Apple to forgive the charge the first time. The second time the child made an unapproved purchase, his mom was stuck with a $2500 charge! Talking to your kids is not enough. Keep your credit card number and passwords to yourself.

Take Inventory

Keep ongoing records of screen devices, apps, games, memberships, and activities to get and maintain control of your home's digital environments.

Don't forget to include usernames, passwords, and passcodes as instructed on your *GKIS Connected Family Screen Agreement.*

Set GKIS Screen Free Zones

Examples of GKIS Screen Free Zones, or location parameters, include no screens in the bedroom, bathrooms, or behind closed doors. Examples of situation parameters include no screens during social and meal times. List location and situation parameters on your *GKIS Connected Family Screen Agreement.*

Surveys reflect that three of the biggest contributors to unhealthy amounts of screen time are screens in the bedroom, background television, and a lack of rules and regulations around screen use.[35] Preschoolers will accept limits better than older children, so take advantage of this time to teach rules. You may not think location parameters are necessary yet, but sooner than parents think kids engage in sneaky and potentially dangerous screen habits. Setting parameters from the beginning increases supervision opportunity, builds habit, and encourages compliance later on. Excessive screen use by children has been linked to increased risk for obesity and diabetes, increased sensitivity to stress, irritability, depression, impulsivity, aggression, decreased attention, motor problems, and sleep problems.[36][37][38][39]

Other recommended parameters include no screens at social or meal times. When parents teach kids that watching screens at the dinner table or when somebody is available to talk is rude, kids learn important rules of netiquette. Also, by practicing tolerance when transitioning between tasks and switching off screens, kids learn important emotional soothing skills. This makes for more polite, social, and overall emotionally resilient kids. Device-free dinners lead to fun, engaging family discussion and *mindful eating,* which refers to attention to food choice, quantity, and taste as well as kinesthetic awareness of the sensations of being hungry and satiated. Putting a GKIS collection basket on the table so screens remain off is an effective way to trigger compliance.

Decide on Blackout Times

List blackout times and days on your *GKIS Connected Family Screen Agreement* (#NoTechTuesday, #NoTechThursday). Preschool age is the best window to set screen time habits. In our house, we called screen blackout days *#NoTechTuesday* and *#NoTechThursday*. My kids are teens now, and I am so happy that I enforced this strategy. These were the days I most looked forward to coming home to dirty kids who were excited to tell me about their adventures. These days pushed them to the limits of their creativity and encouraged self-selected offline skills like initiating projects, cooperation with neighborhood kids, fort building, and tree climbing. Be warned though; these are also the days my kids unburied coyote dens and learned how to fight and negotiate. Because I let them choose their no-tech days, I believe they stayed in sports longer, preferring soccer days to screen-free days. Those extra few years of choosing sports offered more fitness and team-building skills. Win-win all the way around!

Reasonable blackout screen times also include in the morning before school (avoid tardies), a reasonable hour on weekends (so they don't get up too early), ninety minutes after school (so they don't rush through their homework), and thirty minutes before bedtime (to prep the brain for restful slumber). Parental controls, software, and apps can help with boundary setting. Recognize that blackout times will change as your child's age and schedule does.

Create Co-Work Stations

Screens near each other and facing the middle of the room optimizes supervision and cooperative interaction. Not only does this setup allow parents to keep an eye on screen activities, but neighboring siblings often enforce expectations and, in more difficult situations, tip parents off about sneaking and lying. Even more importantly, co-work stations encourage healthy socialization and contribute to healthy sibling friendships. Popular online activities and games, like Minecraft, often allow co-play. Siblings with screens next to each other share emotional response during cooperative problem solving and fun sabotage. Independently working through disagreements is critical for healthy social and cognitive development.

Make sure co-work stations have body-healthy *ergonomics*. Kids are increasingly presenting to medical offices with the repetitive stress injuries detailed in Chapter Eight due to poorly designed workstations and excessive screen use. Avoid injuries like eyestrain and wrist, neck, back, and shoulder pain by paying attention to these simple ergonomic guidelines:

- Eyes level with the top of screen
- Head and neck balanced and in-line with torso
- Shoulders relaxed
- Elbows close to body and supported
- Wrists and hands in-line with forearms
- Feet flat on the floor

- Overhead lighting dim to prevent glare
- Refocus eyes twenty seconds for every twenty minutes of screen time
- Forty-five minutes of play then a fifteen-minute break. Download an app or provide a simple kitchen timer to comply with time limits and body-healthy rest and stretch breaks.

Set Up Creativity Kits and Maker Spaces

Creativity kits placed nearby screens compliment screen activities and encourage multimodal learning. A benefit of screen use is instant access to creative content like images and how-to videos. If your kids are little, dress up clothes and play sets, like a kitchen, castle, or television studio, lead to extended imaginary play. For older kids, art and writing materials make sketching, painting, mapping, and story, poetry, or screen- writing more probable. For more ideas and detailed examples, check out the GKIS Home Starter Online Course at GetKidsInternetSafe.com.

Create Community GKIS Family Docking Stations

Docking devices thirty minutes before lights out avoids screen use in bedrooms after hours. To avoid sneaking, set up your GKIS Family Docking Station in the parents' room. Docking devices helps form habit and accountability.

Eight Healthy Screen Habits for Preschoolers

1. **Co-viewing and co-media engagement are excellent learning opportunities.**
   Just as you must set the stage in your home for safe screen viewing, your kids also need you to set the stage for safe screen learning. By sitting with your child and recommending projects, you are building that critical parent-child connection that is the scaffolding for learning and initiative. Additionally, you are enriching your attachment by enjoying each other along the way. Enjoy every moment. One day these giggles will be the memories that warm your heart.

2. **Teach online skills like netiquette and digital citizenship right from the beginning.**
   The GetKidsInternetSafe (GKIS) blog was created to provide a free resource for parents to quickly grab hot tech topics and digital age

parenting tips. With technology changing rapidly, regulations and supportive resources often lag in reaction to trouble. GKIS provides quick discussions and guides that parents can use to start teaching skills that will help their kids maneuver more safely online. Screen safety discussions teach essential skills like assertiveness, trusting your gut, and thinking before you post. It also provides a forum for kids to teach parents! If kids are raised with easy, informative discussion, sensible guidelines, and consistent, but chill follow-thru, they adapt easily and are more likely to adopt positive viewpoints and values online as well as offline.

3. **Select online content carefully.**
    Young children should not be allowed to view unfiltered content. Exposure to violent or sexualized images is harmful to children. But it's not just inappropriate content that can be damaging. Extended periods of fast-paced superficial content can be over stimulating to a child's nervous system by burning excessive oxygenated glucose, the fuel our brains need to maintain emotional equilibrium. This is why children may tantrum and rage after excessive screen use. These tantrums are more a result of sensory overload than manipulative acting out. Yelling and threatening children during these types of meltdowns is not helpful in that it serves as a further trigger for too much autonomic arousal. Instead, find a quiet room and offer warm, compassionate soothing. Next time, pare back screen use sessions by ten-minute intervals until your kids can independently mood regulate. Psychologists call this technique *pacing*. What content is least likely to result in sensory overload? Choose educational games and programming that have slower-paced narratives with less intensity and novelty. Games that are interactive and encourage unpressured problem solving are best. There is no replacement for supervision, although setting up tech filtering, like a *child-safe browser,* is critical for safety.

4. **Observe your children's use of the media for a probationary period before your mind is made up.**
    When your children get a new device, game, or app, let them know you're just trying it out for a *probationary period.* That means you may change the rules or discontinue use if you see something you don't like (e.g., inappropriate content, excessive frustration, or over-stimulation). Don't cave when your kids say, "but everybody else is doing it." Good parenting starts within your home. Once you cave to pester power, it's a

slippery slope. Kids learn quickly what will make you give in and will escalate to impressive heights when challenged. Don't let them control the parenting playbook.

5. **Maintain a sensible balance between different types of play, face-to-face engagement, rest, and age-appropriate technology.**
There are many types of play, including screen time, three-dimensional, structured, unstructured, passive, and active. Set up work stations where all of these types of play are possible. Selecting appropriate and enriching learning material onscreen is important (what kids view), but so is reinforcing a healthy process (how kids view). Whether we like it or not, most of us outsource tasks to screen technology, like storing information and socializing. Outsourcing is great as long as kids have ample opportunity to master nonvirtual skills as well.

6. **Encourage creative learning by connecting virtual and nonvirtual learning resources.**
The Internet is rich with attention-capturing resources that will spark your preschooler's passion to create. Does your child love animals? Search the web for images of giraffes, sketch from the image, then look up videos and fun giraffe facts in preparation for a zoo trip! Is your child really into Legos? YouTube is full of how-to videos that will show step-by-step how to make a Lego project blossom into a village. Once the Lego village is complete, reproduce it on Minecraft and write up a city charter with a fancy gold seal on word processing software. Plan a family activity where you create how-to videos, write screenplays, sing karaoke, and make movies! Encourage your children to explore fun roles including screenwriter, director, producer, camera operator, set narrator, and the "talent." Lights! Camera! Action! A friend of mine even made a pretend movie camera out of boxes and a workable red light. Introducing your preschooler to movie-making software for beginners will set the stage for the creation of more sophisticated video compilations popular with school-age kids.

7. **Share your creations by video conferencing with family and friends.**
Your supportive village no longer needs to live in your town. The more humans delighted with everything your kiddos do, the better. Not only can online activities help you connect as a family, but you can also reach

out and connect with friends and extended family on video conferencing apps like Facebook's Messenger Kids, Skype, or FaceTime. Expand your love-web using online resources. For example, create a family blog so others can follow your online projects and adventures. Don't forget to share photos of your children's artwork and store it in a digital folder. One day you'll cherish it just as you do family photos.

8. **Once you've set the stage for safety with connection, staging, filtering, and expert parent's strategies, let your children experiment on their own.**

    Parents need their private time too. With the tools for safety sprinkled throughout *Screen Time in the Mean Time*, you will feel safe letting your kids use their screen time in the meantime. They will earn some freedom to surf the net on their own and gain mastery of technology basics (e.g., tech vocabulary and problem solving, essential commands, and how to use the browser), practice problem solving, as well as practicing fine motor skills such as keyboarding, screen touch, and the mouse. There is little persuasive evidence that screen time will dramatically accelerate academic skills for young children. Face-to-face interaction and running in wide-open spaces remain superior for healthy development with young children than hours of screen time.

Developmental Psychology Crash Course: Children Ages Three to Six

The developmental phase of three to six years old marks the progression from parallel play to group interaction in expanding peer and academic settings from preschool through first grade. Learning continues at an explosive rate with rapid brain development (nature) interacting with a protected and enriching environment (nurture). As children become increasingly familiar with and master activities, their cognitive resources are freed up to grasp an increasingly complex understanding of the world around them. During this time, our amazing little beings are blossoming and developing initiative, complex communication, and creativity.

Brain Development

At three years old, your child's brain has reached 50% of its adult size and will reach up to 95% its adult size by six years old.[40] The brain remodels from older to newer brain structures. As lower brain regions develop, they perform scaffolding for later developing, higher brain regions. In other words, when performing a cognitive task, young children must enlist more brain regions for a single task, while older children with more specialization use fewer regions to perform the same task.[41] This progression of mastery frees brain resources for more and more specialized development.

Just as we see a spike in surface area growth of the frontal lobes at age two years, we see another between five to seven years. This is consistent with the dramatic improvements in *executive functioning* (attention, concentration, and organization). Frequent and rigorous exercise, good sleep, sound nutrition, unstructured play, one-to-one parent and peer interaction, and time with nature play important roles in the healthy development of executive functioning. Although educational and prosocial screen activities are a cognitively and socially enriching addition to a well-balanced life, limits are necessary. Too much screen time may contribute to attention problems.[42]

Consistent with the auditory, language, and motor advances during the preschool period, rapid myelination (growth of white matter that sheaths the shaft of neurons to insulate) occurs throughout the brain, particularly in the areas of the hippocampus (memory) and in the fibers linking the cerebellum and cerebral cortex (fine motor skills).[43] More effective connections are also established between the temporal, occipital, and parietal lobes, which are brain areas critical for the synthesis of information and processing of temporal, visual, and spatial information.

Although little research has been conducted regarding screen technology use and brain change in young children, there is evidence of brain structure change with older kids when they overuse screen technology. For example, Hong and colleagues (2013) reported evidence of a significant relationship between Internet addiction and the thickness of a child's medial and lateral orbitofrontal cortex (OFC), similar to changes seen due to drug addiction.[44] The medial OFC is affected by choices involving immediate rewards, and the lateral OFC is affected by choices involving delayed rewards. These areas of the brain also demonstrate similar changes among subjects with obsessive-compulsive disorder.

GKIS TIP: Screen activities targeting children are expertly and persuasively designed to encourage compulsive use. It's up to parents to run a risk/benefit analysis about whether to allow play, to choose appropriate content, and to monitor use time. Stay conservative in your selections for now. There's plenty of time to develop expert digital literacy. Parent-child and peer-to-peer interaction is extremely rich in rewarding intellectual, emotional, and social stimulation at this age. Start restrictive with only one app, website, or game adoption at a time and gradually add more with parent approval as your child grows. I liken this to a funnel __/. Parents who start out overly permissive with screens and then tighten up end up with resentful and sneaky kids. With deliberate planning and good parenting judgment, bad outcome can be avoided.

Cognitive and Motor Development

By preschool age, children's cognitive development has increased ten-fold. They are now able to speak in sentences, follow directions, count, and understand the concept of time. They love imaginative play and will seek out and engage with peers. By age six, they can dance, ride a bike, and climb monkey bars as well as read and write.

Preschool children are rapidly developing a *self-concept*, with both concrete and psychological dimensions. Preschoolers are wildly curious and often focused on gaining independence and self-control. As they collect new experiences, parents can expect new behavioral patterns to emerge. For instance, it is very normal for preschool age kids to become preoccupied with the classification and grouping of things. Clients sometimes worry their children have a clinical form of obsessive-compulsive disorder (OCD). However, lining up toys and insisting on rigid rules and routines is common among the preschool age group. For most kids, this obsessive, cognitive rigidity will pass.

Jean Piaget (1952) theorized that children of this age are in the *preoperational stage* of cognitive development and demonstrate precausal/magical thinking. In other words, preschool-age kids still have a hazy idea of how their ideas and desires relate to the world around them. They tend to accept what can be immediately seen (concrete appearance and reality), yet unable to reason concepts through (precausal thinking). Thus, they are better at grasping short-term rather than long-term outcome. Flaws in thinking during this developmental phase include *egocentrism* (self-centered thinking), *irreversibility* (things operate only one way), and *animism* (ascribes lifelike qualities to inanimate objects).[45]

Preschoolers have limitations in their ability to reason and anticipate consequence. They are better at grasping short-term rather than long-term outcome. Thus, they are not confident in their opinions and may be easily led astray by the influence of others. Six year olds are starting to understand abstract thinking and are shifting from learning through observation to learning via language and logic.[46]

GKIS TIP: Even if you've provided useful information and practiced appropriate response, young children should not be expected to make good choices and are unable to adequately protect themselves against predatory peers or adults. They simply do not yet have the cognitive resources to do it well.

Physical play continues to promote healthy brain development, particularly in the vestibular, proprioceptive, and tactile sensory system, and results in progressive fine-tuning of gross (big muscle) and fine (small muscle) motor skills. That means preschoolers get better and better at running, jumping, and climbing as well as working with their hands like bead-work, writing, and drawing. Free active play not only releases pent up energy, it also allows kids to employ their imagination, creativity, team-building, problem solving, and resourcefulness, ultimately building resiliency and confidence.

GKIS TIP: Give preschoolers ample opportunity for vigorous physical play and provide them with fun, enriching social and sporting activities. Remember that kids develop at all different rates. Your child's sporting success depends on their love for the game. I too often see parents get their egos too wrapped up in their child's sporting performance. This can result in a child who is anxious, resentful, and burned out on sports too soon. Keep it fun and low-key rather than pressured and competitive. Your child's emotional success and skill building depends on it.

Language Development

During the preschool and kindergarten years, children's language ability continues to explode in vocabulary and sentence complexity. Children within this age range are actively learning to tailor their language to their audience.

GKIS TIP: Frequent and rewarding conversation with others is critical to healthy language development. Evidence suggests that excessive screen time, at the expense of conversational interaction, may result in developmental and language delay.[47]

Social-Emotional Development

Sigmund Freud (1940) famously theorized that gender identity forms during this developmental period, with sexual impulse being the primary source of motivation. He believed that gender identity comes from identification with and fear of the same-sex parent as the child increasingly tries to covet the opposite-sex parent. For boys, this conflict is called the *Oedipal Complex* and for girls it is the *Electra Complex.*[48]

GKIS TIP: Don't be surprised when your son tries to take over mom's attention and your daughter openly battles for dad's affection. Working through this conflict is entirely normal. Patient amusement enriches parent-child connection rather than angry shaming.

Erik Erikson (1964) coined this developmental phase *initiative vs. guilt.*[49] He hypothesized that children aged three to six are starting to launch on their own while remaining strongly attached to caregivers. Just as toddlers frequently demonstrate separation anxiety, so do preschoolers. Social learning research has demonstrated that children are more likely to evaluate and regulate their own behavior if they have had lots of in real life playing time with warm, mutually responsive parents. In contrast, kids who have spent less time with parents will comply due to obedience rather than an eagerness to comply or cooperate.[50]

GKIS TIP: It's perfectly healthy for preschoolers to be emotionally needy and clingy sometimes, and other times ready to strike out independently. Be encouraging, cuddly, and patient as your children take two steps forward and one step back. They are still experimenting. Lots of fun playtime with parents to build a mutually warm attachment will result in children having more of a conscience outside of parent supervision.

Physical and pretend play help build *theory of mind* (ability to understand and predict the behavior and feelings of others), social skills, and emotional self-control, as well as creativity and resiliency. There is evidence that solitary play, as opposed to play with others, has a significant negative correlation with overall social skills.[51] When kids start preschool, they can interact with a larger variety of people than ever before unsupervised. However, caretakers still have a lot of influence over whom children spend time with outside of school.

GKIS TIP: Just as too much screen time can cause delay, appropriate technology use can promote individual and cooperative play in children. Remain choosy and vigilant about which peers to arrange play dates with. The quality of peer interaction with closest friends may influence your child's social development over many years.

Preschool children's pretend play is primarily fantasy practice of cultural roles. They spend a lot of time building upon memorized social scripts ("you're the mom, I'm the sister"), progressively becoming increasingly independent.[52] Preschool is a time of playing house and practicing gender roles. One of my greatest joys of my career is watching how fathers have become more nurturing caregivers while mothers have an increasing choice in areas of achieved excellence. Excellent modeling for the little ones!

GKIS TIP: Raising emotionally literate boys and girls means encouraging compassion, nurturance, hard work, and an open mind. Shaming kids to follow overly-prescribed gender roles can stunt learning. Encourage your girls to be assertive leaders and your boys to be nurturing caretakers. We are no longer limited in embracing and practicing valuable societal skills. You'll know what kind of job you're doing by listening to and watching your child during fantasy play. Make the necessary adjustments in your own parenting behaviors as you go, inching closer and closer to your parenting ideal. Particularly look out for messages of *toxic masculinity*, which are oppressive and hurtful ideals attributed to men that can result in pathological shame behaviors (e.g., "men don't cry").

Social curiosity increasingly develops, as preschool children are now able to use social comparison to assess success and failure as well as individual performance. They are motivated to identify with others, such as parents, caretakers, siblings, and peers and learn through modeling and operant conditioning (reward and punishment strategies are detailed in Chapter Ten). During this developmental phase, little ones also learn how to hold a grudge. We see aggression move from simply trying to get ahold of an object to knowingly being aggressive toward a person who's done them wrong.[53]

GKIS TIP: At around three years old, kids start to experiment with name-calling, and tantrums transform from physical outbursts to verbal ones. The tantrums of three-year-olds are often more impressive than the tantrums of two-year-olds. With burgeoning developmental ability comes more impressive tantrum strategy, including threats like "I hate you" and "You're not my friend." Gently counsel a more appropriate response and don't take it personally. As a clinical psychologist, I celebrate a child's ability to brilliantly manipulate others while supporting parents how to stay a step ahead.

Based on the theory of Kohlberg, kids this age choose "the right" for self-gratification and to avoid punishment, rather than knowing what is right or wrong.[54] Preschoolers tend to be impulsive and unsystematic in their thinking. They show little understanding of the need for rules and instead play games to take turns and have fun.[55] Piaget called this the *Premoral Period.* Premoral learners are still only able to hold a few things in memory at once. Consequently, they have difficulty identifying and keeping in mind relevant features of a complex problem. They must rely on what they can see or on hard rules rather than on another's intent, abstract factors, or the spirit of the rule. Outcome counts for little kids, not intent.

GKIS TIP: Many parents overestimate their children's capabilities and give them too much independence too quickly. Then, when they get into trouble and try to scale back technology use, parents meet with child resistance and resentment. Instead of creating an overly permissive tangle that strains parent-child cooperation, set up conservative media guidelines from the get-go. Keep in mind how a twelve year old would use screens in her bedroom when your child is only six years old and choose your most cautious guideline. Rather than giving a lot of rope and pulling it back in response to crisis, instead gradually dole it out as your child develops. That means very little screen time with young children. If they grow up with rules, it is less likely that they will resist it later.

CHAPTER 3: WORLD WIDE WEBBING: AGES SEVEN TO ELEVEN

Brandon is a ten-year-old gifted student. He loves fantasy books and has a few good friends at school. Team sports are not "his thing," but he is in Tae Kwon Do in the winter and swim team in the summer with his parents' insistence. Although brilliant, his grades usually slip mid-semester until his parents get after him to better track his homework and limit screen time. Recently, between his usual video games and YouTube surfing, Brandon searched "DRAGON" in his computer browser for sketch ideas. This led him to a sadomasochistic sexual adult chat room that he compulsively visited for the next two weeks until his parents discovered it. During that time, he met several creepy adult "friends" who solicited sexual text exchanges and nude photos. He even sent a photo to his crush at school. Her parents called the school who then called his parents. The police were notified, who then contacted the FBI. Brandon switched schools. By the time his parents sought therapy for Brandon, they were hoping he wouldn't be charged with child pornography charges and feared how many child pornographers had shared the images online. His family's world had turned upside down. We further worried this experience might change his thoughts and feelings about trust and sexuality forever.

Brandon's Internet compulsions left him titillated, ashamed, and confused. Despite weeks of psychotherapy and increased supervision, Brandon is still distressed and can't concentrate on his regular activities. He struggles with intrusive images and thoughts about violent sex, feels like he is forever different from his peers and is worried about how this experience may affect his ability to have "normal" relationships. His symptoms are similar to those I see with children who've been molested.

Brandon's parents feel guilty, frightened, and saddened by the loss of their child's normal pre-adolescent development. His five-minute browser search simply escaped their notice. Tragedies like these are not often shared outside the boundaries of therapy, which is why I wrote Screen Time in the Mean Time to alert parents to dangers and offer effective prevention. Brandon's situation ended better than many other clients I see. In twenty-five years of clinical practice, I've never seen a more epidemic and distressing danger to child psychological health than poorly managed access to screen media and the Internet.

Screen Guidelines for Ages Seven to Eleven

No more than two hours per weekday and four hours per Saturday or Sunday of screen time.

Time guidelines are not particularly useful, because content and screen activity matters more than time spent. However, my subscribers routinely ask for guidelines. Best guide is to keep an eye on replacement cost, academic and engagement potential, and overstimulation risk.

Gaming devices are a go! But still no smartphones or social media.

Gaming is fun way to develop problem solving skills and socialize with friends. Again, content matters. Follow age ratings and keep an eye out for violent or sexual content, gamevertising and in-game purchase potential, overstimulation, cyberbulling, and privacy and safety issues.

The average age for smartphone ownership is now eight years old; too young in my clinical opinion. Because school-age kids are already experts with touch screens and computers, most are already benefitting from online learning with Wi-Fi-assisted parental supervision. Smartphones work with 4G, outside of Wi-Fi range, making the Internet accessible for kids 24/7. Even if you think you will monitor a smartphone consistently, you probably won't based on survey statistics. Compulsive-use patterns often emerge with smartphones. Additionally, the younger the child, the more mobile screen use replaces important learning opportunity. A caveat to the rule of phone ownership before middle school is a need to contact parents due to extracurricular activities, divorce, or medical conditions. In these cases, I recommend the adoption of a child-safe mobile phone without Internet access.

Set up cybersecurity

School age kids no longer look to parents to guide Internet exploration. They are now exploring, creating, collaborating, and sharing online. Their autonomy is awesome, but it also increases exposure to cybersecurity risks. Now is the time to invest in cybersecurity safeguards like those detailed in Chapter Six.

Prep for filtering and monitoring

Filtering refers to blocking online access to inappropriate content like pornography, violence, and hate. *Monitoring* refers to tracking keystrokes, searches, and usage as well as allowing parents to read social media posts and texts. Filtering and monitoring can be setup through child-safe browsers and search sites, by programming the parental controls on devices and through your Internet Service Provider (ISP) (e.g., Comcast, AT&T, Time Warner, Verizon, Frontier), on individual websites and social media platforms, and through parental control software and routers.

Not only do parental controls block inappropriate online websites, apps, and games, they can also be used to set rules and time schedules, monitor browser searches and online activities, record screen grabs, and even record online talking with a voice-activated sound recorder. Many programs provide remote notification and management, which allows parents to watch use from their online dashboard and override the child's system for blocking, unblocking, and extended time limits.

Make sure you are the administrator on these systems and that your children do not have your usernames, passwords, or credit card information. It's essential that you maintain administrative authority on system controls and new purchases. Schedule a quick weekly maintenance check on your controls (visit the dashboard, update, and take inventory). In our house, we call that #TechCheckThursday.

A controversial issue in screen safety is whether to tell your kids you are monitoring their screen activities. Critics say that "spying" on your kids undermines trust and is destructive for the parent-child relationship. Those in favor of monitoring say it is essential to supervise your child's activities to provide teaching opportunities and stay aware of their activities for safety reasons. I recommend that you let your child know you will be monitoring and talk about it on occasion to highlight how important it is that they remain aware of their online judgment. After all, you are unlikely to be the only adult reading your children's chats. Other parents and school administrators regularly view device content, as well. Kids should be informed of this fact from the beginning.

Although many parents are afraid to admit to their kids that they monitor their screen activity, dishonesty is costlier than letting your child know from the beginning that you engage and supervise their online behavior. Parents are starting to agree. In a 2016 survey conducted by Common Sense Media, 67% of parents surveyed said that monitoring is more important than protecting their children's privacy. It is a myth that kids will hate you for supervising their online activities. In a 2011 survey of teens and their parents, fewer than half of the teens surveyed said were bothered by their parents close monitoring. In fact, 32% said they were "not that bothered," and 22% said there "were not at all bothered."[56] These findings are exactly what I see in my office. If parents are honest, justified in what they do, and warm and supportive of their child's efforts, kids and teens welcome parent involvement and generally understand the need for supervision. In fact, what bothers kids the most is feeling unimportant and unloved.

Monitor more frequently with young kids, and as you child grows, back off and spot check only. Reading your child's activities word for word is overkill and can undermine trust. However, not monitoring at all seems too risky knowing the kind of online perils that I see every day in my office.

GKIS Launch Techniques

Once kids get experience with school, they are likely ready for age-appropriate video games. Video games tend to get a bad rap among parents, but skill-based learning happens during play and expertise can offer social, entrepreneurial, academic, and career opportunities. Plus, it's fun! The majority of play dates among school-age males now happen online or watching each other play in the same room.

Kids are heavily marketed in this niche, because the entertainment value of video games adds up to big money. In 2017, the global revenue for the gaming market reached $121.7 billion.[57] Professional electronic sports, called *e-sports*, also bring in huge numbers of players with lucrative pay-offs. The International 2017: Dota 2 Championship was the first e-sports tournament to surpass a twenty-four-million-dollar prize pool. E-sports tournaments are televised and pull in big viewer numbers. The 2016 League of Legends Tournament garnered more viewers than game seven of the MLB finals and game seven of the NBA finals combined.[58] Universities have even recognized recruitment and talent development potential by creating varsity e-sports programs. A more detailed analysis of the risks and benefits of video gaming is offered in Chapter Six. Here are some tips for parents to launch smart to maintain control of their children's digital worlds.

One adoption at a time.

Progressive, selective adoption of devices, apps, and games will keep you in a position of informed authority over your child's screen activities. Without deliberate planning, kids will adopt screen activities as soon as the impulse grabs them. This will lead to a dizzying digital landscape that will leave you in the dark to regulate. But if you maintain control and authority from the beginning, good parenting will be so much easier. Start with simple, age-appropriate devices with less capacity at first, gradually moving to the more mobile and powerful tools later as your kids learn digital skills and self-control. Also download only one app or game at a time. The *quality* of screen time is as important than the *quantity* of screen time at this age.

Require a *Persuasive PowerPoint*.

If your child wants a game or app, require that they do the research and present it to you. With screen technology in schools, kids learn professional communication skills young. Persuasive PowerPoint presentations are a university staple. By setting your child to task with the research, you both learn and your child takes responsibility and accountability for their request. It also structures the conversation you need to have about each adoption, like identifying embedded neuromarketing techniques and safety measures.

Embedded neuromarketing techniques are game rewards that are sneakily programmed into games to keep you playing, similar to a slot machines *variable ratio of reinforcement* (a reward repeatedly offered after random numbers of plays). Fortnite has become wildly successful by integrating several addicting game features. Arguably, the most addictive feature is what made Candy Crush so addicting, "lose by a little, win by a lot." This means that the game provides opportunity to move through levels quickly by promising that the player only lost by a few moves. Further, when they win it's big, keeping them chasing a hot streak of success. In Fortnite, you know you lost by a little, because you can see the dwindling health bar of your opponent. You lost by only two bullets! This near miss keeps you trying. You win by a lot, because, once you win a gunfight you can avoid other gun fights and climb many ranks on the HUGE Fornite map. These features are particularly good at keeping players playing.

Other addictive game features include celebratory sounds and prizes, pacing with a promise of new features with each new level, bonus turns, and privileged access to new options like other skilled players, realms, supplies, accessories, avatar choices, and skins, extended playing time, extra points and ranks, and addictive reward features like violence, gambling, virtual sex, or pornography. Product placements and advertisements are also commonplace in apps and video games. Proactively selecting screen activities will alert you to these sneaky hooks. Why a persuasive PowerPoint?

It educates you and your child about the new game or app so no stone remains unturned. Let's face it, if left to you, you will either not consider it fairly or cut corners and make a less-than-sound decision. This intervention educates you and your child simultaneously.

It stimulates cooperative negotiation. By addressing each of your concerns point by point, you both feel heard and considered from the beginning. This provides grist for the mill and builds the parent-child connection. Taking a parents' perspective into account is not easy for egocentric kids. Considering the viewpoint of others before oneself takes maturity and practice.

It teaches an incredibly important life skill, the persuasive pitch. You may need to help with the first PowerPoint slide deck and presentation skills, but then set it as a precedent. Research skills, slide creation, persuasive talking points, and public presentation with emotional containment are powerful skills indeed.

It tests your children's motivation to get the new app or game. Believe me, they will not bother to do the research unless they're super motivated to get it. That means they'll drop the less serious requests, which results in fewer apps and games adopted, less pestering, less "no" from parents, and ultimately less resentment.

It puts a plan in place. Maybe you will respond to the presentation with a "never," or "not yet," or "let's give it a try." Either way, it will cut the pestering and both parties feel heard and respected.

What should it include? The presentation should include cost, use details, rating, and safety features. Be sure they are aware that you will still exercise the opportunity to say "no" or "maybe later" to their request. Either way, you'll both be better prepared to make educated decisions and have better understandings about the game, app, or device purchase. Other launch techniques include:

Check ratings and reviews.

To counteract consumer complaints and legislation aimed at enacting regulating controls and preventing child access, the video game industry created the *Entertainment Software Rating Board* (ESRB) in 1994. This voluntary and self-regulating board rates content and classifies video games based on appropriate user age. Most stores refuse to sell video games that don't have an ESRB rating. Similar rating systems exist in other countries. Overall, ESRB ratings have been somewhat successful limiting child access and, unfortunately for parents, preventing and diluting state-sponsored regulatory bills aimed at blocking child purchases, like California's *AB 1793* sponsored by State Senator and child psychologist Leland Lee.[59] Commonsensemedia.org, Parents-choice.org, and Kindertown.com are great resources for detailed descriptions and reviews. If you cannot find your answers online, go to a specialized gaming system store and ask questions. Gaming nerds are smart!

Make adoption probationary.

Once you agree to the new game or app, make sure to go slow and steady with one new addition at a time. *Contain the situation.* Make sure your teen understands that this is a *probationary period*. In other words, for several weeks after the new implementation you will be assessing the wisdom of the decision. If at any time something unexpected comes up that is unworkable, you may pull the privilege. If you do not prepare them for that possibility, it may be a source for escalation and conflict. Finally, when you do implement it, make sure you have their username and password.

Set up and review privacy and safety features with your child.

Review privacy measures like avoiding self-disclosure, and consider if your child is mature enough to draw the line and report before they get too deep into trouble.

Teach how to identify red flags and cope with risks.

If your child is allowed to play with others, teach them what to look out for and how to get out of upsetting or dangerous cyberbully or stranger-danger interactions. Teach the concept of listening to your inner voice, also known as "trust-your-gut." Keep in mind that gaming introduces a new portal for sophisticated and relentless cyberbullying. Reassure them that if they come to you for help, they will not be lectured or receive consequences. You expect they will make a lot of online and offline mistakes and you are available to help them through it.

Limit whom your children game with and keep checking.

Be aware that many gaming platforms allow instant messaging and/or verbal interaction. Even if you do not allow that, kids will seek out instructional YouTube videos or chat rooms to get tips on game play. At what age are you going to cut them loose to play with the public and under what conditions (headset? text only?)? Be aware of *Let's Play videos* that show YouTube celebrities playing popular video games, commenting and demonstrating game strategies along the way. Although some Let's Play videos are safe for kids, others are full of cuss words and inappropriate commentary.

Encourage your child to create anonymous character names and do not hold them responsible for the behavior of others.

You will likely be shocked at the vulgar and brutal social milieu of the gaming community. Hold your kids responsible for their behavior, but don't get mad at them for being witness to it unless you have disallowed that specifically.

Set a Google Alert.

Once kids use the Internet, they are primed to create a digital footprint. Setting up a *Google Alert* with your children's names may be the first indication they are vulnerable. This means that Google with email you the link to any Internet content for the day that contains those words. The downside is that, if your child has a common name, you may get a lot of false alarms in your email.

GKIS Rules and Regulations

In a survey conducted by Alexandra Samuel (2015), one-third of parents surveyed were what she called *digital enablers* ("They've given in to their kids' expertise and allow them to set the family's tech agenda"), one-third were *digital limiters* ("take every opportunity to switch off screens"), and one-third were *digital mentors* ("take an active role in guiding their kids onto the Internet").[60] She further found that kids of digital limiters were "twice as likely as the children of mentors to access porn, or to post rude or hostile comments online; they're also three times as likely to go online and impersonate a classmate, peer, or adult." She concluded, "Kids of digital limiters often lack the skills and habits necessary for consistent, safe, and successful online interactions." Which type of parent are you?

Screen habits used within the home during this age will cement as a way of life. That means it is also the perfect age to establish healthy, balanced screen habits before adolescent oppositionality and defiance kick in. Weave screen smart dialogue into low-key fun conversations rather than dialogue-killing lectures. The more thought you put into your approach, the more credibility and respect you will gain as a parent. The most important goal is to become the person they go to for information and help. Empowerment and education is the goal rather than issuing threats or inspiring fear. GKIS Rules and Regulations are designed to help your child thrive and stay safe online while encouraging a warm and powerful parent-child connection.

Schedule a fun and informal *GKIS Family Meeting* every week to teach skills and reinforce.

Although old-fashioned family dinners are not always easy to manage in a busy household, at least once-weekly check-ins with kind and interested inquiries about your child's offline and online life is an awesome opportunity to demonstrate support, availability, and teach critical skill sets to optimize resilience. GKIS blog topics can help you keep a loose agenda in mind to trigger engaged discussion and offer useful tips regarding online safety.

Create the *no-screen days* and regular *blackout times* mentioned in Chapter Two to model healthy screen management and a balance of enriching life activities.

Don't cave to pester power "everyone does it" and allow your children access to inappropriate screen content, including movies or television programs.

Did you know that young children have poorer *television literacy* than older children? In other words, they are less able to understand and interpret television programming accurately. Because of their inability to maintain consistent attention or interpret abstract connections, children younger than ten years old are unable to follow a storyline and instead only remember a series of disconnected scenes. Unlike older kids and adults, younger children do not follow the arc of the story or the changing motivations of the characters and often accept situations portrayed on television as factual rather than fictional.[61] Research suggests that poor television literacy (the inability to recognize prosocial elements) accounts for children's increased aggression when they've watched violent programming.

Require that your kids ask your permission before they turn on screen devices. Stay ahead of them; don't follow. Be the gatekeeper.

Allowing your child unlimited, free access will become an issue quickly. Instead of giving kids free reign over screen use, get them used to asking permission first. This allows you the opportunity to reason aloud when and in what circumstances screen use is appropriate. Kids will learn that screen time is a privilege that must be prioritized; family and guest time is a priority over games and watching videos. Limit setting should begin from day one.

Discuss important digital citizenship issues as you co-view.

These include netiquette issues like kindness and empathy (cyberbullying and indulging in mean-spirited gossip), content accuracy (fake news), and originality (plagiarism or sharing without the author's permission - including friends and posts of peers).

Don't get in the habit of yanking privileges the minute there is trouble. Be proactive and strategic.

If your kids experience you as the tech-enemy, they will shut down and you will be the last person they seek out for help. By providing calm, deliberate justification for rules rather than abruptly yanking privileges, you will avoid damaging the parent-child alliance. Being strategic also keeps your kids from practicing dangerous habits like sneaking, deleting, and developing dishonest workarounds.

Insist on a balanced media diet.

Require that your children regularly use educational media to provide the foundational nutrition of their media diet. Then encourage the fun media for snacks and dessert. For example, e-books for children are an excellent entrée with complimentary videos as the fun and enriching treat.

Give your kids the opportunity to earn trust with screen devices over time. Praise what you want rather than punish what you don't. Then they will work to please you rather than to avoid you.

Praise is a far more powerful influencer than giving consequences. If you are emotionally neutral, patient, and nurturing the first time your children make a mistake on their screens, they will keep coming to you for help when they need it. Use mistakes as a teaching opportunity. If they make the same mistake again, then it may be appropriate to turn up to volume on your disapproval and determine reasonable consequences. The primary goal is to help your children shape a self-perception of being honest, smart, and capable and working to maintain your children's trust and respect. Joining in your children's digital lives in a low-key, positive way is best.

Studies have found that when children are told they are capable of doing a good job, they are more likely to feel remorse and independently manage their behavior more diligently. Take the time to build your children up by stating your expectations that they will manage their screens responsibly. Your kids will not become arrogant; instead they will work to maintain a positive self-image.

Also, active parenting characterized by reasoning in a warm, supportive way with gentle probing questions has been demonstrated to be a positive contributor to moral growth.[62] When your child does make a mistake, avoid the question, *"Why did you do that?"* Usually children aged seven to eleven years do not know how to answer and their attempts only lead to mutual frustration. A more productive question to ask is, *"What could you have done instead?"* This leads the child to generate solutions and sets you up as a helpful facilitator rather than a harsh interrogator.

Ask parents of play date buddies what kind of screen safety measures they have in place. Share your wisdom and refer them to GetKidsInternetSafe.

Although most play dates happen online these days, when they are face-to-face kids often still engage in cooperative or parallel play screen time. Keep in mind that other parents may have very different ideas about what is appropriate regarding virtual and nonvirtual content and time limits. I once assumed a friend would have similar beliefs as mine when our kids stayed for an overnight. I was horrified to learn they had access to mature game content for endless hours, unsupervised. Don't make my mistake. I strongly recommend a quick, but specific accounting of your rules and beliefs about play content and activities with other supervising parents prior to play date drop off. Also, clarify your expectations to your kids and teach them assertiveness skills so they are empowered to speak up should they be offered inappropriate activity options outside of your home.

School-age kids are eager to build their virtual identity and peer and public following with social media profiles, video streaming, and video posting starting at school age. Avoid these activities until adolescence.

It's tempting to allow your kids to post harmless activities like karaoke and game tutorials online. Not only are these activities fun and creative, but *"everybody's doing it."* I recommend saying "not yet" to these requests, simply because kids too often go off the rails of reasonable discretion to attract online attention and followers. After all sensationalism sells, right? What I mean by "off the rails" is that they may show off and offer disclosures and opinions to their online audience that can be too revealing, sexual, or aggressive. Their natural egocentrism and inability to anticipate consequence make it impossible for them to recognize when they've gone too far. Their mistakes can then be used against them to black mail further inappropriate behavior. Say "no" to public and private posting (like on YouTube or microblogging or vlogging sites).

Developmental Psychology Crash Course:
Children Ages Seven to Eleven

Understanding the basics of school-age child brain development helps parents understand why activity choice can have a long-lasting impact. As we discussed in Chapters One and Two, brain development is less like building and more like "remodeling." It involves neuronal demolition and growth, pruning and tuning. Just because parts of the brain reach maximal volume does not mean the brain is finished developing. Brain volume decreases and increases in various brain regions as children age and reach increasing brain specialization.

When a child masters a task, the brain becomes more streamlined in its circuitry, ultimately forming information superhighways that rely on fewer brain regions per task. Thinking becomes more efficient. A child's preferences (based on personality and experience) leads him to particular environments which, in turn, further affects behavior and ultimately stimulates brain growth, which then affects behavior all over again. This interactive, bidirectional cycle is nature via nurture at work.

An example of neurological specialization is motor memory for driving a bicycle. Remember what it was like when you first started learning? Attending and deliberately not attending to everything at once while using new motor skills, like working the handle bars and pedals while balancing, was initially overwhelming. Your brain was firing in multiple areas at first with tasks competing for cognitive priority. But as the neurological pathways formed and strengthened with learning and practice, those skills became specialized and formed habits that no longer needed competitive, alert brain engagement. Fewer brain areas fire as skills specialize.

From seven to eleven years old, children are independently functioning in a variety of settings offline and online. Not only are they doing their homework and household chores independently, they also start to independently browse the Internet, graduating to email, texting, video conferencing, multiplayer games, and sometimes social media. Increasingly expert digital literacy provides a rich resource for building valuable neurological scaffolding.

Even with their rapidly developing independence, school-age kids need warm, supportive, and engaged parents to develop healthy peer relationships, self-esteem, good judgment, and a strong sense of morality. As you read this crash course, keep in mind how your family's screen use guidelines may interfere with, or enhance, blossoming online skills. As school-age kids become more sophisticated in their cognitive and language skills, adults may be inclined to view them as "little adults" and allow too much unsupervised screen time. This is a mistake. Closely supervising screen time is not about a lack of trust; it's about taking critically important opportunities for guidance with a powerful and potentially dangerous tool.

Brain Development

A prepubescent adolescent has already developed 95% of his brain structure. As children's executive functioning becomes increasingly sophisticated, frontal lobe gray matter reaches its maximal volume in girls at eleven years old and in boys at twelve years old.[63] Executive functions include cognitive skills necessary for higher-order thinking, like self-monitoring, impulse control, emotional soothing, task initiation and follow-thru, working memory, prioritizing, organizing, and planning. The frontal lobe is highly connected to other brain areas and particularly sensitive to traumatic injury. As expected with increasing task mastery, some cortical regions by age ten decrease in volume, especially within the occipital (visual processing) and superior parietal (spatial orientation) lobes.[64]

The caudate nucleus, a brain structure that plays a role in the control of movement and muscle tone and is involved in circuits mediating higher cognitive functions, attention, and emotional states, reaches its largest size at age seven years old in girls and ten years old in boys before it declines in volume.[65]

Myelination is the process of sheathing axons (brain cells) with white matter to insulate them and allow them to conduct the electrical impulses that create efficient thinking. White matter volumes continue to increase throughout childhood.[66] The corpus callosum is the most prominent white matter structure. It integrates the activities of the left and right cerebral hemispheres, including functions related to the unification of sensory fields,[67] memory storage and retrieval,[68] attention and arousal,[69] and enhancing language and auditory functions.[70] *Brain lateralization*, meaning that certain mental processes specialize in either the left or the right hemisphere, continues throughout childhood, allowing subtler and more coordinated motor activity and complex thought.[71]

Cognitive and Motor Development

By now, children have lost their first baby tooth and continue to increase in size and strength. The average American seven-year-old is fifty pounds, forty-eight inches tall and by twelve years old is ninety pounds, fifty-nine inches tall.[72]

Jean Piaget (1952) theorized that during middle childhood the period of *concrete operations* emerge, meaning mental operations (ideas held in memory) better structure thought process.[73] Now children can think flexibly and solve problems, organize ideas, understand social and moral rules, and interpret people's intentions. With increased memory capacity and knowledge stores, school-age kids can follow instructions and be productive on their own with less supervision. Erikson (1964) called this stage *industry versus inferiority*, meaning that as children master skills like chores, homework, and play-dates, they develop a sense of pride.[74]

With more advanced cognitive abilities and increased size, strength, and coordination, school-age kids often become involved in individual clubs, organizations, and sports. Parental roles shift from being caretakers to group leaders, coaches, cheerleaders, and taxi drivers. Parent tasks increasingly revolve around child activities rather than parent-chosen activities. These role changes significantly impact family dynamics and can strengthen or strain the parent-child connection.

GKIS TIP: I've found in clinical practice that parents must surrender the fantasy of who they thought their child *would become* and accept the child *they have*. Engineers learn to embrace their cheerleaders, and football coaches support their chess players. The ease of this transition can profoundly impact ongoing attachment. Lucky for us all, by the time children are school age most parents have fallen madly in love with the unique personalities of their kiddos. With this burgeoning new chapter of acceptance comes a celebration that the real child is preferable to the fantasy child anyway.

Kids this age are also developing *metacognitive skills*, meaning they gain a more abstract and complex idea of who they are, what they like, and what they want. We also see children's interests swaying away from parental influence.

GKIS TIP: At this age, kids know what they want and have skilled strategies to manipulate parents. *Pester power* becomes more difficult to dissuade as your child's arguments get more sophisticated. Internet marketers are experts at developmental psychology and use these concepts to imbed neuromarketing strategies into child screen activities. As a result, kids wear down their parents to purchase games, apps, and devices that are outside of the appropriate age rating. Without a management plan, many kids collect screen activities too rapidly.

Language Development

As *egocentrism* (the inability to see anything outside of oneself) wanes, school-age children are rapidly gaining *metalinguistic awareness* (the ability to think about language and to comment on its properties).[75] Now kids can adjust the content of their communications to the listeners' needs with more sophisticated detail.

GKIS TIP: With these new abilities kids are increasingly able to form complex relationships with adults outside of the family. Sexual predators often target school age kids, because they are highly vulnerable for Internet grooming. Kids on gaming and social media platforms may also be drawn to online relationships that can be intense due to the frequency of contact and ease at which personal information can be inquired about and shared. There is obviously a danger in forming relationships with strangers online. Even virtual peer relationships can be inappropriately intimate.

Social-Emotional Development

Parents expect more of elementary school children and tend to change their discipline strategies from spanking or time out to withdrawal of privileges and reward. These strategies take more self-control, planning, and sophistication to employ successfully. Maccoby (1984) described parent-child cooperation in managing behavior *"coregulation."*[76] Increased self-regulation at school age is consistent with Freud's (1940) assertion that middle childhood is when the *superego* (attending to community values and standards) becomes dominant.[77]

During the seven to eleven-year-old phase of development, children become less egocentric and are better able to recognize that others have different perspectives, opinions, and intentions than they have. They can still be shockingly self-centered, but social skills are developing and friendships are becoming more complex. With this new insight, kids can now anticipate how others may react to what they say or do and better understand potential dangers posed by strangers on the Internet. More specifically, school-age children have been trained to be obedient and polite to adults while still being able to imagine that others may have malicious intent. Parents must emphasize that disclosing personal information or posting unflattering images or actions online can have unintended and dangerous consequences.

GKIS TIP: Although many parents want to protect child innocence and security, it's time to teach children about *digital permanence*, digital citizenship, and online posting. Let them know that it is OK to risk being impolite and assert themselves if somebody makes them uncomfortable. Don't just tell them; *show them* with role-playing and instructive YouTube videos. Once upon a time parents believed that blind obedience was the mark of a well-raised child. Modern parents recognize that blind obedience can be dangerous. Teaching your child to be thoughtfully obedient and confidently assertive makes better sense in the modern world.

Piaget (1952) posited that kids ages five to ten years develop a strong respect for rules and enter a stage called *heteronomous morality*. In this stage, kids make decisions based on consequences rather than considering the intent of the transgressor. By ten years old, kids enter the stage of *autonomous morality*. This means they come to understand that rules can be challenged and even changed if there is good reason to do so (like the transgressor's intent).[78] Kholberg (1984) elaborated that middle childhood marks the development of *conventional morality*, where kids tend to choose "the right" to do what they think is fair or to fulfill the role of a "good person" rather than just acting for immediate gratification.

GKIS TIP: Help your child reason through complex social situations with patience, warmth, and understanding. This means letting them make their own decisions and carry through with their own hypotheses on occasion rather than taking over and doing everything for them. We learn best through trial and error; that means allowing your child opportunity to fail.

Kids within this developmental phase spend increasingly more time with peers than parents. Socializing with other children is essential for learning to assertively negotiate conflict. The closer the friend, the more effort your child will put forth to reach a solution.[79] Kids must have the time and opportunity to develop healthy peer relationships so they can develop *social resiliency.* The challenge is that kids this age will now choose friends outside of their parents' influence for personality reasons, rather than proximity and convenience. As a result, they are exposed to ideas that parents are unaware of and may not approve of. As they improve at incorporating social comparison, they also begin to develop a complex, but relatively stable, *sense of self* based on increasing cognitive, social, and physical competence.[80] As they recognize that effort *and* ability contribute to academic performance, kids become more firmly at risk for developing negative academic self-concepts.

GKIS TIP: Socialization and parental guidance during this period is critical to learning the skills necessary for social and partnering success later in life. Based on the problems families bring to my office, I am seeing more and more situations that interfere with unstructured peer group play time like excessive screen time, overload of academic tasks, online relationships that compete with face-to-face friend time, and misguided attempts to protect that instead isolate kids at home alone. These obstacles may cause developmental delay that is difficult, if not impossible, to remedy later. It is more important than ever for parents to spend time with their kids AND their kids' buddies. Your influence will not only have an impact on your child's decision-making but also on their friends. Sometimes risky activities won't happen because of your child's friend's unwillingness to disappoint you. Keep a balance between allowing your child social privacy while also staying engaged in their socialization process.

Kids between seven and eleven years gradually transition from playing imaginary roles with social scripts to rule-based games. The objective now is not just play to have fun but also play to win. This progression bumps kids directly in the path of conflict negotiation and management of aggression. Girl play is typically more intimate with less direct competition, whereas boy play is in larger groups (e.g., teams) with more direct competition. Parental encouragement and support of a variety of social activities, including team sports, is awesome for social development.

Kids also start to segregate by gender during school age and become more interested in gaining popularity. Play often takes on sexual overtones (e.g., kiss tag and teasing). As kids approach middle school age and puberty, they start to become interested in experimenting with intimate partnerships. Research surveys and my clinical observations reveal that sexting and posting sexually provocative pictures are common, even among supervised, educated kids and teens.

CHAPTER 4: SEXTING, FLAMING, & SURVIVING DIGITAL COMBAT: AGES TWELVE TO SEVENTEEN

Sierra is a fifteen-year-old girl who was brought for therapy after her parents discovered an alarming relationship with another teen online. Sierra lives in California and her friend lives in Iowa. They met in an anime fandom chat room and discovered they have a lot in common. The friendship blossomed quickly as both teens are sensitive, curious, and creative. However, as time went on Sierra's friend, Ryan, disclosed that he was in a lot of emotional pain and was suicidal. Ryan was a female-to-male transgender teen who felt he couldn't come out to his conservative family. He was slowly sinking into a dark depression and had started cutting. Sierra was alarmed and empathetic, affirming his worth and encouraging him to hang in there and keep his chin up.

The relationship had gotten so intense that Sierra and Ryan were sharing their opinions and feelings almost constantly, like a stream of consciousness. They even said they were "like one person," doing their homework on Facetime and falling asleep with each other onscreen at night on the pillow. At first, Sierra's parents were happy to see her so connected and feeling so supported. But over time they recognized an uncomfortable intimacy between them, including sexting and semi-nude photos. Also, Sierra was slowly changing from her bubbly, enthusiastic self to somebody else entirely. She was increasingly isolating herself from friends, dressing in black colors and changing her makeup and hair to resemble the "emo" kids at school. Most alarmingly, she seemed to increasingly distrust her parents and was becoming outright cruel to her little sister. Her parents couldn't decide if they should support her through this "phase," or if she was in a clinical depression.

They also couldn't decide what to do about Ryan. He was so important to Sierra. When they'd taken her phone away, she melted down. Her parents challenged her to let go of this friendship, explaining that Ryan needed professional help and the intensity of the friendship may inadvertently be making his issues worse. Sierra explained that without her, Ryan might kill himself. He'd made suicide attempts before. Her parents explained that threatening suicide to extort somebody to stay connected is a form of emotional abuse. Sierra disagreed and accused her parents of being out of touch, homophobic, and part of the cruel majority culture that oppresses teen freedom. She said she'd kill herself if they took away her contact with Ryan. Because of her intensity, they backed down. Everybody was walking on eggshells while Sierra became more fearful, tyrannical, and emotionally volatile.

GKIS Screen Guidelines for Ages Twelve to Seventeen

Smartphones are a go.

Hold off on smartphones until after their first semester of middle school. By then most kids have phones to socialize and make plans. If you avoid adding the phone during a transition, like first day of school, you avoid it interfering with healthy adaptations to more teachers and higher academic expectations. Start with a mobile phone that doesn't connect to the Internet if they need it before twelve years old. Middle and high school teachers often recommend academic apps and encourage kids to use phones in the classroom. Make your decision based on the strengths and vulnerabilities of your unique child.

Once teens have smartphones in hand, strict time limits are more difficult to enforce, but location parameters are still critically important.

Teen academics and social interaction is almost entirely online these days. Your teen has officially transformed into a cyborg. Offer enticing alternatives to phone time like fun outings, binge watching TV together, and offering to host friends for adventures. Enforce no screens in bedrooms, bathrooms, or behind closed doors as well as situations like mealtime and short car trips to optimize safety and family engagement. Docking devices at night is extremely important, as teens are too often up chatting until early hours of the morning, even on school nights!

Social media is a go.

Thirteen is the official magic age for social media adoption in compliance with the Children's Online Privacy Protection Act (COPPA). Despite meeting the age consistent with social media terms of compliance, I recommend no new adoptions until your child has demonstrated they can manage the increased expectations of middle school, and then only one at a time. Instagram has traditionally been the gateway app. But it is no longer safer than Snapchat with its disappearing storyline and video and instant message capacity. Social media posts can usually be monitored but instant messaging cannot. Most social media platforms allow instant messaging and have shut out third party app monitoring. Furthermore, early adoption of social media exposes your child's brain to dopamine-fueled feedback loops which replace real-life experience. Although it will be challenging, hold off social media adoption until mid-middle school at the earliest. If your teen is demonstrating dangerous signs of addiction potential, wait even longer.

Friends and Fun

Peer relationships take center stage now that family attachment has been mastered. Adolescent socialization is often characterized by multiple, mixed alliances and complex maneuvers for acceptance and popularity. It may feel like your teen is rejecting you as they make this transition, but studies show that teens typically agree with parents on big issues like values, morals, religion, and politics. Even though they may look at you with dismissive disdain, they are likely accepting your influence in profound ways.

Teens are often conflicted about their relationships with their parents. Sometimes they want to be babied, and sometimes they want to be independent. Parents are also conflicted, sometimes wanting to nurture, and other times ready for retirement from child care. With both making developmental transitions, expect rocky roads. It's entirely healthy and normal. The best way to preserve your influence is to be respectful, compassionate, and patient, and keep your sense of humor. Personalizing their attitude and succumbing to anger rarely has a positive payoff.

Successful parents of teens learn to morph their parenting style from demand for strict obedience to calm, controlled negotiation. Teens typically trigger this change by bumping up against limits and demanding change. By accepting their influence, you can negotiate a fun relationship with your teen ripe with conversation, friendly debate, and bidirectional learning. Be prepared for lots of opinions and a sporadic bad attitude. Their occasional scorn for you comes from a brain that is newly able to see hold several thoughts at once and perceive things never before noticed, like the imperfections of their parents. The eye rolls are temporary. Hang in there. They are likely hyper focused on finding and bonding with their same-age tribe and forming an identity independent from yours. How can you best support them on- and offline?

TEACH AND PREACH

Support positive online and offline peer relationships rather than restrict unhealthy friendships.

Teens try out different passions, identities, and friends. On occasion, they will adopt friends you don't approve of. Unless the new friends are dangerous where you may need to step in, parents can provide positive support by offering opportunities to socialize outside of school hours and being a sounding board when complications crop up. It's not effective to take over, demand, and threaten in regard to friend choice. While your taxiing, subtle participation is more welcome than center stage management.

Get to know the new friends by planning teen-centered outings to get smoothies or offering to provide transportation for study groups or club and athletic events. You'll see and hear how the friend choices are turning out while taxiing, and friends may be more accepting of your influence than your teen will be. Be thoughtful by being your less stunningly charming self when your teen's friends are around. They act horrified and embarrassed by you, because they are. Rather than humiliate them by acting over-the-top, dial it back for now. It will bother them sometimes just that you blink and breathe, no need to aggress back by showing their friends your best dance move or responding to their posts on social media. The goal is to respect their boundaries and preserve their respect, not take over or get the last word.

Even though you must trust them to choose their own friends, keep an eye out for HOW they maintain the friendships offline and online (digital footprint and online reputation).

Social skills are not innate, they must be taught. Best-case scenario is that your kids go to you when they feel vulnerable or need help getting through a complex social issue. In the digital age, there is little escape from social expectation and branding. By *branding* I mean that kids use their social media profiles to create a flattering virtual image. Sometimes in an effort to become adult, online behavior slips into overt sexuality, complete with sexy selfies and intimate *sexting*. It can be a slippery slope and is very complicated.

Demonstrate that you are open to discussion, but don't lecture or get too intrusive. Sprinkle in wise comments about good online judgment, and ask for their opinions. Supervise young teens the most and then pull back so that you are not monitoring by their senior year (unless there's a compelling reason to do so). Kids whose parents accommodate too much struggle when they go off to school and may return home mid-semester with an anxiety disorder. Let them practice independence fully by the end of senior year under your roof so dorm life without you won't be so traumatic.

Teach your teen how to avoid cyberbullying by teaching empathy, social and netiquette skills, and complex problem solving.

Not only is it important for teens to consider how they may be viewed by others, but it also important to treat others well. Coping with teen drama offline and online requires a lot of support, problem solving, and a cool head. Cyberbully techniques, like *exclusion* (leaving people out) and *flaming* (trading insults), is common among teens. Often kids bully as a show of loyalty and protection of their friends. It's difficult to recognize you are cyberbullying when flooded with self-righteous indignation.

Not only do kids need support in conflict situations, but parents can also help teens with the fine nuance of social posting. Helping teens build sophisticated netiquette skills requires parents to carve out time from their overtasked lives and balance calm detachment with wise counsel. Don't rant or take over. Instead practice the parent-facilitated problem solving technique offered in Chapter Nine. Trust your child's instincts. They are the experts with the characters and teen culture involved, not you. Validate their experience and trust them to work the problem through. Expect mistakes and failures as critical elements of the learning process. If online cruelty gets destructive or dangerous, consult with school administrators or law enforcement. They have specialized training in digital issues and can be valuable resources. Contacting other parents may result in aggressive retaliatory response; be cautious and thoughtful if you choose this level of intervention.

Keep in mind that all kids make stupid mistakes. Be prepared to help them through it rather than punish them. During brain remodeling at this phase, kids sometimes lose a skill they once had before they perfect their new skill sets, kind of like one step back, two steps forward. This makes for gaps in reasoning and confusing mistakes. Here is an example of how good kids made questionable decisions based on immature moral reasoning.

Recently a twelve-year-old client, Ben, told me a story about his middle school friends, Tim and Amy. Tim texted Amy to tell her he was receiving anonymous texts telling him to kill himself and that he was struggling emotionally. After Amy provided support and suggestions, he ended the texting session with, "Maybe I should just do it. I'm tired. Goodnight," and was no longer reachable. Amy spent the whole night worried that he may have hurt himself. Sure enough, Tim didn't show up to school the next day.

Although Amy didn't want to betray Tim's confidence, she was really worried and told her mom the next morning. Her mom immediately called the school counselor. It turned out Tim was fine, but that was when things got tough for Amy. When my client, Ben, heard that Amy told her mom what Tim had told her in confidence, he group-texted their friends, sharing that Amy had ratted out Tim. The friends were angry with Amy and excluded her in retribution for breaking the "don't tell parents anything" code. Amy was devastated. She knew she'd done the right thing, but her friends didn't agree.

I talked to Ben about the situation in session. We reviewed Amy's dilemma, and I gently challenged Ben to come up with additional solutions to Amy's dilemma. After considering her situation more thoroughly, Ben decided that Amy did the right thing after all. With my careful and calm counsel, Ben eventually understood that his decision to be "honest" with his friends set the stage for the bullying of Amy. After reviewing his options, he ultimately realized that, just as he influenced his friends to turn against her, he could also lead them to repair the rift and provide her with the understanding and support she needed.

After hearing Ben's concerns, the group was persuaded to apologize to Amy. One of the members of the group even ran the situation by her mom, and agreed Amy's choice was a smart one. Tim and Amy ultimately got the support they longed for, but it was rocky for a bit while each teen figured it out. Lecturing Ben about the rights and wrongs of the situation would not have led him to his transformative "aha" experience. Instead, warm and respectful debate did. This is an example of the *pseudostupidity* concept defined later in the chapter.

TRACK AND HACK

Just as parents keep an eye on their teens' school and after school activities, they must also monitor their virtual activities.

It's hard enough for teens to manage their ever-changing nonvirtual identities, but in the digital age virtual identities are also constantly evolving. Virtual identities not only exist on a variety of social media platforms, but they are also reflected on discussion comments, chat rooms and forums, gaming activities, texts, and instant messaging. That means each teen has many selves to maintain, each with different skins and personalities (just like the role-playing games they play).

They experiment with all aspects of the self, online and offline. Online experimentation takes on an entirely new intensity when it is performed in front of thousands of known and unknown viewers real-time and saved for review in the never-ending future. Checking your teens' social media identities and talking to them often about online decisions is critical to help them sift through complex factors of identity.

Recall Sierra and Ryan's intense online friendship described at the beginning of the chapter? Sierra's parents ultimately regretted allowing her constant access to Ryan as their friendship was forming. In hindsight, they realized they should have been limiting her time with him, encouraging other friendships, and talking to her about how unfair it is for Ryan to burden her with very serious emotional problems when he was unwilling to seek adult support. Kind-hearted kids too often counsel friends in pain with the impression that it is their job as a loyal friend. They haven't yet learned that any friendship that makes you feel bad is probably not a healthy friendship. Furthermore, keeping a friend's confidence when he or she is in distress may inadvertently escalate the situation. Unfortunately, I've seen several stalking cases where the victim should have set boundaries far earlier, perhaps saving herself from months of fear and distress. Parents must discuss these specific situations and teach kids to recognize red flags and trust their gut.

Insist on collecting your child's usernames and passwords to gaming and social media accounts and review privacy settings. Insist on being friended.

Looking at your teen's phone real-time and getting backdoor access is the only way you can monitor posting activity and messaging. Kids message almost exclusively on social media now, so commercial programs that allow text monitoring can be bypassed once they have social media and a smartphone. You must rely on education, discussion, and negotiation to teach about issues like privacy. *Microblogging* sites, like Tumblr, and online forums are particularly fertile environments for oversharing.

Recognize that teens often have more than one profile on a single social media app, like having a public, private, and ultra-private profile on Instagram. The smaller, more intimate ultra-private profiles is usually where the most extreme behaviors and opinions are shared. Teens also start group confessional sites that are designed to be anonymous but are often traps for oversharing and phishing and outing (defined in Chapter Seven). The only way you can get access to all their profiles is to check the phone directly from their hand.

Consistently review buddy/friend lists.

Insist that young teens only friend people they know in real life. By getting in the habit of asking teens who is on their buddy lists, parents facilitate important screen safety discussions. It's not unusual for teens to collect large numbers of followers as a reflection of self-worth. Discuss the value of privacy and *real* likes versus a popularity contest among strangers. My clients often have thousands of social media followers. A first step to getting control is to require them to pare down to 300, then 200, then 100 followers rather than deleting the app. When given limits, they tend to keep close friends and cull the creepy strangers. If you're reading this before you kids have social media, limit the number of friends from the beginning.

Organization, Learning, and Education Tools

Adolescents live busy, pressured lives. Along with big changes to their bodies and brains, this generation has more academic expectations placed on them than ever before. College enrollment is at an all-time high, rising from 26% in the 1980s to 41% today.[81] Outsourcing tasks to screens makes day-to-day activities more convenient, like using social media to maintain friendships, calendars to schedule, texting and email to communicate, the Internet to seek new information, mobile maps to navigate, and word processing to store, produce, share, and deliver classroom assignments.

Most of us learned organization and efficiency through the school of hard knocks. However, tanking your grades in high school during this learning period can have serious college opportunity consequences. Instead of abandoning your child to digital overwhelm and long-term academic consequence, start off the school year with a setup day for online tools and encouraging instruction. By teaching effective learning, organization, and study strategies, your teens will not only feel loved and supported with a strong parent-child alliance, but they will also start a trajectory of learning success that sets the stage for excellence. That is a feel-good parenting job that will pay off for a lifetime.

A DUMP STATION AND FAMILY COMMAND CENTER

This sounds obvious, but organization takes preplanning. Assign a dump station for important items like screen devices, backpacks, keys, and shoes. If kids get in the habit of storing items in one space, it avoids a lot of frantic searching and last-minute scolding. A family command center can also be helpful for centralized communication. In our house, this revolves around the kitchen computer, where we calendar activities which automatically synch on our smartphones We also have an inbox/outbox for papers that need signatures and a whiteboard for items that need to be purchased. Along with Siri, helpful calendar and to-do list apps include *iCal, Google Calendar, Outlook, Wunderlist,* and *Cozi*.

GKIS FAMILY DOCKING STATIONS

If you don't set up a docking station for night time storage of mobile devices, kids will be up late on screens, unsupervised. This can lead to sleep deprivation, sexting, and nude photo exchanges. Make docking a requirement and hold them accountable.

STOCKPILE COLOR CODED SCHOOL SUPPLIES

It doesn't take long for folders to rip and paper to run low. By getting your teen's school supplies organized from the beginning and staging backpack checks, you can help them stay organized and avoid missed assignments. Creating digital folders is also helpful for organization and efficiency. With the right support and materials, teens will become increasingly independent with their academics.

ONLINE CLOUD STORAGE TOOLS

Apps like Google Drive, Dropbox, and Picasa are extremely helpful for getting and staying organized. I store my university materials on Dropbox so I can effortlessly pull up slides, syllabi, assignments that need grading, or grade spreadsheets from any screen device. No more heavy book bags, lost flash drives, and aching shoulders. Cloud storage also provides backup for photos and documents in case devices get stolen, damaged, or lost.

PROJECT MANAGEMENT SYSTEMS

Apps like Google Docs, Evernote, Asana, and Trello are excellent systems to track projects and prioritize tasks. You can even work on and share projects real-time so group partners and parents can see progress and help keep track of deadlines.

ONLINE EDUCATIONAL TOOLS

There are incredible online educational tools being developed every day. Longtime favorites include *Skype* so kids can form study groups and share homework information, *Khan Academy* or *Learning Bird* for online lessons and homework help, *iTunes University* for a library of free educational resources, *StudyBlue* for user created flashcards and study guides, *XMind* or *Coggle* for mind mapping and project collaboration, and *Cold Turkey* to block apps, websites, or even the entire Internet until your work is done. Your teen's school will likely suggest a variety of tools at the beginning of the year to optimize parent communication and support. Set it up and use it!

Rest, Rejuvenation, and Self-Care

I have maintained a successful private practice over twenty-five years treating people of all ages with clinically debilitating disorders. My most powerful tool for facilitating positive change is developing a warm and trusting therapeutic alliance with my client. For adults, that means nonjudgmental acceptance and measured counsel. For kids, that means the same with more laughter and game playing sprinkled in. Once that powerful alliance is set, I teach cognitive behavioral, social, assertiveness, and study and organization skills to help my clients meet goals. Here are some quick tips to influence your teens for success.

Five Powerful Life Hacks for Success

1. Model healthy balance and self-care.

As a caregiver at heart, this is admittedly a constant struggle for me. I hate disappointing people and too often put myself as the last priority. But there is one thing that motivates me to selfishly take a step back and meet my own needs; that is the realization that my kids are watching and modeling their lives after mine. I really do not want them putting themselves last now, or when they are parents themselves.

To avoid parent burnout while also teaching your child responsibility and work ethic, assign chores. By adolescence, they are old enough to occasionally clean up, make meals, and do their own laundry. You will have to accept a job not up to your standards. But it's important that they learn, and you go hang out with friends and have a life of your own on occasion. Good sleep, exercise, and good nutrition are key to health. Also try to put your screens down when your kids are around and engage one-to-one in the present. Time alone with your teen is increasingly precious, and they need to know more than ever that they are unconditionally loved.

2. Teach work before play.

Research demonstrates that a consequence of screen multitasking is losing the ability to prioritize tasks. Kids must be taught how to set a goal then reward its completion. Binge-watching videos, movies, and television is epidemic among students. They rationalize that they deserve entertainment viewing prior to, during, and after homework. An immediate gratification expectation comes from caving to addictive screen cravings and indulgent parenting, which leads to procrastination and poor performance overall. Teach them to buckle down then reward themselves for a job well done. Sometimes the anticipation of the reward is what gets you through the task. Reward can be as simple as getting a drink of water, taking a walk, or fifteen minutes talking to a friend.

Of course, it is impossible to control a teenager. The best a parent can expect is to have some impact somewhere down the line. Teens know it all, and you are an embarrassment - you're so out of touch. Don't let their bad attitude scare you off. Set your expectations and make suggestions. Recommend task manager and timer apps, which limits access to screen entertainment until work gets done. On occasion, you may also need to practice the "give me your phone until your task is done" technique to manage follow-through.

3. **Attitude is everything.**

Positive, can-do thinking leads to confidence and achievement. Negative, stinking thinking leads to feelings of hopelessness and quitting. There is an old conundrum in psychology that questions, "Do people get depressed because of negative thinking or does negative thinking cause depression?" It turns out that both are true. Mood disorders are a combination of interacting factors

We are born with personality traits that influence the environments we seek out. We then form perceptions about those environments using our personalities and experiences. Others around us serve as mentors, also altering experience and perception. These bi-directional influences are what psychologists call *nature via nurture*. That means our environment affects our brains, and our brains affect our environments.

Habitual thinking forms neurological pathways and changes brain structure. If one engages in a lot of negative thinking, then those pathways predominate over others. So, with nature via nurture we develop perceptual sets and thinking styles that lean in the positive or negative direction. If we get too negative, we must put forth deliberate effort and use tools to help us lighten up. *Cognitive restructuring* is the act of changing negative thinking to positive thinking.

Start by observing and analyzing your *automatic thoughts* and how you interpret the world around you. When you identify negativity (which is often in the form of absolutes like "never" and "always"), replace it with more moderate and hopeful thoughts. By restructuring negative cognitions ("I can't do it") to positive cognitions ("I might succeed if I give it my all"), depression can turn to hope and eventually happiness.

Fake it 'til you make it. A positive perspective attracts good mood and opportunity.

4. **Practice mindfulness and diaphragmatic breathing.**

To make sound decisions, one must remain emotionally neutral and willing and able to listen. If you get too stressed or anxious, the autonomic nervous system triggers the *flight or fight response*. This response is made up of a series of physiological responses designed for defense. Fight or flight facilitates escape from danger, but it interferes with good decision-making and can be frightening or uncomfortable. *Anchoring* into the here and now by attending to everything you see, feel, hear, and smell is an effective *mindfulness* technique for calming fear and worry. From there, try the cognitive behavioral technique, *diaphragmatic breathing*.

Put one hand on your chest, the other on your belly. Breathe. Which hand moves the most? If you said belly, great. If you said chest, then you need to keep reading. Chest breathing can lead to *hyperventilation*, which happens when one breathes too fast and upsets the balance between taking in oxygen and breathing out carbon dioxide. Too little carbon dioxide narrows blood vessels that supply blood to the brain. This leads to uncomfortable symptoms like light-headedness, dizziness, chest pressure, yawning or belching, and numbness or tingling. In other words, your body distracts you from the task at hand. If you belly breathe, you achieve that balance. It calms the mind and the body.

Now put both hands on your belly. This posture will serve as a conditioned cue for your body that relaxation is on its way. Take one deep cleansing breath in. Exhale for six seconds. Then take an easy breath in. Again, exhale for six seconds. Breathe in easily with six second exhales to the count of ten. In through your nose, out through your mouth.

While doing this breathing technique, imagine on the first inhale that you are gathering in all the stress and tension from the tip of your toes to the top of your head. As you breathe out, imagine the stress escaping into the sky like hot air off concrete. As you breathe in again, melt into the couch. People also like to imagine breathing in one color and breathing out another. Or imagine your body filling with soothing color each time you breathe in. You can also imagine your stress level sinking down the scale, landing you into the perfect relaxation zone. Practice diaphragmatic breathing to the count of three, five, or ten whenever you can until your body relaxes on cue.

5. **Take time out for imagery and meditation.**

Imagery is as simple as closing your eyes and building a relaxing scene in your imagination by constructing everything you would see, hear, smell, and feel. If your mind drifts away, gently guide it back to the scene. Let the scene wash over you and bring peace and calm. I encourage clients to build a library of scenes, both real and fantastical. Some people even like to imagine their favorite people or spiritual beings with them for security and protection. Need more structure to keep your mind on track? The Internet is full of guided imagery and meditation techniques proven to bring rejuvenating energy and peace.

Developmental Psychology Crash Course: Children Ages Twelve to Seventeen

Tweens and teens boldly migrate from safely established family attachment to a spirited pursuit of intimate peer relationships, personal autonomy, and self-exploration and expression. Adolescence is often viewed as a turbulent time, but most teens weather it without significant problems. The challenge for parents is to alter parenting strategies from stringent management to persuasion and negotiation without damaging the parent-child relationship. Adolescence brings a more complex pattern of conflict than what we experienced with younger children. Our admiring, mostly obedient babies start to have their own ideas and carve out their own community and lifestyle, complete with online slang and noon sleep-ins. Understanding brain development during this developmental period will help you be patient during those baffling lapses in teen judgment.

Brain Development

Brain functioning from childhood and adolescence move us from critical windows ripe for learning to increasing skill specialization. With more sophisticated neurological integration, teens start to demonstrate higher order, abstract thinking characterized by better emotional stabilization and the capacity to consider the perspective of others. They can now consider several concepts at once and have increased capacity for insight and planning.

With blossoming cognitive abilities, teens aggressively, and sometimes recklessly, seek experience that will ultimately lead to the wisdom of adulthood.

Temporal (hearing and processing of speech) and prefrontal cortex (reasoning and planning) development is particularly impressive during adolescence. Temporal lobe and prefrontal cortical gray matter (brain hardware) peaks at twelve years for boys and ten to eleven years for girls, followed by a decline in volume.[82] At the same time, myelination and white matter volume continues to increase throughout adulthood. This pattern of neural development fine-tunes brain circuitry resulting in increasingly fast and efficient cognitive processes.

Impulsivity and high emotionality is particularly obvious during adolescence, partly because the prefrontal region and the limbic system (responsible for emotional self-regulation) are the last brain areas to mature. The spikes of hormones characteristic of adolescence affect the raphe nucleus (the area responsible for arousal and mood), typically resetting sleep-wake cycles. As a result, teens stay awake late at night and sleep in late in the morning.

During adolescence, we also see another surge in synaptic pruning much like the one seen during toddlerhood after primary language development. In Chapter One we learned that synapses are the gaps between the neurons where communication between brain cells take place. Synaptic pruning involves the retraction of the neuron from the synapse. By late adolescence nearly half of the synapses that were not used or damaged are eliminated to make brain functioning more efficient.[83] With fewer unnecessary wiring tangles, brain circuitry is regulated and childhood structures are replaced with the complex fibers necessary for adulthood. By twenty years old, the cortex begins to decrease in area, which continues through adulthood.[84] These peaks and declines in grey matter volumes are why parents often observe gaps in teen understanding and capacity before they "get it." Teens regress, as if they unlearned something they used to do, before taking a big step forward. It's all about the wiring!

GKIS TIP: Chronic mental illness emerges during late adolescence and early adulthood more than any other developmental period. This may happen because several risk variables co-occur for teens, revealing vulnerable brain circuits related to the onset of psychiatric disorders and addiction. This perfect storm of potential risk variables includes a high rate of growth and synaptic pruning, stress due to high achievement pressures, and emerging boldness for seeking risky, novel experience that can result in brain trauma (like violence, accidents, or drug use). For some unfortunate teens, alcohol and drug experimentation will evolve into life-long addiction patterns, because the drug co-ops the brain's pleasure center (nucleus accumbens) and simultaneously silences analysis and judgment (still-developing prefrontal region).

Recent research has uncovered a particularly unpleasant relationship between marijuana use and the emergence of schizophrenia. Chronic use of marijuana with high THC content is particularly harmful to the developing brain, because it decreases *brain derived neurotrophic factor* (BDNF). BDNF is a chemical that regulates the birth, survival, and repair of the cells that make up the brain. BDNF is responsible for what scientists call *neuroplasticity*, the adaptive processes underlying learning and memory.

If an adolescent's brain is not developing normally, smoking marijuana may make it worse.[85][86] Unfortunately, it's very difficult to identify genetic brain vulnerabilities before schizophrenia develops. That means any teen smoking marijuana is taking a risk with their mental health. Research has found that the use of marijuana by adolescents increases the chances of developing schizophrenia by 600% for heavy smokers, 400% for regular smokers, and 200% for any smoking. [87][88] Clinically we have found that if we can get clients clean from marijuana soon after they demonstrate psychotic symptomology, they have a chance of recovery rather than suffering a progressive course. This does not mean marijuana causes schizophrenia, but it may increase the chances that it will occur. I caution my patients often, why take that kind of risk with your brain health just to get high?

Cognitive and Motor Development

During adolescence, teens demonstrate a two- to three-year growth spurt that rivals the size of the one that occurred during infancy. Boys may grow as much as nine inches taller and girls as much as seven inches taller, reaching on average 98% of their adult height.[89] Teens also develop secondary sexual characteristics like breasts and hips for the girls and more musculature with wider shoulders for the boys. Girls tend to physically and cognitively mature sooner than boys.

Based on her observations of Samoan youth in the 1920s, famous sociologist Margaret Mead (1928) concluded that adolescence is not a universally volatile time.[90] She believed that cultural and social factors contributed to this belief rather than biology. Sigmund Freud (1940), on the other hand, characterized the *genital stage of development* during adolescence in which sexual drive becomes the dominant motive of behavior. He theorized that the emotional storminess of this time is due to the psychological struggle between *the id* (reawakened primitive instinct), *the ego* (the mediator), and *the superego* (societies rules and values).[91]

Impressive brain maturation enables teens to engage in abstract thinking (metacognition), take the perspective of others (facial expression recognition), and guess what others may think and do ("stepping into another's mental shoes").[92] Jean Piaget (1952) theorized that by twelve years old, kids are entering the stage of *formal operations*. This more complex method of thinking allows teens to hold ideas in mind to operate on and reason more systematically, making it possible to better imagine and plan into the future. This is called *theory of mind*. With these abilities, teens are better able to select and maintain intimate friendships and debate about everything. Theory of mind marks the beginnings of empathy, loyalty, and higher-order moral reasoning.[93]

Erik Erikson (1964) characterized adolescence as a crisis of *identity versus identity confusion*. In other words, he believed adolescents begin to develop a personal identity by reconciling beliefs, abilities, and desires with adult norms.[94] With more teachers, increasing academic expectations, and transitioning from being the oldest, most capable kids at school to newbies who must adapt to a larger social pool, teens use humor, peer pressure, and downright cruelty to coax each other to fit new social expectations. Empathy is not a strong driving force in this stage of development.

Parents of teens also enter the age range where we see the highest divorce rates. Theorists suggest this is because parents go through transition pains of their own (e.g., sandwiched between care of elderly parents and teens, menopause, and retirement) as their kids gain independence. The strain of dual developmental shifts of parent and child may be a contributor to divorce, while others were intentionally waiting to split once co-parenting responsibilities lifted. Teens undergoing family transitions along with increasing academic and social expectations have a lot to deal with indeed. As their observation and insight skills expand, their troubles become more complex. No longer are they in the cozy cuddle of parent-guarded security. They are launching into new psychological territory, which increases feelings of excitement, fear, and vulnerability. The emotions that result from a new capacity for understanding and increased expectations are intense and often overwhelming.

Language Development

With the development of metacognition (thinking about thinking), the ability to think about the past, present, and future emerges. Teen learning style becomes more versatile, with a consistent ability to make alterations in learning techniques in service of more efficiency and excellence. While developing their new identity independent from parents, teens delight in developing their own unique subcultures characterized by iconic symbols, unique styles of dress, special interests (music), private jokes, and unique "slanguage." But what today's kids have that we didn't is online interaction and less face-to-face interaction. Three ways online slang differs from offline slang include:

IMMERSION: No longer is teen social time limited by face-to-face opportunity. Now kids bond with texting and social media most of their waking hours. This means their online relationships are often more intimate and all-consuming than their offline relationships.

IMPACT: When kids post, their content may reach hundreds, thousands, or millions. The more "likes" for their image or post, the more reinforcement. That means kids customize content for shareability and impact. The language used while attaching to teen peers is more intense, shocking, and emotive, reflective of romance and hormone-driven drama.

INHIBITION: We are generally inhibited in aggression when we see our words register on our victim's face. In general, teens are bolder with their sexuality and aggression than adults. When there is a screen between those engaged in conflict, words are more hurtful and claims are more exaggerated. It's tougher to take accountability when you feel emboldened by a keyboard. As a result, cyberbullying and edgy commentary are commonplace online.

Social-Emotional Development

Adolescent interpersonal relationships have increasing influence on self-worth. The new sense of security from peer cliques in place of the traditional family and the "try-outs" and competition for these "family-like" roles can be complicated. For socially successful teens, this social feedback contributes to a global self-esteem. For less equipped or unlucky teens, this may mark an unfortunate decline in their beliefs about competency and ability.

In a study by Adler and Adler (1998), tween socialization was found to operate with the principles of social inclusion and social exclusion. One-third of tweens were incorporated in the *popular* clique, 10% sorted into the *wanna-be* group, half settled into *smaller friendship circles*, and 10% were *social isolates*. Isolates had the lowest self-esteem, followed by the wanna-bes. The popular kids felt best about themselves, and the smaller friendship circles demonstrated the best scores with friendship loyalty, security, and support.[95] These dynamics of exclusion and inclusion drive bullying offline and online. They also drive intimate sharing and connection, which may only be available online for kids unable to join peers for afterschool activities.

GKIS TIP: As peer conflicts arise, directive parental suggestions become less welcome. Advice like "just don't hang out with them" or "go to the school administration" are rarely adequate solutions and often lead to more problems than they were intended to solve. Teen frustration with perceived parent cluelessness can lead to disobedience, blatant disregard, and overall strain on the parent-teen relationship. Best parent support is listening, validating, and helping to generate possible solutions rather than giving advice or taking over. Teens must have many opportunities to try and fail to learn, achieve mastery, and gain independence.

By age fourteen, most adolescents are becoming increasingly sophisticated in their abilities to assess the complex psychological aspects of friendships, including recognizing how different personality and situational factors influence behavior. Teen friendships become more intimate with an emphasis on loyalty and popularity. Cross-gender friendships develop. Primary themes of conversation become gossip, speculation, and sexual flirting and exploration.[96] Competition for romantic partners peaks resulting in tearful dramas and broken hearts.

GKIS TIP: It is not unusual to see teens adjust to new identity issues by shifting peer groups during middle and high school. Elementary school best friends get abandoned, and cliques brutally shut out old members. Feelings of loneliness, rejection, and envy are often reflected in provocative social media posts and microblogging. Teens may try to attract a new social group by promoting a new "image," intentionally releasing racy photos to look more sophisticated or sexually experienced. One moment of lapsed judgment can be shared with thousands of friendly and rival peers, never to be recaptured or controlled.

Developing teen girls are particularly sensitive to body image and maintaining the approval of others. They often display a sizable drop in perceived self-worth and are at higher risk for clinical depression than boys. Other high-risk mental health issues may develop during this time, including mood and anxiety disorders, eating disorders, body dysmorphia, and contagious, troubling behaviors like self-harm.

Academic and athletic identities also take on central roles during adolescence. Teens who maintain sports and extracurricular activities have more positive outcomes in academic achievement, psychological health, and later involvement in political and social causes.[97] As they form identity, young teens assess "what is right" as living up to others' expectations while more advanced moral reasoners believe "what is right" is fulfilling one's duties. While building adult identity, teens take on uniquely bold perspectives and personality traits. Although these are often confusing and frustrating to parents, this collection of defenses provide the springboard for launch from family or origin to same-age peers

Child-self versus adult-self: As teens shift from dependence to independence, they demonstrate the conflict by demanding parent tending (child self) while simultaneously insisting on independence (adult self). This can be maddening seeing your capable teen responsible in some situations and other times blatantly slacking. The adult world is scary. This conflict is behind the passionate quest for security with peers while dramatically rejecting parent input. Furthermore, their new thinking skills allow them to recognize parent flaws for the first time, creating a dramatic fall from our pedestals directly into rude criticism and judgment. Parents feel taken for granted and disrespected, while teens look on baffled with false bravado. While teens can't always accept the advice of parents, other adults can often have impact. Mutual compassion and understanding is key to parent and teen survival.

Imaginary audience: Teens can become extremely focused on their looks and very self-conscious, convinced that EVERYBODY is looking at them. As a result, they pay meticulous attention to clothing, makeup, hairstyle, body shape, and mannerisms. It's as if they are carefully cultivating their brand to fit in and stand out among admired peers. Although imaginary audience has been observed among adolescents throughout history, social media may exacerbate anxiety. I believe compulsive urges to take perfect selfies are a healthy expression of imaginary audience rather than the pathology of narcissism.

Extreme embarrassment and insistence on privacy: With burgeoning sexuality and the intense hope of attracting a quality tribe, teens are often exquisitely easy to embarrass. It can be confusing to want to be their parents' baby while simultaneously taking on the image of an adult among peers. This leads to the double jeopardy of being criticized by everybody for everything. To cope, teens clumsily reject all things parent and adopt all things teen with impressively false bravado.

Theorists point out that sexual attraction makes loving feelings confusing, contributing to the rejection of opposite-gender parents and competition with same-gender parents. Teens haven't rejected kindness and acceptance, they're trying to cope with the intense feelings brought on by hormones and the stabbing pressures of peer recruitment and acceptance. In response to conflicting feelings, boys often withdraw, while girls often provoke conflict as a catharsis. The closest parent-teen pairs often struggle with intense conflict and disengage before forming a more adult-adult alliance.

Pseudostupidity: Because they're new to complex analysis and metacognition, teens often overlook the obvious while simultaneously making other things more complicated and dramatic than they need to be. It arises from brain remodeling maturation factors, losing a skill before gaining a more specialized ability. Their rookie abilities to perceive many possibilities at once without the experience to make good choices makes for baffling oversights and mistakes. It also makes for a lot of sneaking and lying. Teens pivot from blowing something off to overanalyzing. Although this can complicate otherwise simple situations, teens must learn to overanalyze before they realize that complex analysis is not always necessary. They tend to overstep before they settle into more measured, moderate positions.

An example of pseudostupidity is a teen who blows off homework while researching what college he plans to scholarship into. When confronted, he will aggressively insist he didn't blow off homework even though the evidence is there. Prepare to see your teen lying, even if there's only a remote chance he will be believed. Gaps in reasoning and decision-making is a normal consequence of healthy adolescent development, not evidence of poor morals or sociopathy.

Idealism: Not only do teens often naively assume things will work out for the positive, but this perspective allows them to challenge entrenched ideas and think outside of the box. Adolescent idealism motivates young people to courageously challenge and start social movements, as well as self-righteously lecture parents. Again, although frustratingly short-sighted, this is entirely normal.

Omnipotence and egocentrism: Without a fully developed executive control center, teens can't anticipate consequence well. As a result, they are often impulsive and take risks they probably shouldn't while being bafflingly self-involved. It's not unusual for teens to choose aggressive, passive, or passive-aggressive problem-solving means while they master assertiveness. It will be all about them until mid-adulthood.

Apparent hypocrisy: Another manifestation of teen egocentrism is their tendency to accuse others of misdeeds while blatantly dismissing their own. Maddening to parents, an example is how teens often criticize family members for selfishness while making selfish demands, or getting indignant when they aren't believed even though they're lying. Occasional correction with emotional neutrality and humor is critical to keep the parent-child alliance in balance. It's not you; it's them.

Despite their *intentional individuation* efforts from their family of origin, teens tend to share their parents' values and opinions more than you might think. But teens are skilled agents of chaos. Parents can expect moments of warm tranquility inexplicably followed by enraged demands and utter hopelessness. Caught blindsided, parents are often paralyzed - having to immediately decide whether to patiently acquiesce or set firm limits that will certainly escalate the situation. Allowing bad behavior seems like you're not doing your job, but constantly calling teens out is not sustainable and sparks resentment.

During this turbulent time, the more warm, supportive, and clearly communicative the parental support system, the more likely teens will demonstrate resilience. As teens push back, skilled parents adopt a more *democratic parenting style*, patiently allowing teens more of a voice in making decisions. In general, teens DO NOT do well in families where the parents are inconsistently present, have given up (too permissive), or who helicopter intrusively and threaten corporal punishment (too authoritarian). They DO fare well with parents who gradually allow them opportunity to grow and experiment with warm support and understanding (authoritative parenting).

GKIS TIP: In clinical practice, I often see families struggle with the child-to-adolescent transition, especially with families where parents have been highly involved in their children's overall decision making. As teens branch out in search of independent experiences, parents may naïvely perceive adolescent behaviors as intentional defiance and betrayal. For example, teens often become secretive about their peer life and frankly sneaky and defiant, purposely shutting parents out for more opportunity and as an expression of peer loyalty. Parents feel disrespected and may demand that the teen return to openness and sharing. These demands are futile. When parents become too heavy handed and punish teen independence (like yanking screen time), the parent-child alliance can be damaged with resentment, anger, and guilt.

When your teen was younger, you had to turn away from his or her demands to avoid whiney escalation. With teens, parent strategy must change. One must give respect to get it back. Now parents must listen and negotiate with patient authority. Urgent teen plans happen last-minute and their numerous activities and responsibilities often fall to the parents for help with planning, funding, and transportation. Be prepared to have your life waylaid and often! An early-formed parent-child alliance and consistent understanding, faith, and a sense of humor are critical for success.

Did you know the term *parenting* didn't even exist before the 1970s? After all, we don't say wifeing or husbanding or daughtering. In all other relationships, we don't act upon others but acknowledge a bidirectional give-and-take. With the modern concept of parenting, we often overstep our roles as parents and hammer our kids to be who we think they need to be. We take their disappointments and failures too much as our own. It's important, especially during this phase of development, to recognize that our kids are individuals with personalities, dreams, and capabilities uniquely their own. Sometimes their growing pains have little to do with us, and it's not our job to take over or get involved.

Parents of teens still need to set limits, of course, but also listen and consider the situation more thoroughly before supplying an answer. Sometimes teens have to experience failure first-hand to learn, and parents need to let them. Keep in mind, your worth is not dependent on your child's outcome. You need to let them fail sometimes even if it's a heartbreak to watch. A lot of peer support is for parents and teens to pull this off day-to-day.

Despite the challenges they pose to us, teens have the key to my heart. I admire their brash courage and quick-to-trigger vulnerabilities. As they strive for an independent identity and experiment with their power, teens need to know that we won't let go of the rope. They count on us to hold on with our hard-earned wisdom, patience, and understanding no matter how much they thrash and challenge. The struggle will subside. Until then, meet them where they are. Hold them accountable, yet give them safe space to find themselves among the chaos of distractions online and offline. To meet them among the digital debris, you first must be aware of screen benefits and risks.

CHAPTER 5: THE BENEFITS OF SCREEN USE

Screen technology saturates our lives and has exploded our capacity to learn and innovatively produce in ways never seen in history. Science fiction is no longer fiction. We are officially cyborgs. We outsource our capabilities to our screens in ever-expanding ways, to the point that few of us function without screens in hand throughout our waking day. We use our screens to increase our capacity for learning, memory, communication, calculation, and access to information and entertainment. Kids effortlessly and intuitively live multitasking, mobile screen lifestyles, expertly creating and consuming fragments of digital content at lightning fast speed more hours a day than is spent in face-to-face nonvirtual time. Teachers are changing the way they teach, kids are changing the way they play, and parents are changing the way they task. Our brains are rewiring and expanding to accommodate our tech connectivity as we simultaneously manage multiple parallel universes and many nonvirtual and virtual identities, each connected to its own community of networked others. We risk being overtasked and overextended, yet also live richly multifaceted lives because of technology.

Technology has made such a profound impact that it has been used to describe a generation. Born to *X-gens* (born between 1965 and 1979) and *millennials* (between 1980 and 1995), *iGens* are changing the world.[98][99] Other terms for our children's generation include *screenagers*,[100] *digital natives*,[101] *the net generation*,[102] and *risk kids*.[103] This generation has unique characteristics unlike any before them.

Jean Twenge (2014) describes ten trends that shape the iGen generation. These include *in no hurry* (the extension of childhood into adolescence), *Internet* (its profound impact), *in person no more* (virtual identity more prominent than nonvirtual identity), *insecure* (sharp rise in mental health issues), *irreligious, insulated but not intrinsic* (more safety less civic involvement), *income insecurity, indefinite* (new attitudes regarding sex, marriage, and having children), *inclusive* (acceptance, equality, and free speech), and *independent.*[104] IGen kids have been raised largely on a diet of screen content, inspiring a generational divide between kids and parents that has had profound worldly impact.

Corporate structures have also undergone a paradigm shift due to technology, producing innovation, discovery, and service never before dreamed of. No longer are there just businesses with a physical product to sell (*asset builders* like Walmart) or *service providers* (like JP Morgan), there are now companies that develop and sell intellectual property (*technology creators* like Microsoft) and those that bring a network of peers together to collaborate and create a product or service (*network orchestrators* like Uber).[105] Technology is so profoundly influential in today's marketplace that network orchestrators outperform all other business types in revenue and profits. Collaborative ideas have become more valuable than physical products. Automation, robotics, and machine learning has globalized a remote and efficient workforce. Today's smartphone is in the hands of two thirds of the global population and is millions of times more powerful than all of NASA's combined computing in 1969. Amazing! What other benefits do today's families enjoy due to screen technology?

Effective, Ecological, Economical Learning Tool

Recently our local, public middle school issued free electronic tablets to all middle school students for school and home use. Immediately students were offered worldwide information access and creation independent of caregiver and educator mediation. Parents and schools are saving money, fewer natural resources are required, and, most importantly, the kids LOVE IT. They spend more time researching, analyzing, and creating than ever before.

Psychological research supports this shift, conclusively demonstrating that *edutainment* screen activities help us learn. Research concludes that preschool children who watch educational TV are better prepared for school, are more likely to keep up academically, and are higher achievers all the way to high school.[106][107][108] Children who watch prosocial TV programs demonstrate more kindness towards peers and animals. Internet use has also been found to lead to higher standardized test scores in reading achievement and higher grade point averages in the short- (six months) and long term (sixteen months later).[109] Quality screen learning may even be equal to, or better than, nonvirtual classroom time, as illustrated in a 2015 study which concluded that growth produced from watching was equal to learning in a preschool classroom.[110]

Other learning facilitated by screen time include *visual intelligence* (monitoring lots of visual stimuli at once, recognizing icons, reading diagrams, and visualizing special relationships),[111][112] self-monitoring, pattern recognition, and visual memory,[113] multitasking and managing attention,[114] and the development of social-emotional skills like empathy and calming.[115][116][117][118]

Through prosocial interactional experiences in a virtual world, children learn social cues, norms, and skills that they can apply in different settings, as well as identify how their actions affect others. Video games provide a fertile resource for learning team building and cooperative problem solving and connecting kids that may otherwise feel marginalized to valuable others. In a study by O'Connor (2015), online gamers reported feelings of community and belonging while playing online, elaborating that the social support helped them feel more confident and develop a more positive social identity.[119]

It also turns out that, for better or worse, kids intuitively seek different types of content at different ages. With their limited ability to understand complex plots and social situations, younger children choose and watch more educational and informational television programs, whereas older children, who are developmentally mastering social skills, prefer entertainment programming. Because television broadcasters and video game developers know this, there is less educational content and more entertainment targeted at older kids.

In regard to quality of viewing, older children learn more from all types of programming. As cognitive abilities develop, kids are increasingly able to identify factors relevant to the central plot, recognize order as the story scheme, draw inferences about the feelings and motivations of the characters, and recognize cause-effect relationships within the program. Kids most often report learning social-emotional lessons from TV, followed by information, physical wellbeing, and cognitive skills lessons.[120] Because screens contribute to learning, the digital divide between poor and rich families is increasingly concerning. Technological education advocacy and funding is critical to close that gap. Parenting strategies also have a huge impact on how and if kids benefit from screen time.

Factors That Impact Screen Learning

Developmental Match

Make sure your kids are interacting with a variety content created for their age level,. Fortunately, big brand companies like Google, Facebook, and Amazon have recognized the need for specially designed child-centered products. Rather than handing over screen devices designed for adults, parents can provide more appropriate child products designed with developmental match, customized educational feed, and safety in mind. A safer edutainment safety portal, popularly called a *walled garden*, is a relatively new and welcome development. Parents must be particularly discriminating for young children.

A well-managed and balanced digital diet is critical for brain health. There is evidence that age-appropriate media enhances expressive language for infants and toddlers and facilitates learning for all ages.[121] However, too much screen use is also associated with developmental delay, poor self-regulation, and lower cognitive development and academic achievement.[122][123] As we learned from the research that demonstrated the multimillion dollar-earning Baby Einstein series had no educational value, we must not rely on slick marketing information alone. We need more quality research pertain to child screen use in the areas of language, math, functional skills, motor skills, creativity, and more.

Interactive Versus Passive Screen Time

In general, interactive screen activities, like video conferencing and touch media, elicits more interest in learning and drives deeper research and analysis than passive viewing. As your child self-selects more advanced content, she forms neurological scaffolding for later learning. Storing information today leads to better understanding and concept retrieval later. Since our brains "remodel" throughout the lifespan with a "use it or lose it" system, screen can enrich experiences and build new neuronal pathways, resulting in deeper and more varied learning potential. Interactive games may also improve gross and fine motor, spatial, and coordination skills, particularly when outside play is not possible.[124]

Pace and Formatting

Pace matters. Concepts that are delivered in small, organized doses result in more integrated learning than a flood of frenetic, rapidly paced content. Too much frenetic content can hyper-arouse the autonomic nervous system and may even damage brain synapses due to chronic stress.

Have memorization drills preparing for tests strained your family relations? Specially designed study apps and programs can be an awesome option for academic preparedness.[125]

Co-Engagement

Co-viewing and talking through concepts with loving, responsive caregivers enriches learning, teaches important interpersonal skills like empathy and emotional soothing, and deepens the parent-child alliance. The more involved a parent is in mediating screen time, the higher the child's education attainment.[126] Employed mothers have been found to provide more instruction of Internet skills and models of information management with their kids, leading to enhanced opportunities for self-directed cognitive development.[127][128] There is simply no replacement for love and one-to-one attention, even in the presence of screens.

School-Mediated Information Access, Format Variety, and Instructional Skill Building

What once took hours to locate in an encyclopedia series in the library is now available online in seconds. Want to see a neighborhood across the world? Google Earth can provide that for you. How about a video chat with someone thousands of miles away? No problem, just use your mobile phone. Need to access content while video chatting? Your browser is ready and waiting. Expounding on concepts occurs at lightning speed, which creates a vast scaffolding of mastery to build upon.

Not only are kids constantly learning on their own, but teachers have also expanded their repertoire incorporating a dizzying array of online tools geared for improved student learning and communication. At California State University Channel Islands, we use a kit of free online tools, including an online portal, that allows students access to course materials and announcements, discussion boards, collaborative chats, file shares, collaborative living documents, grade books, and opportunities to complete, share, and submit assignments, quizzes, and tests. If students run across an article or video that relates to course material, they can email or post it within seconds.

My curriculum builds real time with content my students self-select and upload. They have access to library materials at a stroke of a key and can upload articles immediately. As a student of the 1980s, I cannot tell you how many hours I spent revising on typewriters and walking the library stacks at UCLA, pulling and packing backbreaking stacks of bound journal articles to copy page by page. I would go home poorer, exhausted, and reeking of fresh ink and wasted time. My students are rescued of these tedious tasks.

Not only do they research online, they also download the product directly with a tool that detects original versus cited or plagiarized content. *Turnitin*, a submission program that compares student work with published content, boasts, "Our database contains 45+ billion web pages, 337+ million student papers and 130+ million articles from academic books and publications." Mind blowing!

Screen content even proliferates the nonvirtual classroom. No longer do students take notes with pen and paper listening to a lecturer at a podium. Professors use multimedia platforms to illustrate complex concepts through animation, images, video, text audio, and graphics, such as mind maps. Slides, complete with embedded video and links, allow students to listen and embellish notes as they listen from their keyboards.

Textbooks are also more efficiently updated, available for digital lease, and cheaper to use. Students can share blog articles, use hash tags to facilitate discussions, and carry one simple tablet instead of a backbreaking load of textbooks and wrinkled notebook papers. I've even had authors and educators teleconference in from other countries, bringing humor and expertise to my California classroom from a flat in London or home in Scotland. Interns have convenient access to me through text and email, and we group teleconference while working on the same document using Google Docs. We edit and comment on each other's writings, offering valuable feedback and supporting each other's confidence. I believe that the most important goal of formal education is infecting the student with a love of learning that will continue throughout a lifetime. Attention-grabbing, fun, convenient screens help that happen in profound and effective ways.

Many schools have even adopted innovate teaching structures, using afterschool time for reading and viewing instructional videos and class time for teacher-facilitated assignment completion. This allows more passive preparation at home and deeper analysis and application in the classroom. Student projects rarely involve poster board presentations anymore. Teachers assign papers, video projects, musical compositions, class presentations, and graphic compositions for homework, all of which are technology-assisted.

It's not just teacher efforts that impact technology-assisted learning. Parent attitude about technology matters too. How a family perceives technology in the home largely determines the expertise and use by the kids. Facer and colleagues (2003) use three metaphors to illustrate family integration of technology into the home. *The children's machine* refers to parents who are largely inexperienced with technology, but understand its necessary role in their children's future. *Computer as interloper* refers to technology resistants who believe computers conflict with family values, creating conflict between generations. *Computer at the heart of the family* refers to technology as a shared and collaborative tool between parents and children.[129] Other terms to describe technology integration within the home include *media light, media moderate,* and *media centric.*[130] *Screen Time in the Mean Time* was written to help parents become collaborative facilitators of technology-aided learning rather than resentful observers. Connection to tech and to each other raises healthy, happy kids. Overcoming the digital divide is important, indeed.

Home Tech Tools for Instructional Skill Building and Career Development

Each student has unique learning potential. No one teacher fits all students, and no one online platform resonates with all kids. Video browsing, binge television watching, and specialty learning sites, like *Kahn Academy* ("For Free. For Everyone. Forever"), allow kids to self-select their learning level and pace, just pause and rewind. Skill building isn't limited to academic subjects. Kids can look up anything from building a radio to whether shampooing their hamster is a good idea. Refrigerator leaking? Skip the expensive home repair call. Joe Schmo from Alabama had the same issue and videoed the solution for you. A blow dryer and a paperclip later, problem solved.

Digital literacy is necessary to be a successful influencer in the career world. For instance, imagine a second-grade classroom that encourages little entrepreneurs to use their tablet to sketch a product, create a business plan, develop a budget, and carry through with public relations and marketing ideas. After accruing money credits, a shopping day is staged where students hold their very own marketplace selling their products to each other! Itty bitty ones are learning to be savvy vendors and informed consumers.

During a recent GetKidsInternetSafe live presentation to parents, a mom expressed that she was sad that teens put so much value on social media likes, suggesting that these aren't "real" quality relationships. With the support of a university student in the audience, I respectfully suggested that social media *like* collections illustrate that teen social media mavens are learning extremely valuable life skills, such as forming relationships and influencing others. What may seem like empty adulation to us is also effective branding practice that teaches students what types of content has value to others. Who among us don't thrive under that type of positive feedback? Passing interests quickly expand into passions, innovative products, and marketable life skills. Education, innovation, design, and marketing with screen technology is readily available and fun and easy to use.

Communication: Access, Clarity, Immediacy, and Dissemination

Each of us, but particularly teens, is networked online as well as offline. Our influence is no longer limited to our homes, schools, workplaces, and neighborhoods. We have access to unlimited numbers of others worldwide, immediately. We are not only connected through voice, we also video chat and game with any set of characteristics we choose for our avatar. Our virtual identities and nonvirtual identities are fluid and constantly expanding.

Kids have access to hordes of potential tribesmen, often forming very intimate friendships with other kids that live far away. Virtual relationships provide limitless hours of contact in a medium that is less anxiety provoking when sharing personal thoughts and feelings face to face. Teens do homework with virtual buddies and fall asleep with them on their pillows. This level of access and intimacy among young people is unprecedented and exposing them to an entirely new avenue of intensity in relationships.

Another modern phenomenon used for connection, discovery, and innovation is crowdsourcing. *Crowdsourcing* is the practice of engaging others online in a task characterized by cooperative directives and information gathering. With inexpensive and immediate access to a diverse crowd, one can work on a collaborative problem with real-time flexibility. *Amazon Mechanical Turk* is a crowdsourcing Internet marketplace that allows individuals and businesses (requesters) to request others (workers) to perform a task unique to human intelligence. Examples of crowdsourcing tasks include missing person searches, research surveys, collaborative art, mechanical, and education projects, medical diagnoses, and third-party programming.

Entertainment

One would have to live in a cave to be unaware that screens are a dominant source for entertainment among kids, teens, and adults. According to a survey conducted by Common Sense Media, teens spend an average of 8.56 hours online per day, with 66% of the time listening to music, 58% watching television, 45% using social media, 34% watching videos, 27% playing mobile video games, and 19% reading. Thirty-nine percent involves passive consumption of media such as listening to music, watching television or video, or reading, while 26% is communicating with others through social media or video chatting, 25% involves interactive consumption like playing games, browsing, or interacting with websites, and 3% is creation like making digital art, composing music, writing, or programming. In general, boys tend to prefer gaming and girls prefer social media.

Documentation and Storage

Shelves that were once packed with books, DVDs, photo albums, and stereo and speaker components are now replaced with screen devices. Cloud backups and flash drives make data backup effortless and seamless. Organization is a breeze. Even materials for artistic, musical, and innovative creation is digital. Access and creative inspiration is at our fingertips.

Not only are our homes less cluttered with learning and entertainment materials, but entire buildings are being repurposed in favor of screens. For example, because technology has provided library materials online, the physical spaces of community and school libraries are being repurposed for new setups called *makerspaces*. These creative work spaces incorporate nonvirtual and virtual elements for creation like 3-D printers, green screens for movie making, tables that come together for cooperation and collaboration, and unique materials for architecture and design. Other activities include three-dimensional model building with blocks, Legos, clock or industrial parts, wood, repurposed computer parts, or cardboard, programming and hacking, sewing or knitting, drawing, writing, or music composing. Makerspace time may be teacher-led or student-led. Maybe it's a time to simply tinker. With space made free from obsolete storage needs, opportunities for designing, engineering, creating, and testing prototypes of manufactured projects has become possible. Many makerspaces even bring in mentors from manufacturing, engineering, architecture, and tech sectors in the community. Exciting indeed.

Safety: Monitors, Tracking, and Data Gathering

Another benefit of screen use is our ability to monitor behavior and technology use (e.g., time on task for children, students, or employees), track progression, and gather immediate data for optimally targeted research or learning. One application for this real-time tasking data is to use it to feed the appropriate learning material to screen users real time. For example, not only can a parent or teacher see WHAT a child is doing online, they can also track HOW the child is problem solving and performing. This data then allows the child customized intervention and paced material level access.

As a simple illustration, if children are reading at a second-grade level and pass a test or illustrate sufficient progress, they can opt to move up to a harder challenge level. If they do not pass the test or show sufficient progress, they will be offered more practice at the second-grade reading level. With this real-time data tracking, each student receives a customized program based on real-time performance without having to wait for others or get left behind. Self-directed learning is more fun and engaging, promising higher levels of mastery. Furthermore, with increased data collection available, we have outcome data that illustrates solutions that work rather than implementing costly solutions we guessed might work, but never had opportunity to test.

Innovation and Discovery: Virtual Reality, The Internet of Things, Artificial Intelligence, and Automation

Einstein once said, "Imagination is more important than knowledge. For knowledge is limited, whereas imagination embraces the entire world, stimulating progress, giving birth to evolution." Today's modern world has already been proliferated by the interdependence between our nonvirtual and virtual worlds. Innovation has no real description when it comes to technology and screen media. Our brains simply cannot anticipate what is possible.

Consider navigation apps and virtual reality. Who would have ever imagined the possibilities of convenient walking or driving apps in all vehicles and in your hand? My first experience with a virtual reality wearable surprised me in its capability for cooperative play. With my goggles directed at the television screen, I scanned a virtual kitchen with my lightning weapon in-hand as my kids, who weren't wearing goggles, shouted where and when to shoot at ghosts visible only to them. My hand-held remote vibrated, the screen flashed wildly, and loud buzzy noises filled my ears. This was a wonderful mix of being isolated in my virtual world while my nonvirtual children hollered tips and tricks from the nonvirtual world. Crazy.

Virtual and augmented reality technology is used for *digital immersion reality training*, to train workplace skills like surgery and law enforcement response. Imagine several police officers in a media room, each wearing 360-degree virtual reality headsets. Each unit shows the perspective of its own officer interacting with the other officers in shooting training scenarios. Each officer is making real-time decisions that affect the decisions of the other training participants. Not only does technology allow immersive training experiences with more intensity and less expense, but it can also be used from the convenience of home.

An interesting debate about the benefits versus the risk of technology arises from the issue of *data mining* the Internet of Things. *The Internet of Things* refers to the Internet-connected network of everyday products (cars, appliances, toys) that collect customer data via sensors, software, and Internet connectivity for corporate and government efficiency, accuracy, and economic benefit. This data is then used to develop new products and skills, improve user experience, or service devices without costly gaps in poor functioning.

Already we have smart televisions that collect conversations from your living room to provide you with targeted programming and advertising. *Smart toys* (toys that simulate intelligence by interacting with and adapting to the actions of the user by gathering data from a microphone, camera, or censors), *connected toys* (toys that are connected via the Internet that collect, use, and share data), and *smart connected* (like *toys to life*, *robots*, and *virtual reality wearables*) are also in the market.[131] These toys act as smart playmates for our kids with teaching capacities far beyond same-age peers. Therapeutic robots are also used for therapy with autistic children or for demented clients in memory care. There are real issues of privacy here, which will be discussed in Chapter Six. Imagine the enrichment these smart, connected objects provide for youth and adults alike.

Machine learning is the technology where machines learn real time from the constant analysis of patterns within collected data. No explicit programming is needed. An example is the driverless car, expected to be commonplace within the next ten years. Imagine how data about mapping, traffic patterns, and potholes or road obstacles delivered immediately could help with city upkeep and driver experience. Immediate and complex delivery targets the problems so solutions can be generated before more cost accrues, no time-consuming and expensive room for human error. In your real life, face recognition technology, credit card fraud detection, and Netflix and Amazon targeted offers are already happening through machine learning.

The human-robot interface really pushes the concept of cyborg. For example, one innovation in development that is literally life giving is *telesurgery*, which offers cost effective accuracy and access. We also have wearable clothing that sends pulses of stimulation between the nervous system and *anthropormorphic robot hands* that move paralyzed limbs for other-abled people is what is called the *hapsuit*. This suit works like a robot skin, moving your limbs and offering function to paralyzed muscles. It can stimulate all senses from movement, temperature, feel, scent, sound, and sight.

There is even a whole creepy industry revolving around simulated virtual sex with a robot, between remotes, or within a virtual reality world with avatars and celebrities. *Cyberdildontics* is an industry aimed at providing mutual remote sexual stimulation for long distance relationships, like advanced phone sex. Sexual gaming, called *3-d Chat,* where players' avatars interact and ultimately have graphic, animated sex, has also blossomed into a lucrative industry. Tired of the drama that results from real life women? No problem. Japanese and American manufacturers of ultra-realistic silicon sex dolls, called Dutch wives, are currently selling at a rate of 2,000 a year. Google it, and you'll see images of men taking their dolls shopping for jewelry and sexy lingerie. The American company, Sinthetics, advertises male and female love dolls with bionic private parts capable of responding to verbal communication "for the ultimate pleasure experience." Is it possible that in fifty years we will prefer computer-simulated or mediated sex over nonvirtual sex? This gives a whole new facet to the computer virus.

Robotic automation has also changed manufacturing, placing robots in factory and service positions that are too tedious or dangerous for human beings. The debate continues whether robots are taking our jobs or filling positions that nobody wants while opening those we do want. Discovery has exploded with possibility with underwater drones identifying new ocean life and satellite surveillance identifying Earth's ancient archeological sites from space.

With technology moving so quickly, it's impossible to guess what will be available in the near future. Telepathy due to implanted chips in our brain? Human cloning for organ replacement? Time travel? Colonization on other planets? Only the future will tell what wonders technology has in store.

The mind-blowing benefits of screen technology ensure that it's not going away. Along with benefits come risks.

CHAPTER 6: THE RISKS OF SCREEN USE: EXPLOITATION FOR PROFIT

Despite the profoundly positive impact of screen technology, there are also three risk categories for digital injury: *exploitation for profit, interpersonal exploitation, and health risks*. When discussing the influences behind new cultural developments with my university classes, there are two answers that crop up most often, "for profit" and "because of individual freedoms." "How did big tobacco get away with so little accountability decades after it was discovered that cigarettes cause cancer?" – "Because of profit." "Why do we continue to lose the drug war despite billions of dollars and decades of committed effort?" – "Because of freedoms." Just as corporate and street thieves and drug dealers successfully peddle products for profit among a population that enjoys protected individual liberties, so do advertisers, violence merchants, and online pornographers.

Product Marketing

Social media operates from the old adage, "If you can't see the product, you are the product." After recent scandals like that involving Cambridge Analytica and Facebook, users have become increasingly aware of how big tech companies collect, buy, and sell disturbing amounts of information about us. Aggregated consumer information is called *big data*, and it contributes to big profit. To keep tracking people once they leave Facebook, engineers created the *Facebook pixel*, which is installed on millions of websites and records what you do online and reports that data back to Facebook. the targeted Ads Division of Facebook can track where you visit online, how long you linger on a page, what is in your website shopping court, and whether you decided to buy or not, among other information.

Websites often have many of these ad trackers surveilling your online activity. The data generated from online tracking has been referred to as *digital exhaust*, because clusters of trackers can follow you from site to site. In addition to information collected from tracking, Facebook buys personal information about its users from one of many services like Experian and Equifax. The specific data purchased is unclear, but may include information like your income, marital status, what you buy and how often you buy from loyalty cards, the square footage of your house, and up to 52,000 personal attributes about you. Facebook can also track where you travel and who you interact with online, and will then repeatedly retarget you with ads about the products and interests you've shown interest in, that are popular in that region, and those that your friends and friends of friends show interest in. Companies like Facebook have not been particularly transparent about the information they collect about us.[132]

Not only are adults targeted for ads, but the digital age has ushered in an increasing commercialization of childhood as well. Because of a dramatic increase in personal screen privatization (child Internet use without supervision) and unregulated corporate marketing, an enormous growth in advertising targets children. In 2006, the Federal Trade Commission reported that food and beverage companies spent 20 billion dollars on advertising targeting children; often involving cross-promotion with movies or popular television programs.[133] With an increasing number of advertising hubs, including YouTube, Netflix, websites, gaming systems, smartphones, MP3 players, DVDs, tablets, and television, that number is now far higher. With that level of spending resulting in a trillion consumer dollars annually in profit, you can be sure that the most sophisticated marketing strategies money can buy are aimed at your kids. What are some red flags to look out for?

Seven Ways Internet Marketers Are Grooming Our Kids to Be Paying Customers

1. Appealing branding, design, and calls to action

When children visit Internet sites with linked cross-platforms, they can expect appealing characters, celebrities, storylines, games, puzzles, contests, toys, group activities, and videos, all branded, to keep them engaged for lots of exposure to different marketing strategies. All are designed to build brand loyalties at an early age. Featured elements, like colorful moving banners and popups, are designed to attract and keep the child's eye. Most powerful are the *calls to action* (CTAs), BUY NOW, GO NOW, SHOP NOW, PLAY NOW, LEARN MORE, with promises of discounts and extra value to start pester power. One quick click on the convenient and attractive merchant buy button, and money is immediately drained from your bank account.

2. **Tricky images and fake news**

Products are linked to healthy images and fake news reports to trick consumers into thinking they are purchasing a product that is healthy, when it actually has no connection to the healthy image (e.g., pairing fruit images with a sugary cereal). Just because it's visually attractive, does not mean it is better quality.

3. **The *illusion of scarcity* and *need for immediacy***

Offers that are limited in number or available "today only" make us anxious to buy immediately, thinking we must buy NOW or will lose our chance.

4. **Neuromarketing strategies and targeted offers**

Neuromarketing research uses data gathered from screen use and brain scans to measure how we react to certain stimuli. Factors like the frequency of visits, time spent on particular sites, how and when we move the cursor, and our cognitive and emotional reactions to what we seek and see are measured, collected, analyzed, and applied. With psychological information about brain response to stimuli and information gathered by ad trackers, advertisers know what we seek and how we respond better than we even know. Adults, and particularly children, are mostly blind to these manipulations.

5. **Variable ratio of reinforcement**

Learning theory teaches us that if you provide reward, it reinforces (increases) behavior. The rate that reinforcement is delivered affects the strength and rate of response. *Variable ratio of reinforcement* means the response is reinforced after an unpredictable, or variable, number of responses. Sometimes you get a reward after two responses, sometimes ten responses, sometimes five responses, etc. There is no set pattern. Slot machines are set with a variable ratio of reinforcement, because it keeps people playing longer. Gaming companies apply a variable ratio of reinforcement within gaming and website design to keep players playing longer and more willing to spend money on products. This can lead to compulsive use and overspending.

6. Surveys and eliciting identifying information

Commercial websites will not always stop at passive consumption from your children. Many survey and elicit identifying information and consumer preference from your children to better target them with content they want.[134]

7. Pester power

Internet marketers aim to create *pester power*, which refers to a child's ability to nag parents into buying. Sadly, that boils down to potential conflict within the family (child anxiety, parental guilt and frustration, and eventual capitulation) to make a buck. If there are profits to be made, advertising dollars are behind it, even if it is to the child's detriment. Examples of unhealthy behaviors heavily influenced by advertisers include dieting and body image problems, processed, high-sugar fast foods, tobacco and alcohol use, excessive gaming, violent entertainment, materialistic celebrity culture, and buying, buying, buying.

Two other issues are worth mentioning when it comes to child-targeted online content and content that may be accidentally viewed by young children. The first is that cartoons are commonly pirated and placed on websites other than the original branded websites. When this happens, the viewer cannot count on quality control when they search for their favorite characters. Pirated content attracts views and inspires troll-created copycat videos full of violent, sexual, and vulgar content, typical of content shared on *4chan* (a website with theme-related image boards frequented by anonymous users). That means little ones go online to see a Peppa Pig Visits the Dentist video and inadvertently view the copycat version of Peppa being tortured by a dentist as Peppa screams.

The second issue is that low-quality, algorithmically-guided content is being created without human input anywhere in the feedback loop. We have outsourced so much to bots, like data generation and content creation, that weird, inappropriate videos combining popular features get created and published without human eyes screening quality. James Bridle's 2017 whistle-blowing article further points out that we can no longer tell when content is computer- rather than human-generated. "Someone or something or some combination of people and things is using YouTube to systematically frighten, traumatize, and abuse children, automatically and at scale, and it forces me to question my own beliefs about the internet, at every level." [135]

Although YouTube recently announced policy changes to disallow monetization of inappropriate content, copycat videos still get through to children even on safety filtered YouTube Kids. To remove inappropriate videos from YouTube, a viewer must flag the content for YouTube moderator review. That means accidental views by kids may happen long before it is taken down.

Young children lack the insight and communication skills necessary to rescue themselves from disturbing content once it is placed in front of them. Even when trained, children under eight years old lack the cognitive ability to view commercials and videos defensively. That means kids will choose commercial and pirate websites for entertainment with equal frequency as a noncommercial site. Developmentally, children have limited ability to understand the vocabulary, sentences, and inference-drawing required for these discriminating analytic skills. For them, visual aspects dominate informational aspects. Education and skill building is worthwhile with all ages, but children younger than eight years old are limited in their ability to protect themselves without active parent supervision and direct participation.[136]

In the last thirteen years, people within and outside the field of psychology have begun to speak out about concerns that young children are being specifically targeted by advertisers, particularly on the unregulated Internet. The *American Psychological Association (APA)* released a special task force report on children and advertising addressing these concerns. They concluded, among other things, that

> *"Advertising that is unfair or that promotes the use of harmful products does a disservice to children"* ... *"Given the significant role played by advertiser-supported media in the lives of the nation's children, it is time to move forward with new policies that will better protect the interests of children and new research that will address the vast array of unanswered questions in this important topic area. The stakes are too high to ignore these issues or their impact on the nation's youth."[137]*

The APA task force made several recommendations to address this Internet marketing problem, including restricting advertising primarily directed to audiences of children eight years of age and under and to develop media literacy curricula for all school grade levels from third through twelfth. Because the *First Amendment* protects our freedom of expression without undue government influence, it is not realistic to expect heavy legislation that will regulate the Internet enough to protect our kids and teens from skilled marketing tactics. Instead, parents and educators must manage screen use with filtering, monitoring, and rules, as well as educate children so they can recognize strategies and build skills for common sense resistance. Remember, however, there is a limit to effectiveness based on developmental capabilities. Expecting that education is enough to keep kids from craving Internet use and purchases puts unfair expectations on children, much like blaming the victim.

Rather than counting on our legislators to take up the challenge, a grass roots movement is necessary. Recent changes in child nutrition are an excellent example of how change can start at home and lead to effective progress within the broader community (e.g., banned soft drinks in California elementary and middle schools and offering healthier food choices in school lunch programs). What do you think about formal Internet regulations? Should government step in or is it the parents' responsibility? How much regulation is too much? Is there enough regulation already?

Existing regulations that help keep kids Internet safe:

FERPA: The Family Educational Rights and Privacy Act (1974)

FERPA is a Federal law that protects the privacy of student education records. The law applies to all schools that receive funds under an applicable program of the U.S. Department of Education. FERPA gives parents certain rights with respect to their children's education records. These rights transfer to the student when he or she reaches the age of 18 or attends a school beyond the high school level.

CTA: The Children's Television Act (1990)

CTA was enacted by the Federal Communications Commission (FCC) to give parents better information, more clearly define core educational programming, and increase the amount of children's television programming. Since CTA was implemented, access to quality children's television programming in the US has improved with genuinely positive result. This regulation was developed due to a grass roots movement by concerned parents.

COPPA: The Children's Online Privacy Protection Act (1998)

This federal law imposes certain requirements on operators of websites or online services from collecting data from or advertising to children under 13 years of age.

CIPA: The Children's Internet Protection Act (2000)

CIPA was enacted by Congress in 2000 to address concerns about children's access to obscene or harmful content over the Internet. CIPA imposes certain requirements on schools or libraries that receive discounts for Internet access or internal connections through the E-rate program – a program that makes certain communications services and products more affordable for eligible schools and libraries. In early 2001, the FCC issued rules implementing CIPA and provided updates to those rules in 2011.

DOPA: Deleting Online Predator's Act (2006)

This bill was proposed in an effort to amend the Communications Act of 1934 to require schools and libraries that receive E-rate funding to create restrictions and the ability to temporarily disable them to block unsupervised children from accessing "commercial social networking sites" and "chat rooms." DOPA was controversial in that it limited access to websites, despite universal agreement that blocking predators was beneficial. It passed in Congress but died in the Senate when Republican majority transferred to Democrat majority.

SOPIPA: The Student Online Personal Information Protection Act (2016)

This bill would prohibit an operator of an Internet website, online service, online application, or mobile application from knowingly engaging in targeted advertising to students or their parents or legal guardians using covered information to amass a profile about a K–12 student, selling a student's information, or disclosing covered information, as provided. The bill would require an operator to implement and maintain reasonable security procedures and practices appropriate to the nature of the covered information, to protect the information from unauthorized access, destruction, use, modification, or disclosure, and to delete a student's covered information if the school or district requests deletion of data under the control of the school or district.

How does regulation impact our kids when they use screen technology at school?

Public schools must meet federal and statutory requirements when it comes to protecting student data and student access to content. As a result, schools generally take student privacy seriously. If student data is required for use beyond its educational aspect (e.g., advertising or research through a digital resource vendor like Google or Discovery Education), school districts must obtain parental consent. It also means that schools must take student online safety seriously. School-issued mobile screen devices can be used for academic use or entertainment. The school district is therefore obligated, to the best of their ability, to filter inappropriate online content.

Schools typically choose from specialty filtering software for all screen content with the goal of blocking harmful material while still allowing ample access to educational material. Types of content typically blocked include pornography, drugs, academic dishonesty, gambling, and specific sites, like particular YouTube channels and videos. The biggest challenge for administrators is keeping up with the countless websites and slang terms that can breach the filter until they are identified. School staff typically have access to a real-time log that shows exactly what each student is working on, complete with aggregate history reports. They receive real-time notifications when students search for inappropriate content. Older students tend to generate more notifications, because they search more controversial topics like legalization of drugs for class projects.

Teachers and administrative staff cannot entirely prevent kids from making bad choices. By teaching digital citizenship in a group format and counseling kids individually, school staff can however determine whether counseling or discipline is necessary on a case-by-case basis. Just like in the home, adult-child relationships are the most powerful tools for safety in schools.

Despite risk, most districts recognize that social media is a powerful medium to communicate efficiently and effectively to parents. As a result, most American school district have Facebook and Twitter profiles for fun and informational posts. Typically, images (and first names) of children are only included if parents signed a consent form in their first day packet. This is a fun way to see school events and keep up to date with educational activities.

Although each district has different requirements, most are building comprehensive digital citizenship curriculums to develop classroom lesson plans. Often lessons are made to match digital citizenship topics with classes (e.g., online searching and researching/website validity for science, cyberbullying for social studies, and academic honesty/plagiarism for language arts). In addition to classroom lessons, complimentary home curriculums are often offered so parents can reinforce digital citizenship concepts at home. These lesson plans bring in writing and communication skills with the goal of being preventative rather than reactive.

Cybersecurity and Privacy

Kids are currently the number one target for identity theft, a cybercrime that involves the theft and fraudulent use of a child's personal information. Stolen information, like name, social security number, address, and date of birth, can be used to carry out crimes like opening fraudulent lines of credit or loans, accessing financial accounts, securing a driver's license or employment, or seeking medical care. Personal information is collected by stealing information from your home, wallet, trash, or mail, skimming information from your ATM card with a special device, stealing electronic data by breaching private data bases, or securing personal information by impersonating a company to process a fake change of address form or application for credit.

Child data is particularly valuable to cybercriminals, because child credit histories are clean and fraudulent activity is unlikely to be discovered until the child is old enough to seek a loan for a car or college. This means your child's private information could be accumulating criminal activity for years before it is discovered. Once discovered, it may take several months or even years of high stress and lots of money and time spent trying to get credit and criminal records cleaned up and sorted out. Your child's financial options may be blocked or delayed when deadlines, like college and employment, are most critical.

Several years ago, I received a phone call from California State Jacqui Irwin's office asking for a statement about a *Child Identity Theft* bill (AB1580) that she was sponsoring and has since been signed into law.[138] The bill "requires credit agencies to allow parents or guardians to create a new credit report for a minor child for the purpose of placing a security freeze on the child's credit. Without a credit report to freeze, protection is difficult."

Assemblymember Irwin was not only asking for my statement and support, but wondered if I knew any child victims of identity theft.

After sending out an inquiry on my GetKidsInternetSafe Facebook page, I quickly uncovered three victims who were willing to share their stories. Two involved child identity theft for financial cybercrime and the other involved identity theft on social media for cyberbullying. My first respondent was a father whose stepdaughter had recently graduated from nursing school. When the family went to their credit union in preparation for purchasing a car, they discovered that the stepdaughter's credit report was pages and pages long with a subpar (mid 500) credit rating. It turned out that a criminal had fraudulently opened several lines of credit with her social security number. From Sprint to multiple department stores, the crook had charged a debt of over $60,000. The family filed a police report and started the long process of calling creditors and clearing her name.

When I spoke to the stepfather, he said he had no knowledge whether the criminal was ever charged. He also said they never discovered how or when the fraud started, but it seemed to be a single party that may have obtained her personal information when she applied for a loan for nursing school. The fraud seemed to stop once the credit agencies were notified and an alert was placed on her account. Ultimately, it took the family over twenty hours of filing time plus another fifteen hours from a private credit fraud service to get her credit repaired. A year after the discovery, her credit score returned to the 700s with letters from the creditors with apologies. Nightmare!

The second identity fraud victim shared a truly tragic tale that has spanned over thirty years. Forty-year-old Jose was thirteen years old when he was first contacted by the IRS and told that he owed over $10,000 in back taxes. Despite all efforts to get clear of fraud, he is still experiencing issues as simple as being denied credit (including a first-time home buyer loan, because it looked like he already owned properties) to having to take paternity tests and go to court for fraudulent child support cases. Jose also shared a story about being pulled over on a fraudulent arrest warrant while he was on his way to become a priest. The officer said if it turned out he was lying about the fraud, he would arrest him and make him apologize directly to his lieutenant. Jose responded to the police officer that if HE was correct, the officer would have to go to church and apologize to his bishop. He laughed when he said the officer lived up to his promise. Despite his resilient attitude, Jose has had to change phone numbers and bank accounts, cannot pay anything with checks, and has elected to put all property in his wife's name.

Considering the decades of victimization he has had to endure, Jose goes to great lengths to protect his children's personal information.

Other Cybersecurity and Privacy Risks

Malware is any software that attacks or captures data on your computer. These include *viruses, worms, Trojan horses* (links that look like beneficial downloads, but are actually malicious), *spyware, adware,* and other malicious programs.

Hacking is unauthorized computer or smartphone access to get data or images or even hijack the camera or mic for secret recording.

Phishing is a type of scamming that is a fraudulent attempt, usually through telephone, email, instant messaging, or a website, to gain sensitive personal information like login credentials or credit card information. Stolen information is then used for fraudulent activities like stealing money, credit card fraud, stealing your identity, or launching further phishing scams. Phishing attempts are often difficult to identify, because the fake website or email can look nearly identical to a legitimate one, such as posing as a popular website, auction site, online payment processor, or IT administrator.

Scamming is a con to get something from an unsuspecting victim. A common scam is posing as the IRS to convince the victim to wire money or be prosecuted for unpaid fees or taxes or suffer frozen bank accounts.

What can you do to increase your family's cybersecurity?

Protect personal information at home with tools such as a locking mailbox, an in-home safe for storage, and a shredder for disposal of personal documents.

Install cybersecurity safeguards on screen devices like passcodes and screensavers, firewalls, antivirus and encryption software, and secure passwords. Good habits include consistently downloading updates for security patches, using strong passwords and changing them often, and not clicking on embedded links or opening attachments from unknown sources.

Educate your children about maintaining privacy and using discretion online. That means cautioning them about disclosing their name, address, school, date of birth, or any other personally identifying information in images (t-shirts with their school logo) or texting or posting. Geotagging on photos and social media should be turned off to hide location.

Setup up parental controls and filtering and monitoring software.

Attach a fraud alert or credit freeze on your child's social security number by contacting one of the three major credit card companies (Equifax, Transunion, Experian). Once a freeze has been implemented, you must order a "thaw" on the account prior to applying for credit.

If you are traveling...

Don't post revealing pictures like travel information, boarding passes, passports, or travel or hotel vouchers. Not only can criminals benefit from knowing the details of your trip, they may also read personal information from barcodes to steal your personal identity. Best option, wait until you're home to post travel photos.

Avoid public WiFi. Hackers can access your private information using a variety of attack and interception techniques, including a man-in-the-middle attack (a fake access point), sidejacking (capture tool at Ethernet frame level), or simply shoulder surfing. If you have to use public Wifi, practice situational awareness and verify the WiFi name with staff at the public site. Avoid online tasks that involve private information like online banking or using private transaction information like date of birth, credit card numbers, or tax id or social security numbers. Always log out when using a hotspot to avoid the hacker continuing the session. Consider setting up a secure virtual private network (VPN) to encrypt inbound and outbound data.

Avoid using public computers for the same reasons it's risky to use public WiFi. Software could be silently running in the background, thus capturing data from your online activities.

If your child is traveling with you, turn off location settings so criminals can't intercept your location data and use it for targeted attacks. On Snapchat, this is called going "ghost mode." Of course, if your child is on an independent walkabout, you may want to leave location services on so you can track them for safety. With information and proactive strategies, you can avoid cybersecurity risk to your family. But psychological risk remains, particularly when we consider the potentially negative impacts of viewing violence on children.

Violence for Profit: Passive Viewing of Television and Video

The United States has long been criticized as the dominant creator and celebrator of violent entertainment. Chalk it up to our fierce protection of the right to bear arms or our thirst for thrilling content, more and more Americans are fans of violent sports, television, movies, and video games. As adults gobble up violent content for entertainment, our children are too often exposed to violence early and often with little regard to the damage it may cause. Everybody is doing it. Right? Right. Yet it has been widely demonstrated that viewing screen violence, passively and interactively, causes aggressive and hostile behavior in children and adults. However, not everybody who watches violent TV or plays violent video games acts aggressively. How much is too much for children who are vulnerable due to immature brains?

First, we must accept that not all screen time is equal. Screen viewing can be *passive* (watching television and videos) or *interactive* (screen touch and video games). In regard to passive viewing of violent screen content, the American Psychological Association Council Policy Manual on Violence in Mass Media (1994) concludes from decades of research that there is correlative and causal risk. It specifically states:

> *On the basis of over 30 years of research and a sizeable number of experimental and field investigations, viewing mass media violence leads to increases in aggressive attitudes, values, and behavior, particularly in children, and has a long-lasting effect on behavior and personality, including criminal behavior;*[139][140][141]

> *Viewing violence desensitizes the viewer to violence, resulting in calloused attitudes regarding violence toward others and a decreased likelihood to take action on behalf of a victim when violence occurs;*[142]

> *Viewing violence increases viewers' tendencies for becoming involved with, or exposing themselves to, violence;*

> *Viewing violence increases fear of becoming a victim of violence, with a resultant increase in self-protective behaviors and mistrust of others; and*

> *Many children's television programs and films contain some form of violence, and children's access to adult-oriented media violence is increasing as a result of new technological advances.*

These conclusions are particularly troubling when one considers that, despite these findings existing for decades, the Internet and screen technology has exploded access to on demand violent content for all ages. The younger the child, the more time viewed, and the intensity and applicability of the content, the more potential developmental impact. Research demonstrates that children who have not yet started talking are affected by screen viewing in ways parents cannot recognize and that impact changes month-to-month, year-to-year. Furthermore, even kids as young as infants who view alongside an older sibling or a parent may still be negatively affected by inappropriate content. Here are some tips to protect your kids from the negative effects of viewing harmful content.

GKIS Passive Screen Viewing Tips

Set up adult- versus child-television viewing with separate devices and parental control programming.

A quick flip through the channels or browse on YouTube will demonstrate the amount of inappropriate programming and content available. It's not just programs geared toward adults that we need to worry about. Most children's programming is designed to attract viewers for marketing potential rather than to provide education. Not surprisingly, broadcasters guided by profit are not great co-parents. If you don't have the luxury of separate devices programmed for kids versus adult viewing, use parental controls for different user log-ins on the device or through your television and Internet service provider, adopt child-safe browsers like Google Safe search, consider installing filtering and monitoring programs, and use child sites like YouTube Kids. Just as you stock your child's reading shelf with children's books rather than adult novels, it's important to shelf age-appropriate screen content. Websites like commonsensemedia.org can be helpful when evaluating program content.

Engage in frequent co-viewing and active guidance.

Take advantage of family time to snuggle on the couch and co-view. Negotiating program choice and discussing issues that come up teaches critical life skills. Schools simply cannot model and teach respectful negotiation and problem solving guided by your specific family values, only parents can.

Regulation has made a difference in availability and quality of children's television, but advocacy is needed for more.

Since the Children's Television Act was implemented, access to quality children's television programming in the US has improved.[143] However, little has been done to protect kids since risk has exploded with Internet access.

Edutainment selections matched with developmental factors can be beneficial.

When making TV program selections, consider that age makes a difference in child choice of programs and the ability to understand complex plots. Younger children choose and watch more educational and informational television programs, whereas older children prefer entertainment programming. Because broadcasters know this, there is less educational content targeted at older kids.[144] As cognitive abilities develop, kids are increasingly able to identify factors relevant to the central plot, recognize order as the story scheme, draw inferences about the feelings and motivations of the characters, and recognize cause-effect relationships within the program. That means younger children don't have the cognitive capacity to connect the dots and recognize story resolution, leaving them with confusing snapshots of disturbing content. This can lead to intrusive images, fears and phobias, separation anxiety, and nightmares.

Violence for Profit: Gaming and Interactive Screen Use

All parents want their children to succeed and live happy lives. We've generally accepted that screens are part of it. But parents often wonder, how much impact does violent gaming content have on psychological process? Too often we are seeing school shooters reference violent video games in their pre-attack manifestos. Do we have anything to worry about?

The five main video game play genres include action, role-playing, simulation, strategy, and sports. Gaming ranges in content and interactivity from simple puzzle games to complex massive multiplayer online role-playing games (*MMORPGs*). In MMORPGs, a large number of people play online together as developed characters in complex, online lands with shared goals in real time. Platforms for gaming include smartphones, tablets, handheld gaming devices, computers, gaming consoles, and the developing market of *virtual reality* (wearable devices with sensors like a helmet, goggles, and gloves where users can "interact" with a three-dimensional environment) and *augmented reality* (computer-generated images superimposed on the player's view of the real world, resulting in a realistic composite of real and virtual life).

Other new, immersive auditory and visual adjunct technologies include *transmedia storytelling* (story content presented across multiple platforms and formats using digital technology), *mini-games* (video games contained within video games), *chrono-* and *geolocation* (identifying the time and location of players), and *object linking* (embedded links that lead the player to sequential digital locations). With multibillions of dollars earned each year from the gaming market, *gamevertising* has also become increasingly prevalent. This means that games are being expertly designed for product placement and with manipulative neuropsychological principals built in to ensure that gamers stay online and spend more money.

Beyond education and entertainment, benefits that can be gained from playing video games include improvements in visual-spatial capabilities, reaction times, attention span, ability to process multiple target objects, and detail orientation,[145] as well as improved visual short-term memory, mental rotation, tracking, and toggling between tasks.[146] Video games can also help with anxiety and mood and improve relaxation and improve problem solving, strategy building, goal setting, and cooperation with others.

Video games also have vocational applicability and can be customized for specific tasks, such as orienting and motivating employees, providing health care benefits like exercise or illness care, or teaching specialized skills like performing surgery or sporting ability.[147] Some gamers compete in profitable e-sport tournaments in person and online, while others learn computer programming skills that can be marketable as a career specialty. Mastery of video games provides opportunity for increased confidence, social connection and networking, and self-esteem. Social benefits are particularly valuable for players who may be isolated by geographic remoteness or physical or mental disability.

Along with benefits come risks. Ninety-seven percent of teens play video games, and more than 85% of video games have violent content.[148] As with all complex psychological phenomena, different effects happen in different situations with different people. Thus, issues like content, time spent playing, and player vulnerabilities due to family life or mental health must be taken into account when considering effect.[149] This makes for messy factors to control for quality research and controversial opinions about the risks of violent video games.

Meta-analytic reviews of research have found that violent video games can cause aggressive behavior, aggressive thinking styles, and aggressive mood, as well as decreased empathy and prosocial behavior. In regard to the effect of violent video games on children, teens, and adults, the

American Psychological Association Council Policy Manual Resolution on Violent Video Games (2015) concludes:

A convergence of research findings across multiple methods and multiple samples with multiple types of measurements demonstrates the association between violent video game use and both increases in aggressive behavior, aggressive affect, aggressive cognitions and decreases in prosocial behavior, empathy, and moral engagement;

All existing quantitative reviews of the violent video game literature have found a direct association between violent video game use and aggressive outcomes;

This body of research, including laboratory experiments that examine effects over short time spans following experimental manipulations and observational longitudinal studies lasting more than two years, demonstrates that these effects persist over at least some time spans;

Research suggests that the relation between violent video game use and increased aggressive outcomes remains after considering other known risk factors associated with aggressive outcomes;

Although the number of studies directly examining the association between the amount of violent video game use and amount of change in adverse outcomes is still limited, existing research suggests that higher amounts of exposure are associated with higher levels of aggression and other adverse outcomes;

Research demonstrates these effects for children older than 10 years, adolescents, and young adults, but very little research has included children younger than 10 years;

Research has not adequately examined whether the association between violent video game use and aggressive outcomes differs for males and females;

Research has not adequately included samples representative of the current population demographics;

Research has not sufficiently examined the potential moderator effects of ethnicity, socioeconomic status, or culture; and

Many factors are known to be risk factors for increased aggressive behavior, aggressive cognition and aggressive affect, and reduced prosocial behavior, empathy and moral engagement, and violent video game use is one such risk factor. [150]

Not only do video games affect gamers in the immediate, but they can also lead to increased aggressive behavior later in life.[151] Furthermore, some players become desensitized to their environment,[152] increasingly spend more time gaming, and ultimately feel more connected to their virtual world than the real world around them. With new immersive technologies being introduced to younger and younger children every day, one can't even imagine true cognitive and psychological impact over time.

Thus far, attempts to regulate and block violent video game content from minors have largely been unsuccessful. Since the 1972 release of the first popular video arcade game, *Pong*, parents have worried about the impact of video gaming on their children. Just like our kids, we have largely become desensitized to its impact. From 1976, when parents succeeded in getting the video game *Death Race* pulled from the shelf due to the little gravestone that appeared when a character was killed, to now, we've come a long way baby. Or have we?

In response to video game players committing violence, several lawsuits have been filed by private citizens and class actions claiming that video game manufacturers were negligent by selling violent content that is harmful to children. However, few have succeeded due to first amendment rights claims and insufficient evidence related to flawed research methodology or correlational rather than causal research. City ordinances attempting to limit violent game play by unaccompanied minors in public places have also largely failed. Law professors and psychologists continue to argue that the evidence is too flimsy to make solid claims that video games cause violence, particularly considering the fact that despite widespread game play, the rate of juvenile violent crime is at a thirty-year low.

A particularly impactful blow against state regulation was the United States Supreme Court ruling in Brown v. Entertainment Merchants Association (2011), which concluded by a seven to two opinion that the California law restricting the sale and distribution of violent video games to minors was unconstitutional. The ruling was based on first amendment rights, stating that "speech about violence is not obscene" and is "as much entitled to the protection of free speech as the best in literature." It's interesting that Americans tend to be horrified about kids viewing sexual content, yet we are somewhat complacent about their viewing violent content. Is viewing online sexual activity damaging to kids?

Online Pornography

Online pornography is popular and easily available. We don't know *how* popular it actually is though, because the large number of pornography websites are reticent to share traffic numbers. Best estimates are that 13% of web searches are for online pornography.[153] What we do know is that the numbers of viewers and time spent viewing is growing. A particularly popular single pornographic site, Pornhub's 2018 Year in Review reported:

> *"Visits to Pornhub totaled 33.5 billion over the course of 2018, an increase of 5 billion visits over 2017. That equates to a daily average of 92 million visitors and at the time of this writing, Pornhub's daily visits now exceed 100 million. To put that into perspective, that's as if the combined populations of Canada, Poland and Australia all visited Pornhub every day! ... When they're not busy watching videos, Pornhub's users enjoy socializing, with nearly 64 million private messages sent and 7.9 million video comments left. ... More than 141 million people took the time to vote for their favorite videos, which incidentally is more people than voted in the last U.S. presidential election. ... Once again, the United States continues to be the country with the highest daily traffic to Pornhub, followed by the United Kingdom, India, Japan, Canada, France and Germany."[154]*

Furthermore, today's online pornography is nothing like the images from our fathers' Playboy magazines. Most pornographic videos are scripted to display fantastical versions of the sexual desires and prowess of men.[155] Most often, that means scenes with women as sexual objects who are seemingly delighted to be the willing and passive victim of demeaning verbal and physical aggression, often by one or more man at a time. Porn content is rich with violent and fetish acts that bear little resemblance to loving intimacy. As customers satiate to milder versions of pornographic activity, clever content developers produce increasingly risqué content to keep their customers browsing. The top seven Pornhub searches for 2018 were *lesbian, hentai, milf, stepmom, Japanese, mom,* and *teen.*

With popularity and ease of access through mobile screens and gaming consoles, many kids and teens intentionally seek, and are being accidentally exposed to, inappropriate sexual images and videos. Based on a set of EU studies, Kierkegaard (2008) states that children have access to Internet pornography at the average age of eleven years old.[156] Not only are kids and teens seeking sexual content for titillation, but many kids are also relying on online pornography as their primary source of sexual education.[157] Alarmingly, I am seeing more and more kids intentionally seeking pornographic content and creating and exchanging nude images and videos. How often are children viewing porn, and, when they do, what kinds of harm may result from that exposure?

Estimates from research studies vary widely, most suggesting that a minority of adolescents actually access online pornography.[158] However, in one study conducted in 2008 with 562 undergraduates, 93% of boys and 62% of girls reported that they were exposed to pornography during adolescence.[159] In my clinical experience, it is quite common due to unfiltered smartphone and tablet use among younger children. Studies show that kids tend to consider what they see online as attractive, normative, and risk-free and may go as far as emulate it.[160][161] The online worlds of MMORPGs increasingly feature virtual sexual assault and pornographic behaviors, and popular television series deliver increasingly violent content and explicit themes.

Who is most at risk for online pornography consumption?

The typical adolescent online pornography user is a boy who is more pubertally advanced, a sensation-seeker, and has weak or troubled family relations.[162] Boys are more likely to be exposed at an earlier age, to see more images, to see more extreme images (e.g., rape, child pornography), and to view pornography more often; while girls reported more involuntary exposure.[163] Statistics demonstrate that female viewing is going up every year. Pornhub's 2018 Year in Review report stated, "2018 saw the proportion of female visitors to Pornhub grow to 29%, an increase of 3 percentage points over 2017."[164] Depression and rule-breaking are also risk factors. [165][166]

What affects does viewing pornography have on kids?

Research demonstrates that pornography use among children, teens, or adults has been associated with:

- Cynical attitudes about intimacy, fidelity, and love[167]

- Stronger gender-stereotypical sexual beliefs[168]

- Desensitization and habituation with explicit content, meaning the user's appetite changes over time from less extreme to more extreme forms of pornography to get the same intensity of enjoyment. This also validates deviant sex practices and potentially lowers inhibitions to engage in inappropriate sexual interactions online and offline[169]

- Attitudes supporting violence against women[170]

- More permissive sexual attitudes, especially in regard to the place of sex in relationships[171172173]

- Greater experience with casual sexual behavior[174175]

- Earlier sexual intercourse[176]

- More sexual aggression, both in terms of perpetration and victimization[177]

- Three times more sexually aggressive behavior when exposed to nonviolent porn[178]

- Twenty-four times more sexually aggressive behavior when exposed to violent porn[179]

- A clinically impairing addiction, called Hypersexual Disorder.

Causal research would require purposely exposing children to pornographic content. Because that is not safe or ethical, all research studies about child exposure to online pornography are correlational. We cannot conclusively say whether online pornography *causes* certain attitudes or behaviors. Obviously, the correlation findings quoted above are concerning. Blocking kids from online pornography is common sense. Not only is viewing pornography an issue, more active sexual role playing online makes kids vulnerable to sexual predators. These attitudes and behaviors are impactful in the short term and may also lead to problematic life-long trauma and intimacy issues.[180]

The Dark Net and Ecommerce

Issues related to screen addiction are becoming increasingly relevant to everyday life. As a result, I assign readings about the dark net for my addiction studies university class. My students are also required to write a paper identifying with and supporting one extremist position or the other, the techno-optimists or the techno-pessimists. Techno-optimists integrate technology maximally, with an eye to the stars as cyborgs. Techno-pessimists believe that technology integration is dangerous, far favoring log-cabin days. Who would you side with?

The *dark net* is a hidden, encrypted overlay Internet network with over 50,000 websites that can only be easily accessed by the Tor Hidden Services browser for no financial cost to the user. From the Tor browser, one's search request is bounced around via several computers encrypting and decrypting as it goes, ultimately making a search untraceable. Anonymous users can then browse and interact with underground websites that, in theory, cannot be regulated or censored. [181]

Interestingly, the Tor browser was originally invented in the 1970s by the United States Department of Defense (Advanced Research Projects Agency Network – *ARPANET*) to browse the net without being recognized. The same technology used for national security is the very software being utilized by users of the dark net. One must always consider that what the US government accesses, any hacker or allied nation may also access. As you may suspect, the dark net is populated largely by those who have something to hide. In his book, *The Dark Net*, author Jamie Bartlett interviews dark net frequenters, including trolls, pornographers, child pornographers, self-harm chatters, political and social movement extremists, and those who participate in black market drug sales.

The Silk Road is an ecommerce site that specializes in the sale of illegal drugs. To shop on the Silk Road, one simply needs to browse for products that are displayed like any ecommerce site, such as eBay or Amazon, with thousands of products offered by hundreds of vendors. One can see a photo and description of the product, read customer reviews to assure the quality of the products, contact the vendor, place an order with your delivery address, and pay with *bitcoin*, which is *cryptocurrency* designed to keep your identity secret. Once ordered, the buyer's money is held in a secure account until the product is on its way. The money is then released to the seller and the buyer is left to wait for the product to be delivered to his mailbox.

Safety, privacy, and anonymity do not fully exist on the dark net. Encryption makes it difficult to locate the server for the website and the creator, but not impossible. For example, in May 2015, the founder of the first Silk Road website was convicted and sentenced to life in federal prison. The federal judge was quoted to say, "What you did with Silk Road was terribly destructive to our social fabric." Silk Road cashed in over a billion dollars in sales between 2011 and 2013. Destructive indeed. The FBI took down Silk Road One, yet within a month, Silk Road Two popped up in its place. The illicit online drug trade was reborn.

Perhaps most concerning about the dark net is the large number of *online child sexual abuse images,* also referred to as child pornography, available on the dark net. Disturbingly, emerging trends reveal an increase in the number of images depicting sadistic and violent child sexual abuse, and an increase in the number of images depicting very young children, including toddlers and infants.[182] With live streaming and gaming platforms, predator accessible is widening. I recently witnessed this very dynamic disturbingly played out when investigating the video streaming social media app, *Periscope.* A popular video stream with lots of floating hearts revealed what looked like a 12-year-old girl playing truth or dare with a hoard of flirting anonymous strangers. She had the demeanor of a hardened flirt, but her vulnerability was dangerously evident. She was talking to men who were daring her to take off her clothes and was quickly in way over her head. Seemingly unaware of the peril, the girl appeared more determined to demonstrate that she could handle it. I was horrified to see this risk first hand, yet it is playing out every day, all the time online. Parents are too often the last to know.

Telling your child a scary story is often not enough to stop them from experimenting with their social power and sexuality online. Bold kids engage in conversation with an online "creeper" as a kind of dare. As digital natives, kids are often overly confident in their control of online situations and even provoke aggressive or sexual banter. It is often a surprise to them when they become titillated or start to trust the guy and ultimately lose control. That is when it gets dangerous. In the sick chess game of online pedophilia, creepers are well practiced and use sophisticated *grooming* methods to manipulate children. Overly confident teens with immature prefrontal brain regions (the seat of problem solving and judgment) are easy pickings for sinister adults.

CHAPTER 7: RISKS OF SCREEN USE: INTERPERSONAL EXPLOITATION

Cyberbullying is destructive and surprisingly commonplace. Recent surveys report that more than half of teens have been victims of cyberbullying. I'd go as far to say that nearly all teens who have access to screens worry about it on occasion. Kids in my practice commonly check social media apps compulsively to stay "in the know," just in case they are targeted that day. Nice kids aren't just victimized; they often become the perpetrators too, striving to be funny or brave, defend themselves, demonstrate loyalty to a friend, or right a perceived wrong. Sometimes they are bored and just want to create *cyberdrama*. Kids and teens are typically unable to take another's perspective and anticipate the potential fallout for online cruelty. After all, it seems everyone is doing it!

Cyberbullying

I am constantly amazed at the innovative forms cyberbullying can take. At first, I worried this chapter may inappropriately serve as a "how-to" for perpetrators, but the truth is teens quickly become familiar with these techniques once online. It's the parents that need to be educated.

Overt Cyberbully Tactics

Flaming is humiliating a victim online by posting harmful content (images, comments, videos, memes, audio files, etc.) with varying levels of malicious intent. If the victim retaliates, the interchange escalates into a *flame war*. Related terms include defamation, libel, and slander. Over time, cyberbullies may escalate to threats, intimidation, cyberharassment, and cyberstalking.

Subtweeting is similar to flaming but the victim's identity isn't overtly named, just alluded to, and it occurs exclusively on the social media platform Twitter (e.g., "Loser goes after a middle schooler, because high schoolers know he's got an STD."). This is also a form of starting rumors and public shaming.

Phishing and outing is inviting private disclosures or images then sharing them with others without consent. This commonly occurs to achieve power, humiliate, and exclude the victim from other peers.

Bash boards or *polling pages* are blogs, chat rooms, social media pages, or online forums used for directive targeting or to invite embarrassing confessions. An example is posting an image and asking the audience to assign a rating, like a score or terms like "F'k, kill, or marry." The social media platform *Ask.fm*, which has been described as a virtual bathroom stall, is commonly used this way. A more recently popular polling app, *To Be Honest (TBH)*, claims to avoid online cruelty by limiting its polling for only positivity. However, anything that encourages personal disclosures or provides opportunity for popularity-type polls can make excluded kids feel terrible. *Confession pages* collect posts where one can anonymously share their own confession or that of a peer. One can imagine how identities are assumed despite being "anonymous." Any online forum that allows anonymity is particularly fertile ground for bad behavior.

Impersonation is cyberidentity theft by creating an unauthorized profile in the name and image of somebody else and then provoking others on it, saying inappropriate things, or making false confessions to make the victim look bad or get them into trouble.

Sextortion is cybercoercion by demanding that the victim submit to sexting or sending nude images under threat of releasing humiliating content to friends, family, or authorities. Threatened content may be fraudulent, collected through illicit means, or from groomed or consensual trading.

Trolling is posting inflammatory comments to provoke others.

Griefing is a strategy of cyberbullying during video game play to distract other players. Examples include playing badly on purpose (e.g., killing your own players), taking over the chat feature with vulgarity and taunting, or sabotaging the game to disruption.

Pranking is when a cyberbully dupes a victim into a setup that is then videoed and publicly posted, like scaring the person with a mask in the window, saying or doing provocative things, or dumping water on their head.

Exclusion is posting get-togethers to highlight who was not invited, even going so far as to tag the missing friend.

Cyberterrorism is convincing a victim that they are under threat from a known or unknown entity. An example is the *virtual kidnapping scam,* where a perpetrator convinces a victim's family member that another family member is in need of rescue or being held for ransom. The criminal might threaten to assault or kill the victim unless the family member sends money or urgently capitulates to exploitive demands. Often these scams integrate a screaming or tearfully pleading accomplice who shares private information gleaned from hacked records or social media profiles or from the victim's stolen smartphone. The criminal may even hack into the victim's smartphone and call from that number even without possession of the phone. These scams are often timed to occur when the victim is vacationing, with the perpetrator calling to convince the victim that he must stay in his hotel room and off the phone to avoid being assaulted or kidnapped. While he is unreachable by phone or text, the victim's family members are shaken down to wire money by ransom. Create an emergency plan today by assigning family nicknames as an alert word to foil a scam in progress should you become a victim.

Covert Cyberbully Tactics

The psychological principal, *The Bystander Effect,* also referred to as the *diffusion of responsibility,* refers to the phenomenon of how an individual is less likely to respond or delay response to a person in distress if there are other onlookers. The larger the number of bystanders, the less likely individual intervention occurs. In other words, people tend to look to others for action instead of taking action themselves.

The most commonly cited illustration of the bystander effect is the case of *Catherine "Kitty" Geovese.* Kitty was a young woman who was brutally attacked and stabbed by an assailant in New York City in 1964. Although thirty-seven people witnessed the crime from their windows and heard Kitty screaming for help, nobody actively intervened and several minutes passed before anybody called the police. However, one man did yell, "Let that girl alone!" causing her assailant to flee and Kitty to crawl to the door of her apartment. The assailant, Winston Moseley, then returned ten minutes later to stab Kitty several more times, rape her, steal $50 from her purse, and then leave her in the hallway to die. The attack spanned thirty minutes. A neighbor finally called the police after the final attack, resulting in an ambulance arriving over an hour after the first assault. Kitty died on the way to the hospital. Later reports revealed that none of the neighbors actually witnessed the attack in its entirety, thus the original report was erroneous. Nonetheless, this incident is typically cited as a classic example of The Bystander Effect. For any single cyberbullying incident, there are various levels of participation, including being a passive or participating bystander.

How Kids Collude with the Cyberbully

- "Liking" or commenting on the mean post

- Commenting via backchannel chat

- Sharing or "favoriting" the posts

- Repeatedly bringing the content back by online sharing, gossiping, or face-to-face bullying (Repeat sharing sometimes goes on for years!)

- Repurposing the content into a humiliating meme

- Viewing and "friending" or remain "friends" with the cyberbully online or offline

- Emulating the cyberbully's technique

- Viewing the cyberbully incident without further action

How Kids Intervene on Behalf of the Victim

- Viewing the cyberbully incident and comment their protest via backchannel chat

- Viewing the cyberbully incident and publicly comment their protest

- Flagging the content as inappropriate or request web mediation

- Requesting adult intervention through parents, academic staff, or law enforcement

Why Kids Cyberbully

There are genuinely rational reasons for staying silent in a cyberbullying situation, even if the result further empowers the cyberbully. Researcher Robert Thornberg (2007) identified seven reasons why bystanders don't intervene:

- *Trivialization:* The child doesn't consider the incident serious (often because cyberbullying is so common children are desensitized).

- *Dissociation:* The child feels he is not involved in the situation or is not a friend of the cyberbully or the victim.

- *Embarrassment Association:* The child doesn't want to make the victim more embarrassed or doesn't want to get embarrassed herself (stage-fright).

- *Audience modeling:* The child looks to bystanders for the social norm.

- *Busy working priority:* The child considers doing other things a higher priority than helping.

- *Compliance with a competitive norm:* The child considers social media etiquette more important than helping behavior.

- *Responsibility transfer:* The child ascribes more responsibility to other bystanders than himself (e.g., online peers who are more involved with the bully or victim or online viewers with more authority).[183]

Another common reason not included in Thornberg's findings is *defensive denial.* More specifically, kids often pretend nothing is happening in fear that by defending the victim, they'd be throwing themselves in the cyberbully's line of fire. Their incentive for silence is fear, fear that predatory cyberbullies expect and exploit by recruiting and speaking for an army of silent minions. Victims often feel the world is against them, this supposition fed with cyberbully comments like, "Everybody thinks you're …" or "We are going to … if you …" Shame and humiliation mix in with the fear for the perfect cocktail of social imprisonment.

The "Typical" Profile of the Cyberbully Victim

Kids aren't the only people who use denial as a defense. Parents often bury their heads in false suppositions as well. Most parents think that the quiet, nerdy types, or the children with poor social skills, are the main cyberbully targets. However, this is not the case online.

The most brutal time for bullying of any kind happens in middle school, usually instigated by self-selected popular kids. Middle school is the time when kids start to differentiate from adult authority and launch bold leadership strategies with same-age peers. Leadership comes in many different forms, but a very effective and primitive form is by self-identifying as "popular" and then controlling peer perception by defining who's "in" and who's "out." To this end, it is common for ambitious, socially skilled kids to enlist a group of followers who support their popular status and then encourage them to shun others on command. Those targeted for the shunning (aka cyberbullying) are often their competition, or other kids who are in powerful positions themselves either due to being superior than peers in looks, assertiveness, academics, or athletics (innately popular) or those who have also self-selected as popular (actively labeled themselves as popular and strategically positioned themselves in an "in" group while excluding competitors).

This means that children who stand out in *any* way (exceptionally high grades or exceptionally low grades, tall or short, loud or quiet), may be targeted for cyberbullying or defend by cyberbullying back. Not only do victims feel ashamed and humiliated by being in the situation, but also loathe to disappoint their parents, fearing the parents will believe the stories being told about them or be angry at their (lack of) response. Furthermore, teens reason that the last thing they need is to be seen as a snitch and have a furious parent clumsily stepping in and making them even more of a mockery. When should parents step in?

How to Tell if Your Child is Being Cyberbullied

- Seems secretive, protective, or jumpy about screen activities

- Isolates from friends or family

- No longer has fun doing things that were once enjoyable

- Refuses to go to certain classes or to school

- Moody, depressed, irritable, or angry, particularly after being on their phone or computer

- Change in sleep or appetite

- Complains about weight or body image

- Complains of tummy aches or headaches

- Acts younger than they are (baby-talk) or becomes jaded or hostile (eye-rolling)

- Changes style of dress or becomes attracted to dark or morose images, reading, writing, or online content

- Quits paying attention to hygiene or appearance

- Becomes particularly hard on herself or expresses feelings of worthlessness or hopelessness

What should parents do?

Empower and Validate Emotion

Be a good listener and acknowledge the complexity of the situation. Working through cyberbullying tangles requires a slow and steady appreciation of nuance. You don't need every detail this second. Let it unravel. Allow your child to take the leadership position in problem solving. Taking a stand, even if it is a silent one, takes extraordinary courage for kids. Consistently give the impression you have their back 100% no matter how they've participated in the conflict.

Don't Shame or Blame

It is a rare instance where the cyberbully victim has not made some attempt to turn things around, only to have those attempts be used as a further threat against them should they seek adult aid (e.g., "If you tell what I did, then I'll tell what YOU did!"). Kids commonly cyberbully back as an expression of loyalty, self-protection, or as an assertiveness strategy. If your child bullied back, be understanding of their difficult position.

Facilitate Problem Solving and Let Them be the Expert

Children need sensible, engaged parents to help them analyze a complex situation and sort through response options. Assess what potential influence they have on the cyberbully. Ask "what if" questions. Coach them to generate a list of feasible options they can choose from. Help them track outcome. Don't take over! You want your children to seek your help in these painful situations. Show them your best, low-key, but effective support. What works in your adult world does not always work in your children's worlds. Ultimately, they are the experts and you are the facilitator. The more active they are in the problem solving, the more independent and resilient they will be in the future.

Don't Rant

No matter how tempting it is to lecture, shame, blame, and yank technology privileges, this will just shut them down and guarantee they won't seek your support in the future. Instead, take their opinions seriously and keep your cool. By staying calm and deliberate, you can seek reasonable options rather than contributing to a very real, painful crisis. Remain skeptical, but don't interrogate, judge, or lecture.

Block Participants and Limit Compulsive Checking

Kids often avoid seeking help, because they are afraid their parents will take away their social media or screens. It's not appropriate to punish your child for the behavior of others. Instead, negotiate a strategy, like blocking and docking, that protects them but still allows them the freedoms they've always had. They need the cybersupport of friends along with your calm counsel until the event blows over.

Save Electronic Evidence and Consult

School administrators and law enforcement officials are expert at handling cyberbully situations. Seeking expert consult is an important skill for your children to learn. Rarely should you approach other children or families. Things can get out of control in ways you cannot anticipate. If they prefer, seek consult anonymously. If your child is so distressed it is getting in the way of school, friendships, or overall mood, consult a psychologist.

Cyberbully Teaching Tips

Public humiliation is never funny.

Do not post private jokes, embarrassing images, or putdowns online. It is best to only use sarcasm or jabbing humor in person, and even then it's risky. Gauging tone or audience response through a screen is impossible, so it is best to play it conservative every time. If it's rude or nude, don't post it

There are aggressive and passive-aggressive methods of cyberbullying.

We all recognize aggressive cyberbullying methods like ridiculing, name-calling, and threatening. Destructive passive aggressive methods include posting group photos to make an uninvited peer feel left out, flaming or mocking an unnamed victim (e.g., *subtweet*), or liking or sharing mean posts or images. *Hashtags* are words following the symbol "#" that then automatically sort onto a page with other images and posts that share that hashtag. Labeling an image with a hashtag is a quick and easy way to sort a collection of mean memes and images from individual profiles to one page for that hashtag (for example, #PattyisaFatty).

Being a participating bystander can be just cruel as being the cyberbully. Be an upstander.

If something mean is going down online, do not participate by jumping in with likes or agreeable comments. Stay out of it, or, even better, be an upstander and intervene on behalf of the victim. This may involve a back-channeled message of support to the victim, a request to the cyberbully to lay off (publicly or privately) or flagging the string for social media or adult support. Be sensitive to the fact that kids are reticent to get involved for good reason. Often the tables will turn on the victim's supporter, so that may not always be the best option. Cyberbullying the cyberbully is tempting but sabotages the process further.

Taking a stand by being proactive shows exceptional digital citizenship.

If your child shows leadership potential and takes a special interest in social justice and friendship, encourage him or her to start a Council for Digital Good at school.

Destructive Digital Footprint and Online Reputation

Most of us have a digital footprint, meaning we live a virtual existence with multiple identities and a path of online activities that can be accessed in real time and in the future, often without our knowledge it even exists. Online maneuvering provides a rich and stimulating landscape, allowing us to experiment with multiple facets of ourselves. Because of the potential for online material to be *evergreen* (always present), it's difficult to anticipate how a momentary decision may live on with reposts and shares. Too often kids present in therapy feeling ashamed and hopeless to overcome the damage from normal developmental mistakes unfortunately broadcast to thousands of "friends" online. Cruel responses can be swift from a multitude of anonymous directions and repeated over time. It's difficult to stage a "do-over" when an online mistake keeps popping up over and over again without welcome or warning.

A famous example of this phenomenon happened to PR executive Justine Sacco, who jokingly tweeted, "Going to Africa. Hope I don't get AIDS. I'm kidding. I'm white!" While she was on the airplane, her racist comment went viral, retweeted 3,000 times and picked up by media outlets. Her three-second lapse in judgement resulted in her being fired and shamed and humiliated by millions in front of millions. No take-backs possible.

Perhaps the most tragic video I've viewed regarding the slow burn of online reputation and vicious cyberbullying is the YouTube story card confession of Amanda Todd. Amanda was a 14-year-old Toronto teen who committed suicide in 2010 when her real and fabricated "transgressions" were purposely re-posted by online harassers every time she moved schools to get a new start. Her attempts to re-compensate were repeatedly sabotaged in the most cruel and unthinkable ways. There appeared to be no escape for her. Poor choices, often driven by humor or an attempt to appear bold and grown up, can haunt us for years online, interfering with reputation, friendships, and college and employment opportunities.

Self-Produced Pornography and Sexting

Amanda Todd's vulnerability was her need to feel connected and socially accepted. Most of us share this vulnerability, especially during childhood and adolescence. My whistle-blowing article about self-posted nude selfies was published by The Good Men Project in 2015. It has been my most popular post to date. Six months after its publication, the Canon City, Colorado sexting scandal hit the news. It's not just Colorado teens that are in the amateur online pornography business, so are your community's teens.

Hey Dad, Your Twelve-Year-Old Daughter Has a "Nude Out"

You're reading with the hopes that this is one of those bait-and-switch sensational articles, right? Oh, how I wish that was true. Unfortunately, I have run across a phenomenon that few parents know about, and those that do are too ashamed to tell anybody. The ugly truth is that middle school girls, with their immature frontal lobes and tender insecurities, are trying to attract high school boys by texting them sexy images of their blossoming private parts. It's like they've invented an unregulated child porn matchmaking profile that doesn't even have privacy settings, terms of agreement, or the option to delete the profile. Just a CLICK and SEND and your daughter's catastrophically nude profile image is available to everybody everywhere forever, no take-backs. Thirty seconds of bad judgment at twelve years old launches a nightmare digital footprint and sullied online reputation. Ouch!

And what about the boys? They enthusiastically log in to this mess too. Some become expert at grooming the girls to send the sexy photos, which they then share with their "boyz" on the wrestling team for quickly growing "<city name> nudes exposed!" collections. And to make things more horrifying, the boldest of the boys proudly share their name lists of the virginity prizes personally collected from girls they intentionally targeted who were too young to know any better. Five seconds and these young women have exposed their vulnerabilities, their reputations, and potentially the downfall of future opportunities. It's like these teens lost their minds and logged in for an on- and off-line pimp-prostitute internship program. All that was needed was a mobile phone with texting ability and a misguided sense of adventure.

How do I know this? Teens tell me shameful truths, truths that trigger pride, shame, sadness, and desperation. They tell me all about how they "released their nude" when they turned 12 years old to attract attention from the older boys. Or how they were duped into it by the soothing promises from entrepreneurial Romeos, only to find out later that they were lied to, and it had been shared over text to the high school football team. There's also the confessions from the boys that get their "ah-ha! I-was-being-a-dirt bag" moment when their frontal lobes come online later in high school. And believe it or not, both genders are capable of being predatory on the other. I hear what most parents don't know.

I remember the first session when I realized this was a thing. I was seeing a beautiful eighth grade girl who was starting to get it and was lamenting about her best friend who purposely "put a nude out" when she was 11-years-old. At 15 years old, the friend was bizarrely proud of it being re-released via texting to "everyone in the county" four years later. My client guessed it was the fourth mass texting of the image. I sat there, horrified and dumbfounded, assessing my ethical requirements to the teens involved and my community in general. As a mother, I began visualizing the creation of a blueprint for Rapunzel's tower in our backyard for my kids, screen-media-free.

So much of my young client's disclosure made me deeply upset for everybody involved. I was saddened that children this young had already learned how to use and exploit sexuality as a cheap commodity. I was saddened that these kids broker power through contemptuous attention catamount to social media "likes." I was saddened that there was an army of teenagers willing to receive these tragic misperceptions of self-worth. And I was furious that some actively groomed their victims to build a sick collection of lost innocence with no more thought than they gave to their Pokémon collections six months earlier. Keep in mind that in many cases these releases are consensual, while in others it is coerced.

I imagine you are thinking, "What kind of amoral community does this writer live in anyway? My kids would NEVER do that!" I'm sorry to tell you that I live in the same community you do. This is not an isolated phenomenon. Participants come from all types of families, families of all income levels and religions with great parents and slack parents. Short of raising your child in a stone tower, there is no family situation where your parenting supervision cannot be breached.

Of course, there are situations where children tend to be the most vulnerable. But the temptation is there for even the most well-adjusted kids. And to make things even more concerning, this pimp-prostitute culture does not always end by college age. The media is rampant with stories of fraternity houses that have private Facebook pages littered with nude photos of non-consenting women and blatant drug deals, not to mention social media and hookup dating sites flooded with sexual trolling. Like it or not, the young have their own culture of sexuality that is different from their parents.

What led us here? Is it the unregulated Wild West atmosphere of the Internet? Perhaps it is the moral decay of the Western culture? Perhaps it is the accumulation of sexualization and objectification of women splashed throughout popular culture over decades? Are permissive parents to blame or the rapid technological developments we simply cannot keep up with? And more importantly, what is going to lead us out?

My university students and I discuss this often, and you might be surprised by how many of them advocate for no social media before age eighteen. I am left to wonder about the sincerity of their self-righteousness. Like them, I am conflicted about what constitutes our "rights" for online liberties balanced with personal vulgarity and decency standards. Until our legislators can fully secure online child pornography portals, some which apparently begin in our own unsuspecting homes, parents must get serious about becoming informed and taking real action. And, believe it or not, waiting until your child reaches the teen years to do this is simply too late.

Shortly after writing this article, I worried that it challenged parents of daughters more than parents of boys. Even though the first article got far more shares, I think this one has more long-time value to parents, kids, and our planet.

Hey Mom, Your Fifteen-Year-Old Boy is Acting Like an Internet Predator

Earlier this week The Good Men Project published my article, "Hey Dad, Your Twelve-Year-Old Daughter Has a "Nude Out," and it's getting some justified attention. As I watched the Facebook share number rise, I realized that my title made the victim (the younger girl) the active agent instead of the predator (the older boy) much like how we say "she was raped" instead of "he raped." That type of language allows the perpetrator to escape accountability, kind of like blaming the victim. Shouldn't the boy be the agent in my title considering he is older, being coercive, and has intent to deceive in this scenario? But then again, *predator* is probably a harsh word for a goofy impulsive teenage boy, or is it? To make it more complicated, sometimes the girls are more willing to pose and distribute their "sexy" image than the boys are willing to receive it. Ultimately, both the boy and the girl may suffer serious moral and legal consequences. Join me in tackling this issue by considering what you want for your kids, and how we might facilitate their delicate and important journey toward good judgment, compassionate morality, and sexual power.

Last week's article detailed an unnerving teen "trend" that I learned from young clients in my private practice. This trend involves a well-traveled digital bridge between middle school girls and high school boys where high school boys deliberately plot and groom middle school girls to send sexy pictures via text. The boys then assign point values, share, and trade with their friends à la human Pokémon cards. Seriously, this topic makes me rant, and for good reason.

Admittedly, I'm somewhat conflicted in my feelings. On the one hand, a boy grooming a girl to expose herself onscreen at such a painfully tender age is manipulative, selfish, and potentially very damaging. The boy sharing the image without her consent is frankly criminal and makes him (and the girl) vulnerable to child pornography and revenge porn charges. But is it predatory? Let's face it, teenage boys are pretty much drunk from a brain newly flooded with testosterone and their frontal lobe won't be done developing until they're around 23 years old. What's more, the thousands of sexualized images of women (and to a lesser degree men) that bombard our kids on screens everyday fuel this objectification. Even our adult culture has a long way to go to responsibly and sensibly deal with issues like intimacy and sexuality. The multibillion-dollar porn industry and lecherous sexual trolling on adult dating sites are testament to that.

I'm also angry with the girls for participating. What does it mean that so many young women willingly release images of their blossoming sexuality for praise, status, and attention? As parents, we want them to value all that they are, but not by posing languidly for the lecherous consumption of strangers. Unlike any time in history, it's too easy to turn a confusingly sexy impulse into a consequence that may be in play for years to come. With this enormous technological power comes enormous risk. In such a complex digital landscape, kids need our involvement in their day-to-day decisions more than ever.

I notice two glaring mistakes that parents make when dealing with these issues. Firstly, they start too late. If you're waiting until your kids are teens before you talk about gender, sexuality, and personal privacy rights, you are starting too late. Secondly, parents only challenge their daughters with discussion and leave their sons out of it. The digital bridge observation illuminates that we must teach girls AND boys to be respectful, nurturing, and responsible. Sexual education and social problem solving must happen with both genders. You would be shocked at how few boys raise their hands in my university class when we discuss who received sexual education in their homes. And the girls admit that most of their parents were only willing to awkwardly mutter quick comments about menstruation and avoiding pregnancy. There's so much more to it than that!

In an effort to "walk the walk," my husband and I staged a discussion about some of these issues over dinner last night. Although it admittedly deteriorated into goofy comments, some awesome insights emerged. My kids asked that I use discretion and not discuss their comments in a public article, but I loved the concept my Navy veteran husband used to help illuminate the issue of assertiveness and social responsibility. The quote comes from Lt. Col. Dave Grossman and Stephanie Rogish's book, *Sheepdog Meet Our Nation's Warriors a Children's and Educator's Book*:

> *If you have no capacity for violence then you are a healthy productive citizen: a sheep. If you have a capacity for violence and no empathy for your fellow citizens, then you have defined an aggressive sociopath—a wolf. But what if you have a capacity for violence, and a deep love for your fellow citizens? Then you are a sheepdog, a warrior, someone who is walking the hero's path.*

A little heavy for our thirteen-year-old daughter and eleven-year-old son perhaps? Initially, yes! In fact, at one point in the discussion my son looked at me and pleaded, "But I love wolves! Why can't I be a wolf?" clearly missing the metaphorical value of Grossman's insights. We persevered in explaining to them what being a "good man" and a "good woman" means to us.

We didn't lecture. We listened and encouraged, knowing that this discussion would happen over and over for years to come in many different forms. We taught them that "wrong" happens the moment you have hurt yourself or another human being, not just when you're caught. Most of all, we reassured them that we will be there for them every step along the way; when they do things they are proud of and when they make mistakes. We reminded them that nobody can do this alone, and we are in it together. Here are some teaching points to address with your kids:

People are far more than their body parts.

Behind every text, image, and idea is a human being with thoughts, feelings, and value. Treating yourself or others as a sexy object instead of a complex, capable person is demeaning.

Screen media is a powerful tool.

Once your hit "send," that text, image, or video can never be taken back. Consider if it would be OK to show it on the screen in a school assembly before you send it to anybody.

Save private interactions for face-to-face relationships.

If posted, it's unlikely to stay private. Assume moms, dads, and school principals may be reading the texts or instant messages, because often they are! Furthermore, tone and meaning is easily misconstrued on text. Any discussion that may lead to hurt feelings is best left for face-to-face contact.

Collecting "likes" is not love.

Sometimes it's even the opposite.

Represent yourself online just as you would offline.

Character matters. Although parents don't want to admit it, romance and sex titillates people of all ages, even children. As adolescent hormones come online those pressures increase. The world gets more overwhelming and confusing as teens learn to drive their new brains. A middle school girl recently told me that a boy came up to her and said, "I can't decide if you're a slut or a nerd." This disclosure launched an important discussion between us about what those words mean and what he was trying to accomplish by demeaning her with them. From this discussion, she insisted she would not cower like a sheep (and I promised to encourage boys not to be wolves). What do you want for your sons and daughters?

Sexual Predators

Online predation doesn't stop at recruitment for nude photos. Many experts assert than consensual sharing of erotic selfies is a normal aspect of adult intimacy. Adults who post on dating sites will tell you that image sharing is very common, even among strangers. However, consent and trust is slippery in that honesty is extremely variable online. One way to provoke sharing is to pretend to be the victim's fantasy partner. Deceptively posing as somebody else to develop a relationship with an unsuspecting audience is commonly known as *catfishing*. Catfishing often occurs on dating and social media sites to gain romantic or sexual favor. Catfishing is nothing new. However, conning people online is far easier than conning somebody in the nonvirtual world. Damage from catfishing ranges from a broken heart to criminal and financial exploitation.

The online environment is ripe for exploitation from pedophiles seeking child victims. The discussion continues whether the Internet has provided opportunity for pedophiles that already existed or if it has recruited adults into pedophilic behavior. Either way, child predators are highly visible on the dark web. In the 1980s, law enforcement considered child pornography, which is more accurately called *images of child sexual abuse*, more or less under control. However, within the last thirty years the situation has changed dramatically. Between 2006 and 2009, the U.S. Justice Department recorded twenty million unique IP addresses who were sharing illegal image and video files.[184] Child predators commonly frequent websites and chatrooms looking for opportunity to snare a victim. The following is a true story from my clinical practice. I have changed names and details to protect my client's confidentiality. "Tiffany" and her parents want her story told if it helps other children avoid her nightmare experience. I have treated several families who have been through similar (and even more terrible) tragedies.

Tiffany's Story

Tiffany was 12 years old when she was referred to me by her pediatrician for psychotherapy. She had curly brown hair and the wise, dark eyes of a young one who's seen too much. I warmed to her immediately. She was curious, feisty, and sharp-witted. She was also NOT charming on her first visit to my office. She had been forced to come by her panicked mother and made it known immediately that she thought I was a waste of her time. But since she was curious, she'd allow the visits...for now.

Tiffany earned average grades in elementary school, but her grades had plummeted a few months into middle school. When I asked why, she spit out, "Because my teachers are idiots, and I really don't care about school," with a look of defiance I didn't yet dare challenge the first day. She had friends, but it sounded like she maintained social status by appearing jaded and aggressive. I remember thinking that it would be a miracle if I could keep her from getting suspended from middle school, as she seemed one snarky comment away from a fistfight.

Tiffany was the only child of a hard-working single mother and spent most of her afterschool time with her tired but devoted grandparents. Her father was murdered during a liquor store robbery when she was only two years old. He worked construction and had an alcohol problem. Her parents' marriage was described as "rocky from the beginning," but Tiffany's mom assured me her dad "loved Tiffany and his loss was hard on her." When his name was mentioned, Tiffany set her jaw but the pain in her eyes broke my heart a little. It was clear this fatherless girl and her vulnerability was something I'd need to keep in mind.

First, I'd need to tackle the crisis at hand. Recently, Tiffany's mom discovered that she had been carrying on a very involved texting relationship with a 32-year-old Internet predator named Billy. Surprisingly, she knew Billy's age from the beginning. She said the relationship started as a friendship and had developed into what Tiffany considered "true love." In fact, when Tiffany's mom discovered the texts, Tiffany and Billy were planning to meet. Billy lived in a neighboring state with his mother and was going to drive in to meet Tiffany for what appeared to be a "romantic weekend." Their texting relationship had become sexual and included an exchange of nude images from both participants. Billy had groomed Tiffany's cooperation with expert finesse, and she was set on championing the relationship to the end.

Fortunately, we interrupted their plans to meet, but Billy already had ownership over Tiffany's trust and emotions. She stated in no uncertain terms, "Nobody can keep me away from Billy. Take my phone. Take my computer, but I WILL find a way to be with him. I love him, and he loves me." And sure enough, our efforts to block Tiffany from contact failed. She used other portals to contact Billy, including school and library computers and the screens and social media apps of her friends. Shockingly, her friends were willing to support the communication, because they thought this romantic drama was adorable and had friended Billy on their personal social media platforms.

Tiffany's mom immediately called the police when she discovered the texts, and a detective interviewed Tiffany and took her phone for evidence. The FBI investigated Billy, and they were encouraging Tiffany to cooperate so they could learn more. Law enforcement referred Tiffany for treatment in the hopes that she could heal and gain insight into the danger she was in. Tiffany had zero intent to cooperate with me or anybody else she saw as an impediment to being with Billy. I spoke to the detective who shared with me that there was preliminary evidence that Billy was in contact with several other minors as well. They considered him potentially dangerous.

Tiffany is a young adult now. She never met up with Billy, nor was he ever convicted. However, even with a support team and accurate information about what a sicko Billy was, she continued contact with him for six months after the discovery. For years after she made a final break from contact, she suffered from issues of grief, shame, fear, and self-loathing that were brutally sad to witness. Her courage kept her resolute in healing from Billy's emotional imprisonment. Tiffany and I formed a powerful therapeutic alliance, and together we slogged through her desolate emotional landscape of pain off and on for several years.

Currently Tiffany is enrolled in community college and hopes to be a therapist herself one day who specializes with adolescents. She is in a healthy relationship and is taking this world by powerful storm. Her resilience and depth of character is an honor to behold, and as a practicing clinician for twenty years, I assure you her outcome is the best-case scenario. I have treated others whose online contact with strangers ended with emotional and physical assault. Abandoning kids to their technology without sophisticated parenting strategies in place can be disastrous.

Empowerment and information are critical building blocks of teen resilience. But when it comes to providing information about sexuality, many parents are so uncomfortable that they simply put it off until...forever. Or, they hand the kid a book or expect the school or peers to handle it. This leaves kids uninformed, hungry for knowledge, and vulnerable. Learning about sexuality is a lifelong process that starts as soon as you become aware of yourself as an independent being. Accurate knowledge allows us to make healthy decisions about our bodies and intimate relationships. If parents model open dialogue early, then kids will come to them for answers. As always, I trust you to custom fit my suggestions into your family with your best judgment. Families and children are unique, and nothing guides better than parental instincts.

Five Things to Avoid When Teaching Sex Ed to Your Kids

1. **Silence**
   Choosing to stay silent and avoid sexual education may cause confusion and shame for your child, which is more likely to lead to later hang-ups about sexuality and irresponsible sexual choices. Being an awesome parent means doing what's best for your child, not making yourself most comfortable by avoiding the issue.

2. **Leaving it up to the same-gender parent only**
   Both moms and dads should provide education to both sons and daughters. It's important for them to hear from both perspectives, and they may relate to one parent's communication style better than the other. Model open dialogue and educated problem solving and start when they are young.

3. **Limiting content to the technicalities**
   Instead of just talking about sex ed mechanics, incorporate family values and beliefs into the discussion. Be persuasive rather than demanding. Your children will learn important skills AND factual information, all the

while having their own perspective rather than being coerced into yours. Eye-rolls aside, kids generally adopt their parents' values. The more complex their understanding, the more comfortable they will be with making the right, and sometimes unpopular, decisions.

4. **Using the opportunity to establish authority**
Your objective is to educate and encourage cooperative dialogue, not scare your children or exert parental authority. That means offering information and listening rather than being intrusive or demanding disclosure. You are not their friend, but that doesn't mean you can't be warm, open, and encouraging. Being heavy-handed will drive them away rather than invite them in to the family support system.

5. **Being rigid and lecturing**
Avoid uninformed, strict, and inflexible standards. It's perfectly acceptable to explore issues prior to sharing your position. It's also OK to disagree. Give your children time to develop a perspective rather than demand that they adopt yours.

Five Opportunities You Shouldn't Miss When Teaching Sex Ed to Your Kids

1. **Be prepared to have many small conversations over time rather than one big one.**
Sex education doesn't have to be a weird, uncomfortable lecture. When it is appropriate to the conversation, engage your kids in dialogue. Keep it simple to start then gradually add more details as your children age and as their questions become more complex. Don't sprint to the finish in one sitting just because you're nervous. Your first conversation may last twenty seconds, then overtime they'll be longer and more complex. Set up the forms today, pour the concrete later, then you still have the finish work. Educating your children is a process over many years to come. Don't rush it.

2. **Teach accurate body-part vocabulary while children are learning language.**
Also teach them discretion about when it's appropriate to talk about those body parts and when it isn't.

3. **Take advantage of everyday activities (movies, articles, storytelling) to bring up sex ed topics, like consent.**

    Recently, there has been several celebrities facing sexual assault allegations. Although contentious at times, the public discussion about consent is important and long overdue. Flirting or looking or acting sexy is not consent to be touched or have sexual intercourse. A "yes" in response to a spoken question is consent. A great teaching tool is the YouTube video titled "Consent for Kids" and for older teens "Tea Consent (Clean)."[185][186]

4. **If you are uncomfortable starting the conversation with your children directly, let them "overhear" a conversation with other family members.**

    For example, you might say, "When I was ten years old, I had no idea how babies were made! Can you believe my first real education was...?"

5. **When your daughter starts menstruation, take her for a special mother-daughter goddess outing to model open dialogue and the celebration of femininity.**

    Too often moms jump right to the challenges of menstruation, like cramping and headaches, rather than talking about the positives of the beauty and strength of developing curves. Encouraging a good attitude from the beginning will launch positive expectation rather than dread. Expecting the best will offer her the perspective of moving forward rather than being set back.

Five Parenting Tips for Making Sex Ed Easier

1. **Understand that it is healthy for even young children to be curious about sexuality.**

    As early as toddlerhood, it is normal for children to masturbate, be curious about the bodies of others (want to "play doctor"), and ask where babies come from. I've worked in preschools, and believe me, there's a lot of jiggling at naptime. Calm, simple instruction without shaming is best.

2. **Some kids are modest about nudity and others let it all hang out.**

    Accept your child's innate personality features and simply teach them about privacy and discretion. Avoid shaming.

3. **Listen as well as teach.**
   Allow your children to have an opinion. Avoid interrupting, lecturing, shaming, and criticizing. Easy conversation is most effective for learning and relationship-building.

4. **If you're nervous, admit it.**
   Have a sense of humor without being silly. Don't be afraid to say, "I don't know, but I'll find out for you."

5. **Focus on skill-based teaching.**
   Storytelling is effective, certainly, but make sure to include tips about decision-making, peer negotiation, and refusal skills. Role-play challenging situations and engage in fun debate.

Five Sex Ed Topics to Cover (plus a bonus that is guaranteed to make uncomfortable)

1. **Tell your kids exactly how their bodies will change as they mature.**
   I know this is difficult, but that means covering topics like erections, wet dreams, puberty, and menstruation. Ask your friends if they were prepared for puberty. You will see why it's important to prepare your kids for what is going to happen with their bodies BEFORE their first pubic hair. Friends and clients over the years have told me how they were convinced they were injured or sick when they menstruated the first time and suffered in silence for months – that means before nine years old for some kids. Boys can get freaked out too and will tend to shut down. By telling your kids exactly what to expect, you'll save them from being confused and afraid. And even better than that, you'll demonstrate that you can be trusted to talk about personal and embarrassing stuff.

2. **Discuss what sexual desire is and how to best manage it.**
   By letting your kids know that sexual feelings are normal, you reduce the chance that they'll feel shame or impulsively act out. Even young children are titillated by romance and sex. If you discuss it openly then you can more fairly hold them accountable for their choices and behavior.

3. **Teach how babies are made and about sexually transmitted infections and birth control.**
   Center for Disease Control 2017 statistics reveal that 40% of high schoolers have had sexual intercourse, and 46% of them did not use a condom the last time they had sex.[187] For most of them, I'd be willing to bet their parents were the last to know. No matter what you think about

premarital sex, your kids must have information to make informed and assertive decisions. That means you must provide education about what sex is, how to prevent sexually transmitted infections and pregnancy, and what you think about teens having sex. Saying, "Just don't," is not enough, which is why abstinence-only sexual education programs in schools have failed. If you've trained your children to be blindly obedient to you, they may be blindly obedient to an exploitive peer or an Internet predator.

4. **Inform them that other kids and adults may try to take advantage of them sexually. Teach them how to assert themselves as soon as they feel the "ick factor."**
    It's not acceptable to scare your kids with stranger danger stories. However, it is critical that you teach them caution. A 2018 published in JAMA Pediatrics reported that sexting is becoming more common. In a review of 39 studies, they found that 15% of teens say they send sexts and 27% receive them.[188] Even with the best filtering and monitoring strategies in place, your kids will eventually be approached by someone looking to take advantage of them. Rather than discover that your child has participated in a sexual online activity AND THEN reacting, be preventative by teaching assertiveness skills. That means boys and girls must be taught to attend to their feelings and respond with confidence.

5. **Teach how intimacy differs from sex.**
    If you've been lucky enough to experience loving intimacy, then you know that online pornography is a poor portrayal. If you don't cover this topic, the risk is that they'll covertly watch online pornography and conclude, "Ah-ha! That's sex." Loving oneself and knowing how to build friendship must come before sexual experimentation with another person, which brings me to the bonus item.

*Talk about masturbation as a healthy but private activity.

I know this is controversial, but hang in and consider my reasoning before you decide what to share with your kids. By the principles of behavioral conditioning, children will become attached to whatever or whomever brings them pleasure. I once had a client tell me he had his first climax climbing a tree when he was eight years old. He said he was convinced that it was the tree that caused the magic for months before he figured out the real deal. First-time conditioning (intense sexual arousal in response to an inanimate object) may be a contributor to later fetish behavior as well.

Rather than leave kids vulnerable to other information sources, doesn't it make sense that you should be the one to let them know they can achieve sexual pleasure on their own without having to find a helper? It is tragic when teens seek a relationship thinking a partner is a required component for pleasure. We all know what happens to our judgment once we are having sex with somebody. If your teens know their bodies and feel self-empowered, then when they're ready to experiment with interpersonal intimacy, the focus can be on mutual affection and friendship rather than sexual pleasure. Accurate information and personal empowerment will help keep them safe and avoid unhealthy dependence on another. By teaching them that you are available for any kind of conversation, no matter how uncomfortable, they'll come to you about sexualized offline and online interactions.

CHAPTER 8: THE RISKS OF SCREEN USE: HEALTH RISKS

Health consequences from poor screen time management include distracting us from healthy relationships and activities, altering our perception of ourselves and the world around us, changing what we do and how we do it, interfering with learning and performance, repetitive use injuries, and rewiring brain process. Keeping screen time and content reasonable allows us to maintain critical building blocks to overall health and wellbeing, including sleep, nutrition, outdoor exercise, relaxation, giving back, recreation, spirituality, and loving relationships.

Distraction from and Replacement of Healthy Nondigital Relationships

Research indicates that the mere presence of a smartphone interferes with interpersonal closeness, trust, and understanding.[189] Many also argue that social skills, like empathy and patience, deteriorate as a result of screen use.[190][191] We've all seen video gamers get hooked to the point that their relationships and life skills deteriorate, leading to more escape into virtual life. But even younger kids with good social skills and a rich social life are opting to spend more time engaging with others online rather than offline.

Nonvirtual play dates are slowly dying in favor of onscreen socializing through video conferencing, social media, and video games. After all, quickly and conveniently sharing likes, memes, texts, selfies, and videos can be creatively stimulating and demands less effort than face-to-face get togethers. One can say and do things online they would never do in real life. The tendency to be more outspoken and less restrained online is called the *online disinhibition effect*. Six factors contribute, including anonymity, invisibility, *asynchronous communication* (reading and responding to texts and videos as convenient rather than real time), *solipsistic introjection* (hearing and imagining text as a voice and imaginary character in one's head), *dissociative imagination* (the relationship comes to exist in an imaginary world with its very own norms and rules), and minimization of authority. [192] Our contacts become an amalgamation of real human and our projection of who we want them to be. Why struggle with the awkward nature of face-to-face empathy and real-time response when one can edit the response at one's convenience?

In my practice, I often treat the fallout from all-consuming online intimate relationships among teens and young adults. With texting, calling, instant messaging, social media posting, and video conferencing, individuals can maintain a convenient and meaningful intimacy over long distances. Often the individuals don't meet for months or years or ever. Other times my clients talk their parents into flying their online dates in for proms and visits. Rules designed to slow down teen sexuality, like watching TV with your date with at least one foot on the floor, are obsolete.

Online relationships can offer much-needed social support, reducing isolation and despair. In most ways, kids are more dependent on these romantic relationships than we were with our nonvirtual boy- and girlfriends, because they are slow building and constantly connected. Your partner being cranky or annoying? Simply sign off. That's rarely so convenient in face-to-face relationships. Avoiding anxiety in the short-term feels good, but in the long-term online relationships can cause the individual to lose the confidence and social skills necessary to attract and maintain a more sustainable, healthy face-to-face relationship. Replacement of nonvirtual relationships can be particularly costly in adolescence, a fertile time for developing social skills with same-age peers.

Furthermore, virtual identity simply isn't as authentic as one's nonvirtual identity. Although aspects of interacting online is fun, our brains don't get the same enriched and satisfying feed from online interactions as we do with nonvirtual eye contact and touch. Virtual interactions eventually leave us feeling vaguely dissatisfied. It's not unusual for my clients to try to "spice" up the relationship with sexuality or add more people to the list. With only virtual connection, many fall into a slow cascade of loneliness and depression without much understanding why it's happening. Virtual relationships can be like using an addictive drug, the first hit is the most powerful and much of the use after is chasing that first high or staving off anxious withdrawal with a quiet, habitual desperation.

YouTube Celebrities and Online Forums

Celebrities and famous YouTube personalities, like Shane Dawson, Trisha Payatas, Jenna Marbles, and Gigi Gorgeous, can also fill this quest for belonging. They specialize in building community and defining culture by sharing stories and opinions, acting out silly skits, creating makeup tutorials, and testing products. Kids become devoted fans, memorizing personal details and impersonating their styles after watching endless hours of curated content. Although many celebrities use their influence to encourage positive social behavior, like Lady Gaga's Born This Way Foundation, others use their influence to market products and introduce child fans to inappropriate sexual exploits and information about extreme plastic surgery. Another strong influencer to behavior are online forums.

An *online forum* is an online discussion group where members share opinions and information. In the 1990s, pro-eating disorder communities (called *pro-ana* – anorexia - or *pro-mia*- bulimia) were born on websites, online journals, and Yahoo chat groups. These days they have moved to blog and micro-blogging sites like Tumblr, in chat rooms like those on the dark net, and on social media apps like Facebook and Twitter. Although these groups most often offer nonjudgmental social support for vulnerable individuals that nobody else understands, it is also common for members of these communities to obsessively share tips and tricks, encouragement, and graphic images that thrust the user deeper into more dangerous behaviors and comparisons that further despairing clinical symptoms (e.g., methods of self-harm, weight loss tips or *thinspiration* images like thigh gaps, and various suicide methods).

Psychologists call copycat contagion online acts *The Werther Effect*, and are rightly concerned about these tight communities revolving around and sharing potentially fatal behaviors. Members often encourage each other to go further, cut deeper, attempt with more lethal means rather than to seek the help they need to recover. Sometimes this misguided support actually distracts the distressed individual from seeking the professional support they desperately need. For example, food diaries are common on pro-ana sites and include challenges such as this one:

Today is the start of my 3-week water fast. I'm only allowing water. I will also be posting weekly to keep you all up to date on my progress, and hopefully I can motivate some of you to fast. If anyone wants to join me on this journey let me know.

Unhealthy Self Comparison and Shame

Screen time can not only distract us from healthy relationships with others; it can also distract us from healthy relationships with ourselves. A *selfie* is a self-portrait typically taken with a smartphone with the intent of sharing through text message or social media post for the purposes of attention seeking, communication, documenting one's day, and entertainment.[193] While the term "selfies" was first coined in 2002, it didn't become popular until 2012. By 2013, The Oxford English Dictionary named it "The Word of the Year."[194] Could increasing exposure to enhanced selfie images be contributing to higher rates of psychological issues among kids and teens?

With photo editing social media apps like Instagram, Snapchat, and Facebook as well as ads online, on billboards, in print media, and on television, kids and teens are exposed to a tsunami of edited images every day, many of their favorite celebrities. In fact, social media has made celebrity worship a common activity among kids and teens. What isn't obvious is how these celebrities and photos are lighted, contoured, surgically and cosmetically altered, filtered, and digitally enhanced, often chosen among thousands of almost identical images. The selfie queen, Kim Kardashian, proudly shared that she once took about six thousand selfies during a four-day vacation. Her celebrity sister, Kylie Jenner, also admitted that it sometimes takes up to 500 photos before she gets the right shot.

Another source of image marketing are *beauty guru* YouTube videos. Beauty gurus are Youtube celebrities who create videos that offer makeup and hair styling tutorials, skincare reviews, and fashion advice. As of 2015, there were approximately 45.3 billion views on YouTube for beauty videos alone.[195] Each month, 50 million people watch over 1.6 billion minutes of beauty guru content.[196] Teens report that beauty gurus are more "relatable" than other celebrities, thus mimicking their carefully crafted and sometimes surgically enhanced looks and adopting their often outrageous viewpoints. With such massive exposures, kids often scrutinize their own appearance, striving to develop and refine the "perfect" face and body.[197] Hyper-sexualized selfies further serve as a negative influence on identity development and perception, attracting "likes" and comments as a reflection of worth and popularity.

Selfie alteration isn't motivated simply by socialization and entertainment. A far more sinister reason lurks behind the manipulation of young minds, namely profit. Each year the beauty industry boasts about 42 billion dollars in annual profit.[198] Add that to the 30 billion dollars brought in by health and fitness and the big business of advertising on social media, and one can imagine the lengths corporations will go to manipulate buyers into buying. The worse we feel about ourselves, the more we buy products to "fix" us.

Do kids adopt unrealistic attractiveness standards from screen media, and can this affect mental health? Although a causal connection hasn't yet received substantial support; anxiety, depression and other mental health issues for young women have been rising at an alarming rate for the past twenty years. According to the Press Association (2014), studies have found "a jump in the number of women aged sixteen to twenty-four experiencing mental health problems and a growing gap between female and male sufferers."[199] Since the 1990s, young women have gone from being twice as likely to being three times as likely to have common mental health disorder symptoms (CMD) compared to young men. CMD refers specifically to "irritability, worrying, depression, anxiety, feelings of panic, compulsion, and trouble sleeping." Estimates from the 2014 National Study of Health and Wellbeing concluded that, "in 1993, 19% of women aged sixteen and twenty-four had symptoms of CMD, rising to 26% in 2014."[200] Researchers conjecture that social media and the pursuit of perfection is a likely contributor.

Body distortion and eating disorders are also on the rise, especially among young children and boys. In the United States alone, twenty million women and ten million men suffer from a clinically significant eating disorder at some time in their life, including body dysmorphic disorder, anorexia nervosa, bulimia nervosa, binge eating disorder, or Eating Disorder, Not Otherwise Specified.[201] In a survey conducted in 2011, 40 to 60% of elementary school girls reported having concern about their weight.[202] Like with women, there is evidence that targeted advertisements play a contributing role. In a study by Leit (2002), men demonstrated significantly more dissatisfaction in their muscular build after viewing advertisements containing images of muscular men than a control group who viewed neutral advertisements.[203] For all genders, body shaming among peers too often starts young and peaks during adolescence. Males tend to be more directly aggressive, while females shame through passive aggressive means like gossip and cyberbullying.[204]

Body dysmorphia (BDD) is a mental illness that describes the phenomenon of obsessively focusing on a perceived flaw in appearance to the point of avoiding social exposure or excessively seeking plastic surgery and beauty treatments. BDD rates are increasing, currently as common as obsessive-compulsive disorder and more common that anorexia nervosa. Patients with BDD tend to seek validation for their attractiveness on social media. Plastic surgeons have recently renamed the specific phenomena of seeking procedures to look more like Snapchat filters, *Snapchat dysmorphia*. With increasing numbers of patients seeking fuller lips, bigger eyes, and thinner noses, experts are positing that frequent exposure to photo retouching technology may be leading to increasing rates of mental illness. In support of this theory, a 2017 survey from the American Academy of Facial Plastic and Reconstructive Surgery sound that 55 percent of surgeons report seeing patients who mention selfies as a reason for requesting surgery, compared to 42 percent in 2015.[205]

How can we inoculate our kids against unhealthy self-perception, distorted body image, excessive consumerism, and mood and eating disorders?

Love and compliment your kids loudly and unapologetically for all they are. This includes their worthiness of love just for being the perfectly imperfect, nondigitally-enhanced them.

Reinforce that the self is made up of far more facets than a beautiful face. Interests, skills, and unique traits make up what's important about a person, not eye size and hair color.

Discuss the fact that we are connected to our bodies for the long haul. We must treat our bodies as our best friends rather than our enemies.

Lead by example. Do you voice your disapproval about your face or body aloud to your kids? If you do, they too will follow suit about themselves. Instead, be loud and proud of the woman or man you are today. Value yourself just as you would like your daughter or son to value her/himself.

Implement healthy eating, sleeping, and exercise habits and explain why that is so important for strength and health. Focus on words like "delicious" and "nourishing" for healthy food to highlight lifestyle factors and frame nutritious food options as a treat, rather than using words like "diet" or "cleanse" or "cheat" that stage junk food as treats and healthy foods as punishment. Refuse to participate in fads focused on fat-shaming that claim quick weight loss.

Remind your teen that what they see on social media and in advertisements isn't always the real deal. Take an Internet browsing journey with them researching this topic by searching "Photoshop hacks" or looking up Jean Kilbourne's groundbreaking work in this area with her "Killing Us Softly" video series, a must see!

Experimental Identity Play

Lesbian, gay, bisexual, transgender, and queer (LGBTQ) kids are at particular risk for social isolation, cyberbullying, mood and anxiety disorders, sexual assault, and suicide. I debated whether experimental identity play should be included in the benefits or risk section of *Screen Time in the Mean Time*. Ultimately, I decided to include it as risk simply because online experimentation with identity is rife with challenges during a tender, complex developmental time. Online communities can provide valuable emotional safety and support and important health information that compliments healthy experimentation. But they can also influence kids in dangerous ways like teaching premature sex and fetish play and glorifying mood and anxiety disorders. Recently several of my teen clients who role-play online have been experimenting with self-identity and gender, sexual, and romantic orientation. It has me wondering, is online role-play healthy experimentation or a dangerous trend?

I once worked with a male-to-female transgender teen, "Via," who was describing frankly psychotic symptoms (hearing and interacting with internal voices) and was prescribed antipsychotic medication from her psychiatrist. Upon further investigation, however, it became clear that, rather than developing a chronic mental illness like schizophrenia which requires immediate pharmacological intervention, she was actually using her creativity to describe a rich experience that was part of her coming out process. With a group of supportive others, she had adopted two alter selves, popularly known as *tulpas*.

A tulpa is a being that lives within the teen's mind that has its own personality and identity. A tulpa is born by willing it into existence. It can be a companion in one's *wonderland*, which is a fantasy world with no limitations, also built by the imagination. This independent, sentient being has access to its *host's* memories and will interact with the host and other tulpas. The host and the tulpas interact like roommates occupying the same brain. A tulpa, or sometimes called an *alter*, can possess, or take control of, the host's body. Group members describe allowing their tulpas to *switch* to act on their own passions, like taking college classes or making their own friends. This dynamic is similar to the mental illness *dissociative identity disorder*, or multiple personality disorder, largely popularized in the 1970s. Chatrooms flourish as the hosts and tulpas share tips and interact with each other online. This type of identity play is a common cultural component among characters in webcomics.

A *webcomic* is a comic published on a website, some of which continue for months at a time. For example, *Homestuck* (2009 - 2016) contained over 8,000 pages and boasted millions of viewers. A *fandom* is a subculture of fans that interact around a particular interest, such as a webcomic. Fans follow complex story arcs while engaging in analytical discussions about the story and the real world, discussions ripe with slang and constantly building upon shared understanding. Many webcomics are pornographic. Fans exchange artistic and costumed images, videos, and memes that relate to their shared passion and form close relationships and subgroups that interact several hours a day. Along with a love of fantasy and creativity, webcomic fans often have a flair for intelligent and vigorous investigation of gender, sexual orientation, and romantic interest.

Within the last several years I've observed that teens are challenging traditional gender and sexual orientations with a dizzying array of alternative sociological concepts and lifestyles. What do I mean? Because webcomic characters are fantasy-based, they can incorporate any combination of state or trait imaginable. One way webcomic authors take artistic license is to create a character of ambiguous gender and/or sexual orientation (e.g., an alien troll who is neither male nor female). As the audience follows these forever growing storylines, they become increasingly tolerant of and curious about character trait ambiguity.

In addition to following webcomic characters with multi-faceted states and traits, many fans go on to act out their interests playing as customized avatars in massively multiplayer online role-playing games like *World of Warcraft*. By experimenting with looks, backstories, and behaviors, players witness the intricate impacts these variables play in social interaction. Not only do the the players' avatars communicate within the game, but the players also interacting privately with individuals or groups of players via instant messaging or with headsets and microphones.

If the immersion into the online world is meaningful to them, or what we call *ego syntonic*, these online cultural attributes may leak into the teen's real world. An example of this is the practice of *cosplay*, or dressing up and taking on the attributes of a character from a webcomic, video game, book, or movie. The most popular type of cosplay is from Japanese comic book and graphic novel genres of *manga* or *anime*. *Gender crossplay* is a type of cosplay in which participants cross dress. One type of cross dressing community is the *furry community*. Individuals who engage in furry play dress and behave as the animal they most identify with. G-rated furplay can provide fun affiliation. However, often furries engage in sexual fantasy and animal sex that can lead to fetish sex. Cosplay gets as outrageous as the imagination allows.

Fandom kids can get a triple load of influence, one as a passive webcomic or graphic novel reader, a second as an engaged fandom participant in chatrooms and video games online, and a third in cosplay activities offline. Many spend more time in these fantasy scenarios and online friendships than as live participants in the non-virtual world. As you might expect, their real lives gradually begin to mimic their virtual lives. I have now worked with several fandom-influenced teens who no longer identify as their born gender in identity, expression, or behavior. Here is some terminology I've learned from my clients:

Agender: neither male nor female

Pangender: more than one gender

Trigender: shift from one gender to another depending on their mood or situation (e.g., male, female, and polygender or any other combination of genderqueer varieties)

Gender Fluid: mix two or more genders at a time (bigender for example)

Cisgender: identify with the assigned gender at birth

Transgender: identify with another gender than the assigned gender at birth

Along with using gender-neutral pronouns, my clients born as girls cut their hair short and wear t-shirts and basketball shorts. Clients born as boys wear their hair long and apply guy-liner. Other times they mix gender-preferred accessories. It's all very confusing, indeed. Now complicate that with sexual orientation (*asexual, pansexual, skoliosexual, bisexual, homosexual, heterosexual*) and romantic orientation (*aromantic, panromantic, polyromantic*), and one's Gen-X head starts to spin. Lest you think it's city living that's creating these issues, think again. The World Wide Web enables anyone with a screen to be the audience and potential participant in these complex sociological and psychological identity principles.

The teens in my office insist that their open-minded exploration is creating the supportive cultural milieu they idealistically envision. Some feel they were born with unique gender or sexual identities and others believe this exploration is a natural result of experience and experimentation. Most love it and seem to be flourishing with the freedom to investigate the many facets of who they are. For many parents, however, it's a challenge as they try their best to make decisions about slumber party arrangements amidst constantly shifting gender, sexual, and romantic orientations.

Parents look to me for guidance as to whether they should encourage or discourage gender and sexual experimentation. They fear how their stance may affect their kids' gender and sexual development. If they whole-heartedly support gender, romantic, and sexual orientation play, are they encouraging behavior that may be overwhelming for teens in the already complex landscape of adolescence? Alternatively, if they forbid experimentation are they creating the kind of shame and isolation that can lead to serious trouble? After all, transgender youth have among the highest suicide rates of any minority group, leading us to understand this is not always "play," but for some a working through of their very identity.

In situations where a teen is alone and closeted among family and friends, one can imagine that the opportunity for anonymity and the support of a positive, affirming community such as a fandom could literally be a lifesaver. Alternatively, game play typically involves provocative themes such as violence and sex. Online peers are friends and strangers of all ages, some with positive and others with predatory intent. The lack of transparency and versatility to manipulate what is seen and said during game play, along with a false expectation of anonymity and privacy adds further layers of risk.

Consider Miley Cyrus' quote in OUT Magazine, "I didn't want to be a boy. I kind of wanted to be nothing. I don't relate to what people would say defines a girl or a boy, and I think that's what I had to understand: Being a girl isn't what I hate, it's the box that I get put into." Like it or not, identity play and gender-awareness issues have hit the mainstream, and our kids are enthusiastically at the forefront of change. Gender-awareness is one aspect, but sexual awareness is another. Sexual exploration on and offline is a delicate topic for even the most open-minded parents. Teens are often curious for information about their developing bodies and urges, often leading them into online chat rooms for information, chatrooms with little to no monitoring for inaccurate or inappropriate information or conduct and virtually no screening of participants. They also look to celebrity idols for modeling and guidance, maybe not the wise parent's choice for a big brother/sister/pansibling.

What should parents do to help their teens through identity exploration?

Become aware that there are potentially life-spinning issues coming through the digital pipelines. For a quick rundown with supplementary videos, check out the CBS News online article by Cydney Adams, "The Gender Identity Terms You Need to Know."[206]

Reflect and untangle your ideas and beliefs about these complex issues before you pass confusion and shame onto your kids. Education and experimentation can be affirming, positive, and exciting. Unsupervised however, exploration can lead to inappropriate risk-taking and exploitation.

Be a willing ear to learn and participate in their lives, on- and offline, whether you agree on these issues or not. If you shut yourself off from these issues, you lose influence and may damage your relationship.

Age and maturity matters. Parents can support identity play while limiting access to sexually explicit or violent material. Keep younger kids safe by filtering inappropriate content, providing gender and sexual education early with ongoing open dialogue, and monitoring online and offline interactions.

When writing this article, I reflected on how different my life would be if I had logged in hours of virtual time with varying gender and sexual identities. When I discussed these issues with my 13-year-old, she responded confidently, "It's always good to be allowed the freedom to be whomever you want to be." Is that true or the ideals of a teen? I suppose it is for each family to work out with an informed, open perspective and the warmth and love only a parent can muster. Whatever your opinion, remember that as kids age it's important that we move from demanding strict obedience to warm, accepting negotiation. If it's a phase, it will fizzle. If it's a true identity issue, the only reasonable option is to love them for being them. Right now, kids have a lot to teach us as well as a lot to learn. This opportunity can lead to a more loving, respectful connection.

Online Radicalization and Recruitment into a Cult or Hate Group

In June 2015 nine innocent people were gunned down in front of their friends and family by 21-year-old Dylann Roof at a historic African-American church in Charleston, South Carolina. During the shooting, he shouted, "You rape our women. And you're taking over our country. You have to go." Dylann was an active participant in online white supremacist forums designed to radicalize youth. Since then we have witnessed several other tragedies due to mass murderer shooters.

Dylann Roof displayed several risk factors characteristic of vulnerable youth. His parents divorced and struggled financially. His stepmother filed court papers accusing Dylann's father of emotional and physical abuse. He dropped out of ninth grade and was reported to be a heavy drinker and user of marijuana and harder drugs. His friends described him as a quiet man who shared a mobile home with five other people. Prior to the murders, friends had become alarmed about his drunken comments regarding a "race war," but nobody suspected he was violent.

Like Isla Vista shooter Elliot Rodger, Dylann posted a hateful online manifesto before his murderous rampage detailing his violent and racist beliefs. Along with photos of him standing on and burning an American Flag and aiming his gun, his manifesto titled "an explanation" details his "disdain" against blacks, Jews, Hispanics, and patriotism. He writes:

> "I have no choice. I am not in the position to, alone, go into the ghetto and fight. I chose Charleston because it is the most historic city in my state, and at one time had the highest ratio of blacks to Whites in the country. We have no skinheads, no real KKK, no one doing anything but talking on the Internet. Well someone has to have the bravery to take it to the real world, and I guess that has to be me."

Dylann Roof was sentenced to life in prison without parole on April 10, 2017. That year the Southern Poverty Law Center estimated that there were 917 known hate groups operating in the United States, an alarming increase from the 602 identified in 2000. When one considers that the Internet is worldwide, the potential for online hate is staggering. Because of an immature self-identity and limited experience and problem-solving skills, youth are particularly susceptible to influence and are the most common perpetrators of hate crimes.

The most frightening aspect of online recruitment techniques is that they are so sophisticated. No longer do hate groups and cults rely on interpersonal contact, newsletters, and rallies for recruitment. Now recruits can be groomed slowly and deceptively from the illusory safety of their bedrooms. Creating websites and social media publicity funnels is easy and inexpensive, allowing big reach and total control over content. Internet platforms are the perfect tool for grooming, behavioral manipulation, and coercive thought control. By the time a teen is ready to pack their suitcase to join the group, they have been expertly brainwashed over months to adopt a radicalized web of beliefs. Because victims are cautioned to keep their activities secret from the beginning, parents are often completely unaware of their teens' online activities.

How might a parent inoculate a teen from this kind of susceptibility?

Filter and block access to inappropriate sites for younger teens and stay engaged and aware of your kids' off- and online activities.

Provide educationally enriched and diverse experiences to decrease susceptibility due to fear, lack of experience, and overly simplistic thinking.

Encourage your kids to think for themselves and research opposing positions. Practice respectful discussion and debate to build assertiveness and reasoning skills with increasing challenge over time.

Teach your kids how to recognize the following signs of online grooming and brainwashing:

Marketing techniques and products designed to be attractive to targeted population segments (like youth and women)

Inducing guilt by providing offers of friendship and gifts to develop a sense of reciprocity leave victims feeling that they owe the recruiter and must give back. Hyped meetings, branding, and merchandizing support the power and exclusivity of the group (e.g., slogans, symbols, colors, mascots, music, video games, and customized slang). Many hate group websites include kids' activities like coloring pages, puzzles, animated mascots, videos, and downloadable music and video games (sometimes with racially intolerant content like torturing or hunting the target populations of their hate) for early grooming.

Sensational messaging based on deception and false facts that trigger intrigue, suspicion, and paranoia

For example, "Did you know that Martin Luther King Jr. was not a legitimate reverend?"

Attempts to isolate the subject by exploiting emotional vulnerabilities and destabilizing friend and family support

Isolation starts with probes that assess susceptibility ("Where is your computer?" "Are you alone?") and attempts to validate emotion and join ("I know what that feels like." "You can trust me."). Once victims show interest and openness, the recruiter challenges their belief systems and attacks the credibility of family and friends. If the recruiter can tap into fear and insecurity, they can then start to target blame ("Do your parents overlook and dismiss you?" "Do you feel lonely and misunderstood?" "If they loved you, they would not control you like they do.").

Promise of a cure for emotional pain in the form of service and secret sanctuary

Examples include secret intimacy, romantic unconditional love, belonging to a community, wealth, fame, power over others, escape, a spiritual "answer," and protection.

Intense unrelenting pressure to build trust and a sense of belonging

Online blogs are highly effective for nurturing belief change with long narratives dispersed overtime among cyber communities bonded by belonging, shared values and practices, and a fierce sense of elitism and pride. The goal is to tempt subjects into slowly sacrificing free will and becoming increasingly reliant on the group to do their thinking for them. Hate groups thrive through members who are willing to hop on a radical bandwagon based on personal ideologies, rather than factual or scientific evidence, and actively cyber bully or censor others who don't agree with their message. Teach your child how to recognize confrontational, combative, and abusive comment threads as well as exploitive and extortive threats ("If you don't, I'll show your friends and family the texts and pictures you've sent me."). Teens with a high desire to please others and those who are convinced they are too tough to influence are vulnerable. Kids who feel their parents are too intrusive or controlling may also rebel. Nobody is safe from the charm of a skilled recruiter.

Tests of loyalty and intimidation, inducing guilt for opposition to achieve blind obedience

"We have direct authority from a divine power."

Invitations and offers for travel

Perhaps you're thinking government surveillance and regulation will keep your family safe? Unfortunately, regulation to block hateful cyberconduct is only in its infancy. It is not unusual for teens to launch into a quest for individual identity, even if it means joining somebody else's civil war. Rolling Stone magazine wrote of three Muslim teens who were taken into custody at the airport on their way to join ISIS after a long period of online grooming, all without their parents' awareness. It's impossible to know how many people have been radicalized on the Internet. The records of prosecuted teens are sealed due to minor status.

With teen spirit characterized by idealism, omnipotence, and egocentrism, youth will always be at the forefront of the fight for social justice. Their powerful need for spiritual fulfillment, meaning, and a sense of belonging during a high-pressure time also makes them vulnerable to those who promise black and white answers in a confusingly nuanced world. As parents, our best hope is to provide them with a loving, enriched, and protected environment where they don't fear marginalization and failure. If we love and accept our children during their search for independence and identity, they're less likely to seek the mentorship of dangerous others.

Distraction from and Replacement of Healthy Nondigital Activities

Researchers have long cited studies that demonstrate that our brains are attracted to new and striking stimuli, which psychologists call *salience*. But never before has anything captured our attention like screens. Like heroin, our attraction to screens can even hijack our most basic instincts toward connection and activity. I'm seeing more distraction among clients presenting in my office, not only from our primary relationships, but also from our most essential activities like sleep, food, and exercise.

Rejuvenating Sleep

Have you ever wondered why sleep is so important? During sleep our brains conduct general housekeeping and memory strengthening duties.

Housekeeping tasks necessary for neurological health include the pruning, repair, and regeneration of neurons and the removal of toxins. Memory strengthening, called *memory consolidation*, occurs by stabilizing memory traces that were acquired while awake. Memory consolidation occurs with both *declarative* (fact-based) and *procedural* (how-to) information. *Rapid-eye-movement* (REM) sleep is particularly important for stabilizing complex or emotionally charged memories.[207]

When we don't get enough sleep, our brain's housekeeping and memory consolidation tasks remain undone, leaving us unable to efficiently acquire or retrieve information. Sleep deprivation not only stunts learning, it can also cause mood volatility, negative mood states like depression, irritability, and anxiety; fatigue, confusion, attention problems, motor impairment, and overall impaired cognitive performance.[208] Furthermore, sleep deprived individuals often fail to recognize impairment. In other words, they don't realize the costs and keep burning the candle at both ends.

Missing out on much-needed sleep and staying up all night on screens is called *vamping*. Teens with chronic sleep deprivation demonstrate lower achievement motivation, more teacher-child relationship problems, a poorer academic self-concept, and poorer school performance.[209] I believe that the digital age has contributed to sleep deprivation, one of the most common and insidious threats to mental health.

How might parents decrease the risk of vamping and encourage healthy sleep?

Stage the room to be restful.

I know it's nearly impossible to motivate kids to unclutter their rooms. But a soothing environment contributes to a soothed mind. Offer your support by helping your child create a more restful environment with a fresh bedroom makeover. Light paint colors, soft textures, organized closets and bedside tables, soft lighting, white noise makers, and yummy smells can turn a chaotic hovel into a relaxing paradise.

Recognize that nutrition, exercise, and screen content impacts the quality of sleep.

Research has demonstrated that young children who watch violent television content have more sleep problems, particularly delayed onset of sleep, than children who view age-appropriate content.[210] Furthermore, kids who get adequate nutrition and exercise, especially outdoor exercise because of sunlight setting your circadian rhythm, also get better quality sleep. In practice I find that teens, in particular, benefit from the mood benefits of regular cardio and cooperative team play.

No screens in the bedroom.

Why? Because screens wake up our brain! The blue LED light from the screen stimulates the photo sensors in the retina that signal the brain to suppress melatonin production (our sleep-regulating hormone) and makes us more alert. Less melatonin disrupts our natural circadian rhythms, which can lead to sleep during the day and wakefulness during the night. Using screens before bedtime has been found to cause people to go to bed later, prolong the time it takes to fall asleep, delays the timing of REM sleep, reduces the amount of REM sleep and sleep overall, reduces alertness in the morning, and causes more daytime sleepiness.[211] Use alarm clocks with red-lighted numbers in bedrooms rather than screens for time keeping.

Screens also condition us to be awake in bed. If we are often awake in bed, our bodies will automatically be *conditioned to cue*, or believe that the bed is an "awake-only" zone. Alternatively, if we only rest and sleep in bed, our bodies will be cued that bed is a "sleep-only" zone. In psychology, we call this type of cued learning *classical conditioning*. By these principals, we must resist the urge to do anything in bed but sleep to develop good expectation and habit. Make the *No Screens in the Bedroom Rule* BEFORE it's necessary. It's asking a lot to say no TV, video games, tablets, or smartphones in the bedroom, but vamping leads to sleep deprivation. Sleep deprivation leads to impulsivity and risk-taking.[212] Impulsivity while in intimate spaces leads to intimate gestures like sexting and viewing inappropriate online content.

Encourage a soothing nighttime ritual.

We are creatures of habit. Habitual activity during the thirty-minute bedtime wind-down signals the body to anticipate rest. Components of a soothing ritual may include soft lighting; quiet, repetitive, or white noise sounds; and comforting activities. Sticking to a consistent bedtime schedule is also important.

Screens off thirty minutes before lights out.

As our brains sort through our memory caches, information is prioritized to either forget or remember. Because experiences that trigger emotion are typically important, evolution has shaped our brains to prioritize memories infused with emotion. Based on cognitive science theories, looping on a troubling experience is thought to be the cause of nightmares.

Just like the response to fright when we're awake, stress hormones like cortisol and adrenaline dump into our blood stream when we have nightmares. If we are troubled upon falling asleep, agitated dreaming and tossing and turning may result, leaving us tired, irritable, and cognitively scrambled the next day. Over time, this can seriously impair mental health.

Although emotionally triggering and arousing screen activities like gaming, texting, or viewing activating content aren't as troubling as real-life trauma, they still stimulate the same brain regions activated with chronic stress, often for hours at a time. The hangover from chronic stress has been referred to as *mental brownout*. Limiting activating screen activities at night and giving your children time to soothe prior to bedtime will result in better quality sleep overall and pave the way for healthy learning during the day. Particularly avoid eating, triggering discussions, video gaming, and intense exercise before bed.

Teach sophisticated self-soothing strategies.

The opportunity to spend time with a relaxed parent is another factor critical to self-soothing. From birth, a child's brain synchronizes with a responsive parent. Eye contact, narrative moment-to-moment comments with emotion words, and general conversation teaches kids what emotions are and how to deal with them. We cannot provide this kind of synching and teaching if we are focused on screens instead of each other. Also, if you don't sleep well one night, don't stress about it. Getting anxious or angry will wake you up more, and most of us get poor sleep here and there and simply make it up later.

Cognitive-behavioral exercises like those detailed in Chapter Four (diaphragmatic breathing, progressive muscle relaxation, mindfulness, imagery, and cognitive restructuring) can fend off even the most persistent sleep disorders. Exercising one's mind to relax is critical to self-soothing. Another option for overcoming some of the negative effects of sleep deprivation is napping. A full cycle of sleep takes about ninety minutes and provides the cognitive rejuvenation that improves procedural memory and creativity with no *sleep inertia* (grogginess). Sixty to thirty minutes is good for *slow wave* sleep, which helps with fact memory and retrieval, but may still result in grogginess. Twenty to ten-minute *power naps* are shown to increase alertness and energy. If you have time to nap, it's best to spend ninety minutes to complete a sleep cycle or just power nap for ten.

Mindful Eating

Good self-care is tough for even the most disciplined of adults. A key element to healthy living is developing an awareness of brain and body cues, like hunger and satiation, thirst, discomfort, and emotion. If kids are distracted by screens during mealtimes, they will also be distracted from the very brain and body sensations that regulate healthy eating. Screens at mealtime are associated with poorer family communication and poorer nutrition choices overall. Alternatively, screen-free family dinners provide opportunity to strengthen the parent-child relationship and facilitate learning. Old-school family dinners have also been found to decrease the risk of adolescent mental health issues and cyberbully victimization.[213]

Exercise and Non-Electronic Play

Screen time can interfere with non-electronic play activities like pretend and physical or competitive play. *Pretend play* is defined as the act of playing the role of another person, creating an imaginary friend, or visualizing a new play setting or adventurous scenario. Pretend play helps kids learn social and emotional competence, like how to form and maintain friendships, develop *theory of mind* (understand and predict the behavior and feelings of others) and verbal ability, perfect emotional awareness and empathy, develop social adaptation skills, and build self-esteem and resilience.[214] Learning from non-electronic play is a primary foundation of successful education by encouraging curiosity, creativity, motivation, and initiative. Furthermore, peer acceptance and social competence is correlated with more successful life outcome.[215]

Physical and competitive play also offers developmental benefits. More specifically, "rough and tumble" play, running, and structured ball games offer gross and fine motor development like balance, strength, and hand-eye coordination. Rule-bound, organized play that requires practice for mastery also teaches kids grit and work ethic. Direct competition contributes to emotional control, moral reasoning, cooperation and negotiation, empathy, and overall resiliency.[216] Children who do not learn resiliency are vulnerable to bullying, drug use, and have trouble dealing with everyday life challenges.[217]

Injury, Distraction, and Performance Deficits

Is Wi-Fi dangerous to our health?

The average American spends eight hours and forty-one minutes a day on screen devices, with Wi-Fi-dependent mobile devices making up most of that time.[218] The demand for increased Wi-Fi availability and speed has caused many businesses and nations to vastly increase production. In India, for example, the government is working on a Wi-Fi program that is estimated to cost sixty-two billion dollars. This vast sum of money will be used to create 1,050 new Wi-Fi hotspots in areas that currently lack Internet access.[219] With global interests focused on increasing public access to Wi-Fi, mobile device use will continue to increase among users of all ages.

Wi-Fi, or *wireless fidelity*, is a wireless technology that uses radio waves to transmit information across a two-way wireless network; information received from the Internet and from the Wi-Fi-enabled electronic device. Smartphones have adapters that translate data into a radio signal, which is then sent to a decoder, called a *router*. Every router has a unique *IP address*. Once the data is decoded by the router, it is first sent to the Internet through a wired Ethernet connection. Returning data from the Internet will pass through the router a second time for decoding, then on to the smartphone's wireless adapter.[220] Wi-Fi enabled devices include smartphones, gaming devices, tablets, printers, appliances, toys, cars, robots, and computers.

There are two kinds of radiation, ionizing and non-ionizing. *Ionizing radiation* is the radiation that we fear, high-intensity radiation that is emitted from x-rays and nuclear bombs that is strong enough to penetrate our cells and damage our DNA. The radiation emitted by Wi-Fi enabled devices is *non-ionizing radiation*. It is the same low intensity radiation that is emitted by the sun. Cancer research has clearly shown that the radiation from the sun can harm you. However, the sun's radiation is at a vastly higher level than the radiation emitted from our Wi-Fi devices.

The World Health Organization (WHO) has classified mobile phones as a "possible carcinogen," meaning that current studies are not conclusive enough to show that cell phone radiation does or does not cause cancer.[221] A study conducted by Moskowitz and colleagues (2015) revealed that rats who were exposed to high levels of cell phone radiation were at higher risk for developing brain and heart tumors.[222] However, the radiation used in this rat study was much higher than the radiation experienced when on the phone or using Wi-Fi. Other studies have shown that high levels of Wi-Fi exposure cause hormonal shifts and oxidative stress, which can promote cancer and brain diseases.[223] High exposure to Wi-Fi has also been hypothesized to cause neurodevelopmental issues and reproductive harm in humans, especially among the vulnerable like pregnant women and children.[224] However, when considering the bulk of research that exists thus far, there is no persuasive evidence that our everyday Wi-Fi exposure is dangerous to our health.

The ability to connect your device to the Internet via Wi-Fi has allowed us to entertain ourselves and be more productive on the go. However, utilizing unsecured Wi-Fi sources exposes us to hacking dangers. If there is a username and password on the network, then you are using a *secured network*. This network can be hacked but requires more work. An *unsecured network* that is free to access without a password, like you would find at your local coffee shop, is riskier. When you connect to an unsecured Wi-Fi network, your device's IP address can be seen, which is how hackers infiltrate your device. Once the hacker has infiltrated your device they can add malware or steal personal information.

How to Limit Wi-Fi Risk

- Employ common sense safety measures like not sleeping with your phone by your bed, not storing your phone in pockets near your heart or reproductive organs, and keeping routers out of the bedroom. Also, use your headphones or a Bluetooth device if you spend many hours on your mobile phone.

- Track and set limits on how many hours you spend using Wi-Fi (time management apps can help).

- Use filtering, monitoring, and control apps with kids, especially to turn off phone activity while driving.

- Develop screen-free skills by setting time and blackout day limits, like GKIS #NoTechTuesday and #NoTechThursday.

- Only sign on to secure Wi-Fi sources.

- Avoid screen fatigue by limiting multitasking.

- Turn off Wi-Fi when not in use.

- Most of all, disconnect and spend time with the people you love doing things that are fun and rejuvenating.

Repetitive Strain and Distraction Injuries

Have you heard of *text neck*? This refers to premature degeneration and malformation of the neck and spine caused by looking down at the screen for texting. In the past, these types of injuries were common among aging dentists and welders. Now physicians are seeing these injuries in teens. Hanging your head at a sixty-degree angle while texting places sixty pounds of force on the neck. This is far beyond the ten pounds of force your neck is designed to support when your head is in the neutral position. Poor texting posture can be particularly problematic for young users whose spines are still developing and could lead to arthritic changes in the spine, bone spurs, or muscle deformities. Research findings indicated that *kyphosis*, which refers to S-curve of the spine, or rounded back, can be caused by the loosening of ligaments in the spine aggravated by screen use.[225] Other repetitive strain injuries from excessive screen use include tendonitis in the shoulder, elbow, forearm, wrist, or hand, back or neck strain, carpal tunnel syndrome, hearing loss, and eye strain.

To avoid painful and costly repetitive strain injuries, set up your *GKIS Co-Work Stations* with the body-healthy ergonomics detailed in Chapter Two. Teach your kids to be aware for awkward or twisted body placement, slouching, loud earphones, high glare screen settings, or pounding the keyboard or gripping the mouse. Recognize that sitting and texting is particularly problematic. Also show them strategies for proper setup, awareness, and frequent breaks and stretches. Finally, have a discussion how texting distracts one from being aware of their environment. The Internet abounds with videos of people walking into traffic, fountains, and even bears while texting. I'm particularly scarred from hearing about a gruesome accident where a woman got her hair caught in an escalator while texting. Avoiding injuries due to repetitive screen use and distraction is a perfect GKIS family dinner topic.

Pranks and Challenges

Online modeling of dangerous pranks became popular with the MTV series, *Jackass*, where a group of young men dared each other to carry out stupid stunts for fun and humor. With the omnipotence and idealism of youth, kids don't recognize risk as readily as adults do. Furthermore, participating in a risky or funny dare can give an insecure teen street cred with peers. Because monkey see, monkey do, enthusiastic kids often copy stunts to create sharable videos; the more shocking the stunt, the more dramatic the outcome, the more social media likes. With viral sharing on social media, pranks and fads have hit hard over the years. Even pranks that appeared mild occasionally turned dangerous. Here are few of the most popular pranks that have resulted in injury or death:

Planking – laying rigidly straight, face down with arms to your sides in an unusual location. This one is only dangerous if one is planking on a ledge, for example.

The Cinnamon Challenge – eating a teaspoon of ground cinnamon in under sixty seconds without drinking anything. The thrill is watching the victim cough and sputter in a cloud of cinnamon as they gasp for breath, gag, vomit, or wipe their nose from irritation. The risk is choking, pneumonia, or a collapsed lung.

The Salt and Ice Challenge – pouring salt on one's skin then applying ice and pressure to see how long the victim can tolerate the pain. Exposure can cause first- and second-degree burns.

Swatting – making a false 911 call claiming bomb threat, gunman, or hostage held so the SWAT team will respond, usually to an unsuspecting victim's house. This is considered a third-degree crime and can result in injury or death or legal consequences, such as a fine or jail time. Gamers often naively brag about swatting conquests and use it to retaliate against gaming victors.

The Choking Game (aka *The Fainting Game*) – choking oneself to unconsciousness to wake up to a state of euphoria. Oxygen deprivation to the brain can cause permanent disability and falling can cause bodily or traumatic brain injury.

Texting and Driving

Motor vehicle accidents are the leading cause of death for children, and texting while driving is the cause of 25% of all driving accidents.[226][227] Texting and driving has become a bigger hazard than drinking and driving. Ninety-five percent of drivers disapprove of distracted driving, yet 71% admit to doing it.[228] In the five seconds it takes to respond to a text while driving 55 mph, one travels the entire length of a football field.[229] Not only does texting take your eyes off the road, but it is also takes your hands off the wheel and is a cognitive distraction.

Because teen drivers are inexperienced and tend to overlook risk, draw up a safe driving contract with your teen so they are aware of distracted driving risks and agree to safe driving practices. Make sure they recognize that texting while driving is illegal and may result in fines, license restriction, rise in auto insurance rates, and even prison time. Critical safety measures include setting a good example, limiting the number of passengers, investing in a safe-driving course, and using a parent-controlled tech tool like a pause button that freezes smartphone capacity.

Multitasking

Multitasking is defined as toggling back and forth between a primary task and an interrupting task. For our purposes, I am specifically referring to doing schoolwork while attending to interrupting screen tasks like instant messaging, texting, or social media. Although most people think of multitasking as simultaneously performing competitive cognitive tasks, that's a myth. The brain doesn't work that way. It only engages in one demanding task at a time per mental module. If two tasks require the same cognitive resources, they're in competition as we toggle back and forth very quickly. Toggling attention can have a significant cost to learning and performance.

Because teens have grown up with technology, they are well practiced and fully immersed in the multitasking screen culture. Within the past decade, we've witnessed a 120% increase in the time youth multitask with media.[230] Not only are kids multitasking during home hours; we have introduced screens into the very sanctuaries where we build the scaffolding of reasoning, our schools. Kids often need screen access to complete schoolwork and homework. The challenge is discriminating what screen activities help get the task done, and which are distracting by feeding our compelling hunger for escape, socialization, or entertainment.

Of course, there are learning benefits to screen use in schools. Kids are no longer limited to passive consumption of single-source information like books or documentaries. With the Internet, digital storage, and many consumption options, they can creatively and actively seek content on demand. They are learning more, faster than ever before with *breadth-based cognitive control*. Because the brain creates superhighways of neuronal pathways for efficient learning, screen content consumption is customizing brain wiring. Heavy multitaskers demonstrate a superior ability to switch between tasks and manage multiple streams of information at once, while also being better at identifying distracting cues while working.[231] It seems that practiced multitaskers either toggle without fatigue cost or have, in fact, formed a wider mental pipeline.[232]

The mental flexibility of digital learning has created a different type of learner. Younger people are better than older people at multitasking.[233] Outsourcing to screens means less need for memory or spatial skills and less cognitive effort. By practicing fewer depth learning skills, resources are freed up for breadth learning skills. But the question remains:

How does multitasking interfere?

The answer is complicated. Some types of limited multitasking are healthy for learning, other types not so much. Furthermore, we cannot trust our judgment. Though people insist they get more done, better and faster when multitasking, they are wrong.[234] They don't recognize the response cost, kind of like a drunk driver saying he drives better while under the influence. We even attribute Google-searched facts to our own intellect, taking false credit while feeling smarter with less fact memorization or independent thinking.[235] Research demonstrates that certain types of multitasking have a cost to our performance and overall well-being.

One such cost is *brain drain* when our phones are around. In other words, once interrupted we often struggle to re-engage with and focus on our task. A study conducted by Stothart and colleagues (2015) found that smartphone notifications hijack attention and distract us by launching distracting thoughts whether we've checked notifications or not.[236] Furthermore, when smartphone users are unable to answer a notification, their pulse and blood pressure increases, they feel anxious, and their problem-solving skills decline.[237] The more dependent subjects are on their phones and the closer their proximity to them, the more severe the effect.[238]

Not only do we feel the distraction and distress of notifications, they also consume time. When people are interrupted, it takes an average of 23 minutes 15 seconds to return to work, often getting distracted by two or more tasks after the interruption.[239] Subjects have even demonstrated that they're less likely to encode a fact to memory if they know it is published online, a dynamic now called the *Google effect*.[240] This effect is kind of like the diffusion of responsibility introduced in Chapter Seven. However, in this instance, instead of relying on our neighbors to do the work for us, we quit thinking or taking responsibility for learning, because we expect our smartphones have it handled. Why bother to take the effort to remember the date if a press of a button will get the job done?

Not only do we get distracted and stressed out, our performance also suffers if we are multitasking between tasks that compete for the same cognitive resources. Results are consistent across studies that multitasking results in a small but significant decrease in test scores (4-5%) with brief interruptions (e.g., IMs or text messages) and a somewhat larger deficit with extensive interruptions.[241][242] Perhaps a 5% decline doesn't seem like much, but it is half a letter grade. If two tasks require different cognitive resources, like walking and talking, then the performance decline is smaller. If tasks require similar cognitive resources, like talking and texting – which both require language centers, then the deficits are larger.[243]

Not only does the quality of performance deteriorate with multitasking in the short-term, so does productivity, speed, GPA, and overall cognitive performance in the long term, especially in the areas of working memory and attention. Among college students, Facebook users and heavy Internet users tend to perform worse on memory recall tasks and have lower GPAs.[244] Similarly, the amount of time spent on instant messaging was found to be negatively correlated both with cognitive performance in lab tasks and with GPA.[245] A recent large-scale study found that heavy media multitaskers performed worse than light media multitaskers in several cognitive tasks that involved working memory, selective attention to task-relevant information in visual search, and surprisingly, task switching.[246] It's been hypothesized that multitaskers may permanently lose these skills, because they are getting less memory practice overall, evidence of the use-it-or-lose-it model of brain development.

With more app adoption, we are being conditioned to check our phones more often with the random schedule of reinforcement described in Chapter Six. Studies have found that the boundaries between work and home have blurred. Overall, our work and school days span more hours and our jobs have become more demanding, leading to more stress and dissatisfaction and less connection to the things that are meaningful to us.[247] Not only have we changed the boundaries around our work day, but research suggests we have trained ourselves to self-interrupt, leading to worsened task prioritization and poorer sustained attention overall.[248]

The cognitive overload from multitasking can take a toll on mental health. Research has shown that toggling between mental tasks burns the brain's fuel, oxygenated glucose, at a rate faster than concentrating on a single task.[249] We think we are saving time and energy by fracturing our attention, but we are actually draining the very energy necessary to do the work and taking more time to do it! Factors that make us most vulnerable to rapidly switching tasks are neurotic or impulsive personality traits, stress, and sleep deprivation.[250] Without downtime, mental stress and fatigue can lead to poorer learning, irritability, and mood and anxiety disorders, especially for teens.[251]

How can we overcome the depleting effects of multitasking? Drinking coffee or adding an entertaining screen task into the mix is not the answer. Not only should we focus on one task at a time and batch notification checks instead of toggling back and forth, but we need to take frequent screen-free brain breaks. To rejuvenate, we must let our minds wander or stare off for fifteen minutes every couple of hours, without an organized task like Facebook or YouTube. Workplaces have learned that setting boundaries around work hours and providing brain-healthy activities, like yoga, group hikes, and nutritious snack times, pay off in regard to productivity and satisfaction. Autonomy with task choice and vacations help as well. In preparation for pushback when you encourage more efficient study habits with your kids, here are the facts.

Watching TV or videos while doing schoolwork interferes with performance.

Watching TV and doing homework are both demanding tasks that compete for visual and verbal cognitive processing. As a result, the toggling required to attend to both tasks will impair learning and homework quality. Research studies have demonstrated that watching television, or even just having it on in the background, impairs reading performance,[252] recall and recognition,[253] and even your memory of what you've watched on TV.[254]

How about music and homework?

It was once widely believed that listening to classical music makes you smarter, known as *The Mozart Effect*. However, this theory has largely been debunked. Studying in a quiet environment results in better performance than studying with music.[255] Furthermore, learning disruption is equal with liked and disliked music.[256] Kids think they do better while listening to the music they like and worse while listening to music they don't like. But performance is poorer in either condition. As with other multitasking scenarios, subjects fail to recognize that their performance on cognitive tasks deteriorates with music on in the background. However, music does have a positive role in learning if you listen to music you like before homework or during breaks due to a bump in arousal and mood (called the *Stephen King Effect*).

Every brain is different. If your teen insists on listening to music while studying and is earning good grades, perhaps he'd be willing to choose a genre that is the least likely to compete with cognitive resources like nonlyrical selections. Consider that it's not just his performance on homework that matters, so does the cognitive energy and mood he's left with when homework is done!

Is using a laptop during lecture OK?

In a study by Hembrooke (2003), college students who did not use any type of technology outperformed those students who used some type of technology during the lecture.[257] Researchers explained the results in terms of a *bottleneck in attention*, in which off-task use of technology impaired students' ability to remember lecture information.[258] Moreover, Sana (2013) found that laptop use during lecture not only distracted the user, but also distracted the student's neighbors.[259]

In conclusion, pumping yourself up to learn before homework and relaxing during breaks is a good thing. But distracting yourself during homework with anything that may compete for cognitive resources is a bad thing. Interestingly, there are exceptions to the rule. Approximately two percent of the population, called *supertaskers*, defy statistics and demonstrate an extraordinary ability to screen out distractors and interference, as if they have enhanced synaptic plasticity.[260] Supertaskers can maintain these exceptional abilities by practicing excellent brain health habits, like good organization and time management and refueling with emotional and cognitive control strategies that are screen-free like mindfulness, imagery, and meditation.

If we are trained to self-interrupt tasks due to our screen habits, do we all have AD/HD?

Attention-deficit/Hyperactivity Disorder (AD/HD) is popularly described as a mental illness, behavioral disorder, brain disorder, chronic condition, or neurodevelopmental disorder of childhood. It is clinically diagnosed when, prior to the age of twelve, a child meets a set number of diagnostic criteria that is significantly impairing compared to same-age kids across settings (like school and home).

Criteria for inattentive type of AD/HD include impairment due to an inability or reluctance to give close attention or sustain attention; trouble with listening, follow-through, organization, and forgetfulness; losing things; and high distractibility. Criteria for hyperactive/impulsive type of AD/HD include impairment due to fidgeting and getting out of seat; excessive running, climbing, and talking; interrupting, blurting out, and trouble waiting his/her turn; and often "on the go" as if "driven by a motor." There are three types of AD/HD, predominantly inattentive type (ADD), predominantly hyperactive type, or combined type.

Mental health professionals typically diagnose AD/HD with a thorough clinical interview with the parents, child, teachers, and other caregivers. Neuropsychological testing results provide further evidence of impairment on frontal lobe tasks that require attention, concentration, visual and auditory discrimination, and executive functioning (planning, organization, working memory, and cognitive flexibility). There are no clear biomedical markers for AD/HD; thus, no single test can be used to diagnose, including blood tests or brain scans. We do know that AD/HD primarily involves the prefrontal region of the brain and imbalances in the neurotransmitter dopamine.

How common is AD/HD? What Causes It?

Experts estimate that 11% of American children have AD/HD. However, diagnostic rates vary considerably between populations.[261] AD/HD is most commonly diagnosed in the United States and is less prevalent in other parts of the world.[262] There is controversy about the rising rates of diagnosis, with explanations ranging from over-diagnosis due to drug company marketing pressures to neurotoxin exposure in our food and environment. There appears to be multiple contributors to AD/HD rather than a single cause.

What we know for sure is that there is a strong genetic component (passed down from first-degree relatives) and that environmental, social, and cultural factors can contribute to impairment or may be mistaken for AD/HD. For example, other mental illnesses like anxiety and depression, as well as sleep deprivation, dietary allergies, stress, chronic pain, poor nutrition, and brain injury are common contributors to attention problems. It is hypothesized that Western expectations for children to sit still at school for up to six hours a day with little opportunity for sunshine or exercise may be inappropriate for adequate stimulation of the growing brain. Screen time has also entered the conversation, making us wonder if our hyper aroused, hyper tasked, hyper rushed lives are driving us to distraction.

AD/HD Kids and Screen Time

Research has demonstrated that the symptoms underlying AD/HD are associated with early television viewing and addictive social networking and video gaming.[263][264] Individuals with AD/HD typically have difficulty attending to boring tasks while also hyper focusing on arousing tasks that trigger dopamine release, like screen time.[265] Further, motivational models show us that children with AD/HD are less stimulated by reinforcement and reward than kids without attention issues. That means increasing quantities of novel reward is required to support optimal performance with AD/HD subjects.[266]

Screen activities are programmed to reward the user in just the way AD/HD brains crave, with escalating amounts of increasingly novel content that keep the Internet user using (and spending).[267] Screen time also offers an escape from the constant barrage of verbal corrections and disappointing outcomes that too often burden AD/HD kids. Whereas many tasks require AD/HD kids to doggedly "swim against the current" only to fail anyway, screen activities allow them to exercise independent choice without failure and enjoy limitless mastery among similarly impassioned peers. For kids with AD/HD, the nonvirtual world simply cannot compete with the virtual world. As a result, they too often self-medicate with screens resulting in excessive, and sometimes addictive use patterns.

Does screen time cause AD/HD?

The short answer to this seemingly simple question is, "Screen time does not appear to cause AD/HD, but excessive use can be a strong contributor to clinically impairing symptoms. That means for some of us, yes screen time may contribute to impairment. For others, it will not." Recent research showing structural brain changes and escalated behaviors from excessive screen time means that we may start seeing even more AD/HD symptomology as screen use increases, especially among the young whose brains are still developing and vulnerable. Excessive screen time puts kids at risk for psychological problems and overwhelm. This overly aroused, overly fatigued, and overly tasked state can be impairing and is preventable with parent oversight.

Why can't I conclusively say excessive screen time causes AD/HD? Unfortunately, the type of research that demonstrates causal connection between screen time and the development of AD/HD is very difficult to do. Imagine trying to find the control group of young adults (no screen time) with similar environmental factors to a matching gaming group for comparison. Or even more difficult, finding the study subjects young and then following them over time, exposing one group to gaming and preventing the other from the same screen opportunities. In today's digitally literate world, that would be nearly impossible. As a result, we must rely on correlational studies that have raised significant concern.

Clearly, we must manage screen use or risk our children's neurological, psychological, and socioemotional development. Banning screens from our kids, especially those with AD/HD, is not a real option and may cause unnecessary distress. After all, the virtual world gives them social capital, learning opportunity, and reward in ways the nonvirtual world does not. However, management is key to avoid hazards like attention deficit and even addiction.

Screen Addiction

Let's face it, most of us are already screen addicted. According to Apple, we check our iPhones an average of 80 times a day, 30,000 times a year.[268] Sixty-seven percent of smartphone owners find themselves checking their phone for messages, alerts, or calls even when they don't notice their phone ringing or vibrating. Forty-four percent have slept with their phone next to their bed, because they wanted to make sure they didn't miss any calls, text messages, or other updates during the night. Twenty-nine percent describe their smartphone as "something they can't imagine living without."[269] Nearly 60% of parents think their teens are addicted to their mobile devices.[270]

In 2018 the World Health Organization opted to include gaming addiction in their June, 2018 publication of the 11th International Classification of Diseases. Symptoms must be present for twelve months and include impaired control over gaming (frequency, intensity, duration), increased priority given to gaming, and continuation or escalation of gaming despite negative consequences.

Currently, *gambling disorder* is the only behavioral addiction included in the most recent edition of the *Diagnostic and Statistical Manual of Mental Disorders – 5 (DSM-5)*. However, even as early as its publication in 2013, enough research had surfaced about screen addiction that the substance use disorder work-group opted to list *Internet gaming disorder* (IGD) as a potential mental illness in need of further study. The main concern was that researchers hadn't agreed upon standardized diagnostic criteria across studies. They argued that, for screen addiction to be considered valid, further scientific information must be gathered about prevalence, course, treatment, and biomarkers.[271] At the time of the 2013 DSM-5 publication, there were over 250 reviewed publications from Asia and fewer from North America that described mostly youth and young adult subjects who engaged in extended Internet game play without sleep or eating that resulted in severe consequences, such as seizures and death.[272] They further found that the studies that compared different types of Internet use (social media use, online gambling, pornography viewing, etc.) concluded that gaming was distinctly more disabling.

From these publications, the work group identified the following nine criteria for diagnostic classification (five are necessary for diagnosis):

- *Preoccupation:* Do you spend a lot of time thinking about games even when you are not playing, or planning when you can play next?

- *Withdrawal:* Do you feel restless, moody, irritable, angry, anxious, or sad when attempting to cut down or stop gaming, or when you're unable to play?

- *Tolerance:* Do you feel the need to play for increasing amounts of time, play more exciting games, or use more powerful equipment to get the same amount of excitement you used to get?

- *Reduce/stop:* Do you feel that you should play less, but are unable to cut back on the amount of time you spend playing games?

- *Give up other activities:* Do you lose interest in or reduce participation in other recreational activities (hobbies, meeting with friends) due to gaming?

- *Continue despite problems:* Do you continue games even though you are aware of negative consequences, such as not getting enough sleep, being late to school/work, spending too much money, having arguments with others, or neglecting important duties.

- *Deceive/cover up:* Do you lie to family, friends, or others about how much you game, or try to keep your family or friends from knowing how much you game?

- *Escape adverse moods:* Do you game to escape from or forget about personal problems, or to relieve uncomfortable feelings such as guilt, anxiety, helplessness, or depression?

- *Risk/lose relationships/opportunities:* Do you risk or lose significant relationships, or job, educational, or career opportunities because of gaming?

Recent studies using these criteria conclude that IGD prevalence rates are around 1-5% and is most common among single young males.[273][274] Male Internet addiction most typically involves video gaming, cyber-pornography, and online gambling. [275][276][277] Women are more likely to show addictive use patterns with social media, texting, and online shopping.[278][279][280][281] IGD is commonly comorbid with a variety of psychiatric disorders, including depression, anxiety, AD/HD, self-harm, obsessive-compulsive disorder, oppositionality, suicidality, and personality disorders.[282][283][284][285][286][287][288][289]

Other risk factors among European youth include living in a metropolitan area, not living with biological parent, low parent involvement, parent unemployment, and not having a reliable friend.[290] Consequences of IGD include pathological behaviors like skipping school, lower grades, family conflicts, lack of offline sociality, sleep problems, and unresolved developmental problems.[291] These factors, along with escalating emotional problems, often result in a deprivation of the very resources necessary to break out of this vicious cycle.

Not only are there behavioral and psychological consequences to IGD, neuroimaging studies are increasingly finding evidence of distinct neurobiological changes similar to those seen in subjects with substance addictions.[292][293] In other words, the more we play video games, the more our brains adapt. Activation pattern changes that result in brain tissue changes is a process called *adaptive neuroplasticity*. More specifically, IGD subjects show gray and white matter atrophy (loss of tissue volume) and reduced cortical thickness in various areas of the brain, including the prefrontal, inferior frontal, corpus collosum, and supplementary motor areas. Studies have also found evidence of dopamine release, volumetric differences, less dopamine receptor availability, and higher activity in the striatum (the brain's pleasure center) when playing video games, the same mechanisms seen with all behaviors and drugs of addiction.[294][295][296] The patterns of brain activity while playing reflects how heavy-use players process rewards and losses differently than nonplayers, which may lead to riskier or more cautious decision-making overall.[297]

More recently, the federal government has funded a large study through the National Institute of Health (NIH) looking at how screen time impacts the adolescent brain. With a $300 million price tag, researchers have started to give interviews and brain scans to more than 11,000 nine- and ten-year-old subjects over a ten-year period. The first wave of MRI brain scans of the first 4,500 subjects have revealed that kids who use screens seven hours a day versus kids who do not show premature thinning of the cortex and lower scores on thinking and language tests.[298] Although it is too soon to interpret what these findings mean, they do suggest cause for concern. What isn't yet clear is if these differences make us vulnerable to screen addiction in the first place, or if brain changes are the result of excessive use.

Behavioral changes correlated structural brain changes due to screen use appear to mimic what is seen with substance abuse subjects. [299] These include impaired risk evaluation, [300] decision-making, and regulation of emotion; increased craving, impulsivity, [301] cognitive inflexibility, [302] and compulsivity; and increased reward sensitivity and decreased loss sensitivity.[303][304] Furthermore, the longer the duration of playing, the more significant the brain structure change.[305]

In response to impairment and distress, American families are increasingly seeking help for child screen addiction. Increasingly inpatient and outpatient treatment facilities that specialize in the treatment of screen addiction are cropping up in the United States and Europe. Such facilities and "boot camps" have been commonplace in Asia over the last ten years.

CHAPTER 9: THE PARENT-CHILD ALLIANCE: ATTACHMENT

Although parenting is deeply fulfilling, it's also hard! Everything is a moving target. Our kids are growing up so quickly, while at the same time, we also face new, unexpected adult developmental milestones. This while school, work, sports, and friendships throw us challenges. We are constantly impacting each other and reworking our parent-child synchronized dance of love and communication. Parents with kids of varying personalities recognize that there is no such thing as a one-size-fits-all parenting strategy. For that reason, I typically teach parenting models instead of offering situational tips, so parents can expertly tweak strategies real time rather than becoming dependent on my day-to-day advice. The truth is, parenting is a journey full of hits and misses. The keys to success are to have an open heart, keep learning and re-evaluating, and soak in every imperfect moment as it is, whether it be the noisy chaos of toddlerhood or the eye-rolling hilarity of adolescence. A sense of humor about yourself and about your kids is the number one requirement.

There are few resources available to parents that comprehensively address the challenges and skills needed for best managing screen devices and Internet access. In general, media literacy experts posit two types of interventions: protectionism and empowerment.[306] *Protectionism* generally involves media management, which is blocking and filtering kids from online content. *Empowerment* generally involves education and skill building with the goal of helping kids be informed and capable consumers of media. Both protectionism and empowerment are necessary for Internet safety. This chapter focuses on parent and child empowerment with an emphasis on communication skills that simultaneously strengthen attachment while facilitating the child's ability to independently solve problems and build resilience.

Strengthening Attachment

The foundation of good parenting is a healthy attachment with your child. Attachment begins the first moment you learn of that little baby in mom's tummy and continues to grow throughout the lifespan. The good news is that most of us are predisposed to nurture and be nurtured, so the instincts are there if we carve out quality parent-child time for attachment to flourish. Good parenting strategies can make a difference, but no technique will work without parents who are willing to open their hearts and devote the time. Here are the basics of attachment, demonstrating that the parent-child connection is one of nature's greatest miracles.

Attachment is a foundation of trust between two or more people based on consistency, warmth, and reliability. As explained in Chapter One, babies and parents form the foundations of attachment quickly. From the nuanced harmonies between parent and child, each party learns how to communicate and meet the needs of the other. If the baby's physical, social, or emotional needs aren't met consistently, behavioral issues may emerge including, in extreme cases, developmental delay, apathy, depression, and acting out behaviors. In less extreme cases, babies can develop different types of attachment like those described in Mary Ainsworth's work using the *Strange Situation* research paradigm.

Types of Attachment

Securely attached infants consistently use their caregivers as secure emotional bases while they intermittently explore their surroundings. They tend to seek out their caregivers if a stranger is around, gradually warming to the stranger if their parents are encouraging and positive.

Insecure/avoidant attachment is characterized by children who ignore or avoid their parents and treat strangers with avoidance.

Insecure/resistant attachment is characterized by a tendency to cling and then reject parents while hiding from strangers.

Disorganized attachment is characterized by toggling between reactions, sometimes clinging and other times avoiding the caregiver in the presence of a stranger.

Factors That Optimize Healthy Parent-Child Attachment

Nature has paved the way to make sure kids and parents stay connected. Because human beings have a long time span when a child is reliant on the parent for survival, it is to everybody's advantage to have the foundational elements that optimize healthy attachment.

Sufficiently Mature Cognitive Development

Jean Piaget's (1952) theories beautifully illustrate that no amount of environmental enrichment can facilitate child capability if his or her brain infrastructure has not yet developed.[307] Remember from earlier chapters that the brain is constantly remodeling well into adulthood. As children age, they become increasingly capable of developing specialized abilities. Until children's brains are ripe for task adoption, these specialized abilities are outsourced to loving parents. Well into late adolescence, our kids need us to do much of their reasoning and decision-making for them, slowly encouraging them and providing safe and developmentally-matched learning opportunities that stretch them to progress as they mature.

Although Piaget's body of work is too extensive to review, the three basic components to his cognitive theory include:

Children develop *schemas*, which are critical building blocks of intelligence that are constantly revising and changing based on brain maturation and interaction with an enriched environment.

Children demonstrate *adaptation processes* (equilibrium, assimilation, and accommodation) that enable them to transition to more advanced stages.

Children must go through set, sequential *stages of development* to reach full cognitive maturity, including:

- Sensorimotor (birth to 2 years old)
- Preoperational (2 years old to 7 years old)
- Concrete operational (7 years old to 11 years old)
- Formal operational (11 years old to 16 years old)

Learning, Modeling, and Mirror Neurons

Our biology sets us up for success with attachment. In the 1980s, Giacomo Rizzolatti and his team of researchers discovered that when monkeys observed the behavior of other monkeys, the same neurons in their brains fired as if they themselves were performing the behavior.[308] In other words, the monkeys had specialized brain cells (called *mirror neurons*) ready to fire by observational learning. They learn and get practice by watching as well as doing.

Infant humans also have mirror neurons, which are not only key in learning specific chains of motor behaviors but may also be what's behind complex emotional learning like empathy and attachment.[309] This genetic advantage means we are neurologically prewired to understand the intentions of others and unconsciously respond.[310] We not only recognize logically what others are doing and feeling, but we also experience it with them. We are prewired to mimic, learn, and connect with each other.

Imprinting and Oxytocin

Konrad Lorenz, zoologist and father of ethology (the study of animal behavior), also contributed to attachment research by describing the process of learning in ducklings and goslings. He called this process *imprinting* which involves a critical period upon hatching where the baby bird will instinctually follow and imitate its parent. He demonstrated this phenomenon by being present for a hatch and quacking like a mom duck. From that point on the ducklings persistently followed him around in a little line, not unlike our toddlers do with us. Imprinting is another example of how we are genetically primed to imitate specific types of behavior necessary for our survival.

Human infants and parents are also prewired to connect with each other. The neuropeptide, *oxytocin*, is involved with multiple issues related to attachment including initiating maternal and paternal behaviors, promoting social affiliation over the long term, reducing stress, falling into romantic love, and enhancing social competence.[311] Newly smitten parents become obsessively interested in teaching and protecting their offspring at birth and throughout life due to this bio-behavioral synchrony between parent and child. Our neurology is designed for a powerful, bidirectional attachment that maintains us through decades of family love and protection. The infant-parent attachment sets the stage for their romantic relationships as well as their attachment success to their own children. Good parenting pays off for generations to come. It's THAT important.

Physical Contact and Nurturance

I'm a devoted lover of babies and animals, suggesting I have a lot of oxytocin. As a result, telling you about Harry Harlow's deprived baby rhesus monkeys makes me a little depressed. But Harlow's work teaches critical psychological concepts in support of the importance of maternal touch, skin-to-skin contact, and nursing. Controversial today because of the deprivation his research subjected baby monkeys to, his animal model demonstrates why psychology experiments that demonstrate causality among humans is somewhat crippled by our righteous insistence on treating research subjects humanely. We can't expose human children to unsafe research conditions, so we often have to rely on animal models or correlational research.

Harry Harlow was an American psychologist who studied the effects of maternal deprivation on rhesus monkeys in the 1930s. Harlow discovered that when baby monkeys were taken from their mothers and raised in isolation, they demonstrated significant social impairments and remained reclusive and clung to their cloth diapers. This finding led him to set up a research scenario where he raised baby monkeys in nurseries with a wire mother that supplied milk and a cloth mother who didn't provide food. Surprisingly, the baby monkeys far preferred the cloth mother to the wire mother with milk. Furthermore, when a fearful stimulus was introduced (e.g., noise-making teddy bear), baby monkeys with a cloth mother explored with more confidence than monkeys in a nursery without a surrogate mother.

These findings demonstrated that infant monkeys, like humans, do best with an attentive, affectionate mother rather than a sterile environment devoid of maternal warmth. His work went on to incorporate the importance of paternal attachment on child wellbeing. Believe it or not, his work was met with considerable hostility from the professional camps of the 1950s who believed snuggling and soothing babies was a form of "spoiling" and could lead to unwanted outcomes like a lack of initiative.

Fortunately, modern day psychologists endorse Bowlby's findings that warm responsive parenting is important to healthy attachment and learning. Furthermore, recent research demonstrates that babies who receive less physical contact are more distressed and may end up with changes in the molecular process that affects gene expression. In their 2017 study, a team from the University of British Columbia found that, at four years old, children who had been snuggled more as infants displayed differences on five specific DNA sites compared to the kids who received less touch and were more distressed.[312] They also found a gap between the epigenetic age and chronological age for the "low-contact children." Although too soon to tell, this could reflect "less favorable developmental progress" and possibly even future health problems. That means parent attentiveness and snuggling impacts the very genetics of their baby. Further, too much parent and child screen time replacing face-to-face interaction and snuggling could feasibly result in a similar type of unfortunate outcome seen with affection-deprived monkeys in the research setting and parent-deprived children in orphanages and institutions.

Parent-Child Fit and the Importance of Warmth, Consistency, and Gently Guiding Communication

Parent-child fit also has an impact on the quality of the attachment. Parent and child must learn to recognize each other's bidirectional bids for attention to communicate effectively. As kids age, bids and responses change in form and complexity. Both parties' responses and environmental situations serve to reinforce or punish certain patterns of engagement. Furthermore, kids and parents continue to learn communication skills throughout the lifespan, while neurological and environmental facilitators and distractors wax and wane in influence.

As parents, it is our obligation to lead with warmth and responsive nurturance in a home that provides the safety our kids need to thrive. Typically, a home is made up of multiple family members nested within a neighborhood, a community, and a culture. Families operate as an interdependent system with many moving parts. When one member of the system is affected, other members respond. Every family has unique roles, patterns, explicit rules, and implicit rules that are influenced by the family's culture and values. Some rules are negotiable and others are not. Because of this interdependence, the quality of the interactions and communication affects all aspects of family life.

In general, implicit (hidden) expectations create confusion and unhealthy communication patterns. Parents, as well as extended family members, teachers, friends, and other caregivers, establish rules for kids. With so many factors influencing a child's world, consistency can become challenging indeed. For example, let's consider screen technology culture. If parents resent and excessively block child screen use, but do not discuss their feelings, reasoning, and expectations, kids are left to wonder and guess why their parents make, or don't make, the rules that they do. Guessing and insecurity can result in pervasive anxiety and intermittent avoidance, sneaking, or acting out. These behaviors can damage attachment both temporarily and permanently. GKIS parenting strategies are designed to make the implicit rules in families explicit (spelled out) to optimize skill building, efficiently resolve conflict, and strengthen attachment. If rules are not planned and explicitly communicated, families may develop rigid roles (e.g., the "perfect" child, the "black sheep/scapegoat" child, the "strict" parent, and the "permissive" parent) and maladaptive behaviors.

Parent-Facilitated Problem Solving

As children gain awareness of themselves and the world around them, they press for autonomy and independence. These normal developmental undertakings can strain the parent-child alliance. It's important that parents recognize that these behaviors result from burgeoning ability. Even though pushing back can look bratty, disrespectful, and provocative, your child is not hatching diabolical schemes to disarm or thwart your authority. They're trying out new skills on the person they feel the safest with, you!

The developmental aspects of growing up covered in Chapters One through Four will help you recognize normal, healthy developmental process. Armed with this knowledge, it is easier to accept and best manage a child's propensity to test rather than slip into toxic parenting reactions like discounting, teasing, or intimidating your child. Responding with patience, understanding, and emotional neutrality is key to preserving a positive, hard-earned attachment. Supportive conversations about challenging situations help children learn from experience rather than avoid seeking help or internalizing shame. If kids feel parental acceptance of mistakes and failures, which ultimately lead to important new learning and skills, they will be more transparent and come to you when they run into challenges. Parent-facilitated problem solving provides the scaffolding necessary for resilience and independence. There is no better compliment to a parent than being your child's go-to person when they're scared or hurting.

Step One: Identify and Gather Intel

Most parents don't know they have a screen safety problem until their kids are already buried deep in trouble. A better strategy that doesn't result in psychologically injured kids is to proactively learn about online risks and assess your child's potential for running into them. *Screen Time in the Mean Time* is designed to inform you about potential screen risks and give strategies to best manage them.

Step Two: Get and Maintain Cooperative Engagement

Once you've educated yourself about important screen safety topics, now you face the challenge of getting your kids interested in the conversation. That requires three essential ingredients: fun, validation, and respect.

The fun part isn't as simple as you might think. Without fun, you cannot sustain the child's interest. It is the aspect of generating fun (I call it throwing sunshine) that is my therapeutic superpower. Research has consistently revealed that the most important element necessary for therapeutic progress is the quality of the relationship between psychologist and client. In other words, if you don't like each other, therapy will not work. Building this alliance starts with an enthusiastic greeting and consistent demonstration that I'm interested in learning who they are and what they want. The key is warmth and listening. A similar but far more profound attachment process exists between parent and child.

How can parents form a fun alliance? Get to know your child's quirks, characteristics, and special interests, and join them where they are. As basic as it sounds, the fun banter that happens in my office over board games is a critical element to building the rapport necessary for exploration and skill building. In a laid-back, warm, and accepting environment, kids will reveal their feelings and create situations that are the foundations for engagement and complex cooperative problem solving. It's really that simple, sitting crisscross applesauce on the carpet and play if your kids are little. For teens, it's more about having an open mind, an open heart, and a willingness to listen, usually while in the car to buy them a smoothie. A sense of humor is also critical to sparking fun.

Validation is another ingredient in forming a healthy one-to-one connection. *Validation* is the act of compassionately making the child feel seen, heard, and understood. An easy recipe for validation is to simply reflect how the child is feeling, ("You're sad, because you think you've lost a friend"). By validating a child's feelings, the parent creates a safe, accepting environment for exploration and discussion.

Respect refers to a parent's willingness to listen and let the child take the lead. That requires us to put our screens down and provide opportunities for conversation. A balance of informed inquiries ("Did you end up playing with Emily today?") and storytelling ("When I was in third grade I lost a friend too") can lead to mutually satisfying and respectful engagement.

Step Three: Facilitate the Generation of Options and Work Through to Solution

At this step, you're generally screen savvy and the parent-child conversation has been initiated. Now it's important for you to help identify and simplify the problem and guide your child through a sequence of problem solving steps toward resolution. Due to less developmental capacity, more active engagement is necessary with younger children, while less active coaching and more negotiation and quiet supervision is appropriate with teens. At any age, this must be a collaborative process. If you lecture or provide all the answers, you'll lose your children's interest and deny them the opportunity to come up with their own solutions. The goal is not to prove you are right, but rather to help your children discover their own competence and mastery. Decide together what problem you're going to address, then actively elicit tactics that may lead to solution. Be sure to throw in some silly, ridiculous strategies to keep it fun.

I am constantly approached to debate whether kids today are more resilient or less resilient than we were at their age. Although these discussions are stimulating and important, the answer is not so simple. Kids today may be less street savvy than we were since we keep them safely tucked in at homes rather than letting them roam the neighborhood independently solving spontaneous problems, but they are still informed and skilled problem solvers as the result of the resources available from adept screen use. Rather than being contemptuous of their generation's different perspectives and problem-solving approaches, we must support that they are willing to think outside of the box. The learning journey is far more important than outcome. The key to good problem solving is working things through in an atmosphere of warmth, respect, encouragement, fun, and recognition of a job well done. Kids who are allowed the freedom to develop their unique spirit develop the confidence to take personal accountability, have a sense of humor about themselves, and tend to be more adaptive, flexible, and positive along the way.

During this phase, facilitate the generation of a whole list of possible problem-solving strategies from ridiculous to most sound. The more options you consider the better. Then prioritize them from most to least likely to be effective. Encourage them to go forth and execute the number one choice, even if it wasn't your pick. Agree to resume the conversation later to see how it went.

Step Four: Reflect, Evaluate, Revise, and Relaunch

Once you've discussed several possible problem-solving strategies and your child has executed the chosen best, you are ready for the step that only the best problem solvers get to, analysis and reevaluation. Even if the problem was successfully solved, there is still learning to do. Ask for a recap about how it went, then analyze and reevaluate. Flexible evaluation without shame or fear builds the scaffolding necessary for self-directed, advanced problem solving. It may lead to an even better list of options next time!

Children may have difficulty staying engaged during this stage of problem solving since outcome is no longer imminent. Because the secretary of their brain (the prefrontal region) is still developing, kids tend to be impulsive and impatient. They need us to slow them down and consider options rather than plough forward with the first option that comes to mind. Don't forget to praise their efforts and reward a job well done with a mini-celebration like a family activity or outing.

Step Five: Innovate

With a fun, safe, and encouraging learning environment, you can move your child from simple problem solving, to re-evaluation, and then innovation and creation. Continuing to explore the issue even after the problem is solved is the arena of wizards, magicians, and inventors. It involves adding higher-order creativity to the knowledge already gained. While kids get silly and generate new ideas and projects, parents have yet another opportunity to express delight and positive feedback. During this problem-solving process, kids and parents get to know each other and kids are more likely to adopt your family's beliefs and values while creating some new versions of their own.

A working example:

Problem: *My fifth grader is begging for Instagram. Most of her friends have it, and they seem to be using reasonably good judgment. My daughter is a great kid, but I hear these stories about social media dangers. Thus far I have said "no" to Instagram. She's starting to get angry with me though, and I'm afraid it will damage our relationship. How should I handle this?*

Step One: Identify and Gather Intel

The key to credibility and confidence is being informed. Do your homework. Gather the WHATS and the WHYS about Instagram for 11 year olds. The

GetKidsInternetSafe blog is an awesome spot to begin. Simply use the search window at the middle right and enter "Instagram." Then go to the Instagram Help Center to get the details about basic information, safety, and security. Invite your child to create a persuasive PowerPoint to get in on the information-gathering game.

Step Two: Get and Maintain Cooperative Engagement

This step (fun, validation, respect) is a little bit harder to facilitate, because creating fun depends on what your child likes to do. I'd be willing to bet though that a fifth-grade girl wouldn't mind a quick trip for the smoothie of her choice. While you're sitting down with your mango banana surprise (fun), have a calm discussion that starts with why she wants it so much (validation). Really listen to all of her reasons. Take it in and consider it as she speaks. Don't plan what you're going to say or interrupt. Take it all in (respect). After she slows down, and it's clear she really feels understood, talk about your real concerns. Mention that it has nothing to do with trust. Rather, viewing, posting, and access to others (including strangers) are risks you take seriously since she means so much to you. Provide a few examples of the risks you learned about from your research.

Step Three: Facilitate the Generation of Options and Work Through to Solution

Invite your daughter to plot out the risks and benefits of Instagram, and look over them together to see what you can negotiate without jeopardizing either party's concerns. It might look something like this:

Problem: You want Instagram, but I have concerns for your safety.

Options:

1. No Instagram for now
2. Shared Instagram with mom
3. Instagram with a limited monitoring + username/password + friending me
4. Instagram with friending me
5. Instagram free rein

Risks:

- Instagram's Terms of Agreement state that you must be 13 years old to use the service

- Posting mishaps (list all that you can think of)
- Viewing mishaps (list all that you can think of)
- Mishaps due to access by strangers (list all that you can think of)
- Distraction potential (include why this is a problem)

Benefits:

- Entertaining and fun (list all the ways that you can think of)
- Social (list all the ways that you can think of)
- Creative (list all the ways that you can think of)
- Building digital responsibility (list all the ways that you can think of)
- Opportunity to learn and share concerns with mom > *GKIS Connected Family Screen Agreement*

The GKIS recommendation for Instagram is wait until at least the second semester of sixth grade or when your child is 13 years old. However, kids can get socially marginalized if they have no social media available to them by mid middle school. However, there is always risk. Some parents choose to allow Instagram sooner than 13 years old and others never allow it. Because each situation and each child is different, parents are the ultimate experts when it comes to their family. But after a patient and calm discussion about options, choose one on a probationary basis with the agreement that you will come back to the discussion over and over. This is a perpetual problem that needs to be frequently negotiated, not a resolvable problem that is solved with one discussion.

Step Four: Reflect, Evaluate, Revise, and Relaunch

A few weeks after a decision has been made and executed. Go back and review the problem and see if concerns have surfaced. If it's working, proceed. If it isn't, go back to the drawing board.

Step Five: Innovate

This is the most amazing step in that it pushes kids to think outside the box and be extraordinary. If one of the solutions turns out to be less than ideal, brainstorm and entertain crazy possibilities. Maybe the first Instagram is family only, or maybe posts can focus on a particular interest. Maybe limit the friends list to five besties only. The sky's the limit on ideas in step five. It may just be the one thing nobody's ever thought of before! Here is a bonus tip list about how to sprinkle screen safety skill building into everyday family conversations.

Tips for Getting the Conversation Started

Create an open, honest, and positive family environment. If your kid's opinion differs from your own, have a sense of humor and go with it. Don't scold or shame them. Encourage them to try out different perspectives.

Play high-low. Each person shares the HIGH part of their day and the LOW part of the day. If they don't have an answer, don't sweat it. Let them skip their turn. This is a tried-and-true conversation starter.

Start young, but recognize it's never too late to get started. Consider the age of your child and simplify your language accordingly, but don't be afraid to talk to little ones about hot topics. Sharing your values, opinions, and problem-solving style is an awesome opportunity to connect and teach. Kids have access to information younger and younger due to screen use. You'll have to be brave and start open dialogue earlier than our parents did.

Get out there and get tech-savvy. Before your child gets a social media app, test it out first so you know the ins and outs. Be eager to let them teach you.

Seek them out to share funny memes and videos. This will quickly become a fun two-way street; an awesome opportunity to engage and stay engaged.

Initiate the conversation with the intention to listen. Don't lecture, shame, or threaten. If you start with "kids these days...," you're headed in the wrong direction. Connect rather draw lines between you.

Inform them about hot topics. Scare tactics do not work. Give them the facts, as complicated as they may be. Kids know exaggeration when they hear it. It's best to tell the truth and explore the black, white, and gray areas together. Get in the habit of collecting current event "stories" from the GetKidsInternetSafe blog. ("Did you hear about the Dad who posted a video on YouTube publicly shaming another dad?")

Structure conversations about complex situations as a series of legitimate options. Stress that there is rarely one "right" way to respond and that you celebrate mistakes and failures. That's how we all learn.

Recognize that, in fact, "everybody" IS doing it even if you won't let them.

Have empathy, but still stay firm.

Praise. Look for demonstrations of good moral reasoning, assertiveness, and leadership and be generous with worthy compliments.

Don't scare them, but share how often people are inappropriate and unsafe to talk to online. Role-play how to assertively manage these situations. For example, teach them how flattery is used as a manipulation technique.

Figure out how to bring up an uncomfortable topic. Let your kids "overhear" a conversation with your partner at dinnertime. Yes, the walls do have ears.

Be patient. Be prepared to have many small conversations over time rather than one big one.

CHAPTER 10: EXPERT PARENTING STRATEGIES FOR RAISING THE DIGITAL NATIVE

In earlier chapters, we explored child development as it relates to screen media, risks and benefits of screen use, and the critical importance of building a powerful parent-child connection for love, education, and skill building. This chapter covers parenting from a common sense, strategic standpoint. The GKIS Parenting 4-Square, the Bennett Box Challenge, the GKIS Connected Family Agreement, and Dr. Bennett's Top Ten Parenting Tips are techniques and strategies developed over twenty-five years of psychology practice working with families just like yours, some who needed light emotional and parenting support and others in crisis. Plus, I use them with my own family. These techniques work for kids of all ages, even the feisty ones!

GKIS PARENTING 4-SQUARE

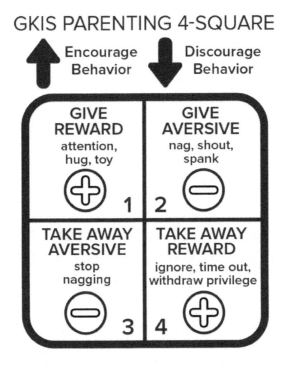

The GKIS Parenting 4-Square

In my private practice, the primary therapeutic modality I use is *cognitive-behavioral therapy* (CBT). We covered some CBT techniques in Chapter Four (diaphragmatic breathing, mindfulness, and imagery) as recommendations for teen self-care. The "cognitive" part of CBT is cognitive restructuring (replacing stinking thinking with can-do thinking). The "behavioral" part is what I'm covering in the GKIS Parenting 4-Square. The primary mechanism behind this 4-square is what psychologists call *operant conditioning*. Operant conditioning was described by BF Skinner in the 1930s and refers to the factors of reinforcement (encouraging behavior) and punishment (discouraging behavior) as a means to effectively change child behavior.

Definition of Concepts

- *Encourage Behavior* (two left-side boxes) = make the behavior happen more frequently (increase favorable behaviors)

- *Discourage Behavior* (two right side boxes) = make the behavior happen less frequently (decrease unfavorable behavior)

- *Aversive* = something unpleasant for the child (e.g., disapproval, yelling, or hurting)

- *Reward* = something pleasant for the child (e.g., approval, attention, food, toys, or money)

- "**+**" signs = interventions that I recommend.

- "**-**" signs = interventions that I do NOT recommend.

BOX 1

"Give Reward" is encouraging behavior by giving the child something they like, like turning toward your child with warm eye contact, praise, affection, or a material reward like money or a toy.

Giving a reward to encourage (reinforce) the behavior you want is, by far, a parent's most powerful intervention. I'm fond of saying that parents should implement this box nine times more than Box 4 (and avoiding Boxes 2 and 3). Providing reward not only increases the behavior you want, but it also doubles as fuel for a positive parent-child relationship. Also, kids have an easier time doing what they are told to do directly("do this"), rather than having to stop the behavior and then reason what else to do instead.

Give Reward Tip #1: Praise is better than a material bribe.

If eye contact or an appreciative smile is enough reinforcement for a behavior, keep it at that. Save bigger rewards, like material items (toys, food, money), fun activities, and reward charts, for more challenging behaviors. Kids love appreciation and affection, which is typically enough to encourage behavior. Fun family activities, like movie night, bowling night, or craft day, are the best cash-in for reward charts. Money or toys typically need to increase in value over time to continue to incentivize kids. That means cleaning your room starts at one dollar and eventually leads to $80 remote control helicopters. This increased value requirement is not sustainable and leads to demanding, entitled behaviors, a potentially unfortunate side effect to a reward intended to build values and good judgment. Fun family activities work consistently.

Give Reward Tip #2: Eye 'til comply.

This simple strategy is extremely effective. When you give a command, keep your eye on your child until they initiate the task you requested. Too often busy parents command then get distracted. Kids take this as implicit permission to blow off the command. However, if you eyeball them until they start to obey, then they will do as expected. If they don't, you will consistently follow-thru, reinforcing the habit for immediate compliance.

Give Reward Tip #3: Providing extrinsic reward for an intrinsically rewarding activity is a mistake.

If your child loves to do something just for the sake of doing it (*intrinsically rewarding*), don't reward them with a material bribe (*extrinsic reward*) like money, toys, or food. Research shows that by extrinsically rewarding your child for something that is intrinsically rewarding, they may lose their enjoyment of it and instead focus on the material reward. It's better to let them enjoy their activity and save your extrinsic reward options for things they don't like to do. An example is paying kids for grades when they already work to achieve them on their own. If paid for those grades, the letter grade will decrease in meaning while the focus will instead be on the money reward. For the child who could care less about grades, however, a material reward may be effective.

BOX 2

"Give Aversive" is discouraging a behavior by giving the child something they don't like, like nagging, yelling, or spanking to discourage behavior.

Punishing a behavior by giving an aversive is my least favorite intervention. Research has conclusively demonstrated that exposing a child to something unpleasant, like spanking, may stop the behavior you are targeting, but it also may cause unpleasant effects. More specifically, kids who are frequently exposed to aversive are more likely to increase the undesired behavior outside of the punisher's presence or develop a problematic psychological problem like anxiety, depression, anger, or acting out. It's pretty simple to see that hitting and hurting the people you are tasked to love and protect doesn't make much sense. It models aggression and breaks down trust and security. Giving or withdrawing reward is all you need to parent effectively. When there are better options, it is not worth risking those potentially destructive side effects.

BOX 3

"Take Away Aversive" is taking away something unpleasant to the child, like nagging and then stopping when the child finally does what you want to encourage behavior.

Similar to Box 2, I suggest you avoid this intervention due to the potentially harmful side effects of an aversive. This box is particularly unpleasant, because all the child has to look forward to when they do what is desired is the absence of discomfort. Nobody wants to consistently cause their child discomfort, as they will learn to avoid you entirely. It's very easy to fall into this with teens, which results in resentment (e.g., "clean your room. Clean your room. CLEAN YOUR ROOM!").

BOX 4

"Take Away Reward "refers to taking away something the child likes, like turning away or ignoring, implementing a time out, or withdrawing a privilege to discourage a behavior.

Box 4 is also a powerful intervention in that it interrupts whatever is reinforcing the bad behavior in the first place and gives the opportunity for changing the channel on the situation. It's like a do-over. Kids love attention, which means annoying others may occasionally be reinforcing. Getting a parent to lose his temper is particularly reinforcing for teens, because it is developmentally appropriate for them to start experimenting with personal power. If parents are unable to maintain emotional neutrality (which is ideal when executing a behavioral intervention), then kids win. By stopping everything and removing the reinforcement from that situation, rehabilitation is possible.

Take Away Reward **Tip #1: Emotional neutrality is key to success.**

Practice the mood management CBT tools from Chapter Four. That way when your little precious tests you (and they will), you are prepped to be your most effective. Kids respect and feel safe with parents who maintain calm, deliberate authority. If you lose your temper, kids get anxious and sometimes learn to enjoy triggering you. If you consistently maintain your control and authority, your kids will take you seriously. I just had a fourteen-year-old client tell me yesterday, "Why would I keep working hard to mind my dad if he doesn't even try to keep his temper?" It is a slippery slope once you lose your child's respect. Of course, all parents freak out on occasion, but you'll have the best authority and credibility if you practice emotional neutrality while giving a command. If you are consistent, switching from silly to serious can be a cue to kids that you mean business and increase immediate compliance.

Take Away Reward Tip #2: Give a concise command with a 1-2-3 warning.

When your children misbehave, give them a concise command (five words or less if possible) followed by a "one" (e.g., "brush your teeth, one"). If they still don't comply, repeat your concise, no-nonsense command ("brush your teeth or you'll have a consequence, two"). Repeat to a three then give a time-out. For younger kids, a time-out is sufficient (one minute for each year old they are). For older kids, you may need to withdraw a privilege.

Take Away Reward Tip #3: Don't give them the plays from your playbook until the situation calms.

When you're delivering your threat of consequence, say the word "consequence" instead of detailing the consequence you're thinking of delivering. By keeping your consequence choice vague, you maintain power and prevent them from negotiating. You also avoid escalating the situation by triggering them further. When things are calmer, go back to tell them the consequence they've earned. Kids are less willing to gamble with more bad behavior if they're not sure of the consequence.

Take Away Reward Tip #4: Create a go-to list of consequences.

Make a go-to list of rewards and privileges, from smallest to biggest. That way when your child earns "a consequence," you have a go-to list to help you make an immediate, deliberate, well thought-out decision. This way you won't undershoot or overshoot the mark and can follow through every time. Consistency and fairness will earn you valuable credibility and respect.

Take Away Reward Tip #5: Keep consequences simple and short, with an end date.

Consequences that span long period of time require a lot of parent supervision, which often leads to more episodes of limit testing and negotiation. Rather than providing triggers that escalate the situation, only take something for a few hours. This also has the bonus of keeping your parenting toolbox full for additional consequences. Short time spans also give kids more hope and incentive to pull it together. Also, tell them when they get their privilege back so they're not soaking in resentment. Too often I've seen kids give up, feeling like the they have nothing left to lose. An end point keeps them from anxious wondering and asking if it's time yet for the privilege to be returned. Nobody likes to feel like a dancing monkey for authority. Explicit expectations from both sides are best.

Take Away Reward Tip #6: **Always follow through.**

If you don't have opportunity to consequate, don't threaten with a 1-2-3. It's critical that you have consistency to condition your kids to comply and maintain your credibility and authority. Many consequences can double as rewards as well.

Examples of Short-Term Consequences

- Bedtime fifteen minutes earlier
- Fifteen minutes shaved off TV time
- Dinner at the table instead of a fun porch picnic
- No Legos tonight
- No earphones tonight

Take Away Reward Tip #7: **When you implement a new parenting intervention, expect your child's unwanted behavior to escalate at first before it gradually decreases. Stay consistent, and the new habits you're hoping for will anchor in.**

Family members are all connected into one big system. In general, systems resist change. If one person in the family behaves differently, other family members will adjust their behavior as well. They will also unconsciously cooperate with each other to return to the familiar way of functioning, even if old habits are unhealthy. That means that new parent strategies sometimes trigger tantrums before behavioral improvements set in. With warmth, consistency, and patience, kids will eventually develop better habits. But don't be surprised if a new tantrum pops up after weeks of better behavior. Psychologists call these out-of-the-blue tantrums *extinction bursts*. Stick to your best strategy and your child will go back to acting better once again. One slip, and they'll return to escalating tantrums.

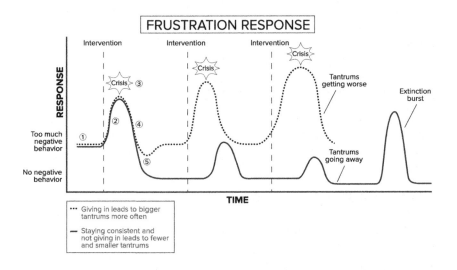

Bennett Box Challenge

Behavior Reinforcement Schedule: Immediate Goal + Habit-Building

In over twenty years of clinical psychology practice, I have seen practically every mishap a family can stumble into. One of my favorite tools to use to incentivize child behavior is the *Bennett Box Challenge*. This reinforcement chart is doubly powerful. It not only provides same-day immediate reinforcement for positive child effort, but it also reinforces habit and consistency by rewarding the child for meeting their goals for days in a row with escalating reward levels. That means the child is pleased to get a Bennett Box for effort that day and extra pleased to get extra boxes for days in a row! Here's how this works:

Getting Started

Introduce Bennett Boxes as a fun way to reinforce compliance and encourage good habits.

For young children, decorate the chart with stickers and crayons/markers, and hang it in a central location. This will increase their investment and anticipation for success.

Choose your *Target Goal.* Make sure it's an easy one to start. You want your children to be successful the first time so they fully buy into the concept. If the first goal is too hard, they'll association the chart with frustration and it will lose its hook.

Write the Target Goal as the desired behavior, followed by a behavior you want to avoid. For example: "Set timer & stayed within tech time limits (no forgetting or sneaking)."

Commit to a daily Bennett Box cash-in time (e.g., before dinner) when you review the day and fill in the Bennett Boxes. Don't skip days. Your parental commitment to the rewards will determine your child's commitment to the goal.

Agree on a super fun activity as the final reward (e.g., family game night, craft day, bowling night, date night with parent(s)). Keep it reasonable, not an epic trip to an amusement park. Avoid material rewards like money, toys, or food, because they quickly lose their reward power, called *habituation*. When that happens, kids demand bigger and bigger rewards. Then charting becomes undoable and parents end up with demanding, disappointed children. Kids habituate less quickly to family activities than material rewards.

Bennett Box Parenting Strategies

Use a friendly and warm tone that communicates a firm expectation of cooperation, rather than a timid request or authoritative demand for compliance. Parent emotional neutrality (keeping calm) is key to success. Don't let them see you sweat even if they get oppositional.

For some kids, frustrating the parent is a better reward than what they get for Bennett Boxes. In other words, your children may try for the opposite of what we are trying to accomplish (making you mad instead of meeting the target goal). Anticipate this and patiently outsmart them.

Praise success instead of nagging or threatening. Once a box is earned it cannot be taken away. Bennett Boxes are intended to provide reinforcement, not punishment. Examples of praise include, "You're on Level 3; at this rate, you're going to fill your chart quickly!" Bragging to others so the child can overhear is also an awesome reinforcement.

If your children do not meet their target goals, do not lecture or remind them other than a quick comment at Bennett Box cash-in time (don't demoralize them). Also, it is perfectly acceptable to withdraw a privilege for excessive defiant noncompliance.

If your child seriously stalls and does not receive a Bennett Box for several consecutive days, wait a few weeks then renegotiate a new chart. Allow time between charts to avoid burn out.

How Bennett Boxes Work

Level 1 - The first day your child meets the goal, date one Bennett Box.

Level 2 - The second consecutive day your child meets the goal, date two new Bennett Boxes.

Level 3 - The third consecutive day your child meets the goal, date three new Bennett Boxes .

Level 4 - The fourth consecutive day your child meets the goal, date four new Bennett Boxes.

Level 5 - The fifth consecutive day your child meets the goal, date five new Bennett Boxes.

Level 5+ - Each consecutive day your child meets the goal after that, date five new Bennett Boxes for each day (no higher level than 5).

The first day the goal is **not** met, your child does not get any boxes dated that day, and that missed date is listed at the bottom of the chart (Level 0). The next day the goal is met, simply go back to one Bennett Box awarded (Level 1) and work your way back up to Level 5.

There are 60 Bennett Boxes on this chart. With perfect consecutive compliance, this chart will take 14 days to complete. For imperfect compliance, it can take far longer. You may want to cross some boxes off to start to make it easier for younger children. Also, award a single bonus box here and there for exceptional effort.

BENNETT BOX CHALLENGE

Name _____ **Target** _____

date:_____	date:_____	date:_____	date:_____	date:_____
date:_____	date:_____	date:_____	date:_____	date:_____
date:_____	date:_____	date:_____	date:_____	date:_____
date:_____	date:_____	date:_____	date:_____	date:_____
date:_____	date:_____	date:_____	date:_____	date:_____
date:_____	date:_____	date:_____	date:_____	date:_____
date:_____	date:_____	date:_____	date:_____	date:_____
date:____	date:_____	date:_____	date:_____	date:_____
date:____	date:___	date:_____	date:_____	date:___
date:____	date:___	date:_____	date:_____	date:__
date:____	date:___	date:_____	date:_____	date:___
date:____	date:_	date:_____	date:_____	date:___

List the dates of days missed below:

GKIS Connected Family Screen Agreement

How to introduce the GKIS screen agreement to your kids:

"I found this guide to help us stay connected as a family and still use our screens. With an agreement we'll know what to look out for and what's expected. After all, if we don't have an agreement and learn to talk about it, our rules won't make sense, parents will get mad, and kids will get in trouble too often. None of us want that!"

"Let's cover a few items today, and others on other days. I won't torture you with long lectures, just cool conversations and negotiations. If we can't agree, we might have to revisit that item a few times until we make a decision. It is a "living agreement," which means we can renegotiate and change items at any time. The goal is to learn from each other in a fun, loving way. Let's get started!"

Commitment

☐ This agreement applies to all screen use everywhere, including home, school, in the car, and at a friend's house.

☐ If you want something changed, we can discuss it. This is a starting point. Your opinions and values matter too. I want to hear them.

Love & Protect

☐ We promise to honor and respect each other online just like we do offline.

☐ We promise to use good judgment, kindness, and discretion when posting. We will not post embarrassing photos or quotes of each other or share private information.

☐ We will answer each other's texts and calls quickly and politely.

☐ We will talk to each other instead of getting lost on our screens. We will keep track of each other's interests and occasionally share screen activities (videos, articles, games) together.

☐ Everybody makes mistakes off- and online. If you feel uncomfortable, come to me for help. We will work it out instead of lecture or punish. We are a family and have each other's backs, 100%, always.

☐ What adult, other than your parents, can you go to about uncomfortable online issue that comes up? _____

Honesty & Transparency

☐ All screen devices, apps, games, and software are owned by parents, not kids. We will purchase them, track all usernames and passwords, and give permission about use.

☐ We agree to be open and honest about online activities. We will not delete browser history without permission.

☐ We will never disable or deliberately work around parental controls.

☐ We agree to dock our screens at _____ am/pm on weekdays and _____ am/pm on weekends.

☐ There is no exclusive right to privacy with screen activities. Adults in authority (parents, school staff, law enforcement) may check any screen content at any time. However, we promise to monitor for safety rather than violate our mutual trust or be overly intrusive between you and your friends.

☐ We agree to follow screen rules of others and ours whenever we're at somebody else's house or at school. We are aware that schools and workplaces often require passwords to social media accounts.

Screen Smarts & Digital Permanence

☐ We will listen to our instincts and trust our gut online just as we do offline.

☐ Warning: Anything online may be shared or altered without permission. There are no take-backs. Even disappearing or deleted images are stored on a server somewhere. We agree to think ahead and use good judgement before browsing, texting, commenting, or posting online.

☐ We agree to never share personal identifying information online via text or photos on public posts (like name, age, or location), and be careful of photos with clothing or backgrounds with school logos.

☐ We won't over-share, including with photos, texts, or questionnaires (quizzes).

☐ We will use anonymous user and screen names if our content will be viewed by anybody off of our approved friends lists.

☐ We will turn off geo-tags and face recognition when possible.

☐ We will not chat with strangers online. We understand that nobody can be trusted online even if they tell us differently, even if we think it's fun or we're feeling brave.

Cybersecurity

☐ We will support our family's cybersecurity measures, including:

    ☐ Activating firewalls

    ☐ Updating protective software and parental controls

    ☐ Never sharing passwords and regularly changing them

    ☐ Not joining unknown Wi-Fi connections

    ☐ Never opening unknown emails or downloading, copying, or installing unknown attachments

    ☐ Frequently backing up data

☐ We are aware of cybersecurity risks: tracking, malware (viruses, adware, spyware, Trojan horses), scamming, phishing, hacking, and identity theft.

Digital Citizenship, Online Reputation, & Netiquette

☐ We agree to be kind online just as we are offline.

☐ If a difficult situation comes up, we can resolve it together. Parents agree not to take over, unless the situation is dangerous and needs immediate intervention.

☐ We will apply the *grandma test* prior to texting or posting anything. This means you would be fine with any post or text being viewed by grandma. If you aren't comfortable with that, don't post it.

☐ We won't participate in cyberbullying actively or passively. It hurts people deeply. We won't ever be cruel online, even when we think the person deserves it.

☐ We will not view or participate in porn, sexy photos, cruel humor, or excessive violence. Ever. Once images or texts are in cyberspace, you lose control over what happens to them.

☐ We will make a serious effort to be present and experience real life and face-to-face relationships instead of only virtual ones.

☐ We will be considerate of our safety and of those around us when using screens. No texting and driving!

GKIS Launch Techniques

☐ I agree to create and present a *Persuasive Powerpoint* if I want a new device, app, game, or Internet activity. My research will include an overview of the product, cost, ratings, privacy settings, reviews, and safety and reporting features.

☐ I promise to only adopt one new digital activity at a time.

☐ We will setup the new technology together with on eye on privacy and safety features.

☐ We understand that the first several weeks with a new screen activity are probationary. We may need to retire it if something unexpected comes up.

Friends Lists

☐ We agree to occasionally go through friends lists to make sure that you know each person.

☐ We agree to allow parents on friend lists.

Blackout Situations & Times

We agree to follow these Blackout Situations:

☐ While driving

☐ Behind closed doors

☐ In your bedroom

☐ In the bathroom

☐ While you're doing your homework

☐ During meal time

☐ 30 minutes before lights out

☐ Mornings before school

☐

☐

☐

☐

☐

We agree to follow these Blackout Times:

☐

☐

☐

☐

☐

Social Media Apps & Instant Messaging

☐ I will supply all usernames and passwords.

I will not use instant messaging:

☐ At all

☐ Outside my friend list

☐ Without good judgment

Approved screen devices (with passwords) (* if has webcam):

☐

☐

☐

☐

☐

☐

☐

☐   Approved apps, games, and activities (with passwords) (* if has instant messaging):

☐

☐

☐

☐

☐

☐

☐

☐

Child Signature   Date   Parent Signature   Date

_____   _____

Dr. Bennett's Top Ten Parenting Tips

1. **Respect**

   Allow your children to maintain their dignity by providing choices and an opportunities to recover whenever possible. Being harsh may produce an immediate result, but the consequences can be damaging to your children's sense of self over time. Avoid humiliating or shaming. If you have good relationships and expect them to do the right thing, they usually will. Set a good example by apologizing and talking about your feelings when you've made a mistake.

2. **Lighten Up, Slow Down, and Connect**

   Set aside time for casual conversation often. Let your kids know they are important and you care what they think and feel. Demonstrate your enjoyment them by *lighting up* when you see them. With little ones, this means play; with teens, it is discussion and shared activity.

3. **Give Nine Times More Positive Than Negative Feedback**

   It's too easy to ignore things when they're going right and then comment when there's a mishap. Avoid this mistake. Turn toward the behavior you want and away from the behavior you don't. Turning away is a little time-out, called *extinction*. Even more powerful than extinction is rewarding compliance with a smile and praise. Just like adults, children need to feel important and appreciated. If you praise more than scold, they will learn to parent themselves with celebration rather than criticism. This will benefit them throughout their lives and the lives of their children.

4. **Don't Assume Your Children are Little Adults**

   Kids vary in their ability to reason and solve problems at different ages. Teach children how to soothe and comply, rather than demanding immediate and blind obedience. Give them permission to fail by explaining to them that every failure is a learning opportunity. Give them room to have feelings and work things through.

5. Pick Your Battles

Not every issue is worth tackling. Coach toward solution rather than taking over. Consider the developmental level of your child with each intervention and increase expectations of self-reliance as he or she ages. Promote independence and responsibility.

6. Remain Emotionally Neutral

A negative emotional response from the parent sets a bad example and may accidentally reinforce manipulative behavior from the child. Avoid escalating the situation by being too harsh or yelling. Practicing anger management techniques.

7. Be Clear and Concise

Before you speak, be sure the child is listening and is not distracted by establishing eye contact and asking her to repeat the request. Give your request in five words or less, and explain yourself only once. Although the child deserves to know why he should do something a certain way, don't nag or repeat yourself over and over. That only provides opportunity for argument. You may have to remind your child about the limit later, as children learn best with consistent, neutral repetition. Avoid lecturing.

8. Don't Intervene Unless You're Prepared to Follow Through

Children frequently respond emotionally when they don't get their way. For a young child this is a tantrum, for an older child this may be intimidation, badgering, threatening, pouting, or sweetly cajoling. Keep in mind that such displays are meant to express emotion and manipulate the parent to change course. Expect this reaction, ignore attitude, correct more inappropriate behaviors (e.g., with time-out or withdrawal of privileges for verbal or physical aggression), and don't give in. You may find relief in the immediate (phew, they've quit tantruming), but in the long run you just rewarded your child for being difficult to get his way. Reinforcement (even one time out of ten) can be a powerful motivator for more tantrums. After your initial intervention, expect your child to still have tantrums on occasion in the future; this is called *spontaneous recovery*. If you are consistent and don't give in, the amount of spontaneous recoveries will decrease. Remember that, despite their protests, children need to have firm, consistent limits to feel safe and achieve mastery. When you give a request, keep your eyes on your child until they move to comply. If you don't, they won't obey and you'll be repeating yourself over and over.

9. Choose the Lowest-Level Reward Possible

Use praise and affection rather than material rewards whenever possible. Avoid putting yourself into a position of bribing the child when a simple request followed by praise will do. This not only allows you the opportunity to have more options for reward choices later, but it also lessens the risk of the child becoming satiated and no longer needing or wanting more reward. Telling another person how proud you are of your child's accomplishment with your child within hearing distance can be a powerful reinforcer and avoids the opportunity for him to discount your comment in embarrassment. Also, do not be put off by protests about praise and affection from older children. They may have dignity to uphold, but still need love and support. If praise isn't enough, have a list of privileges and rewards, from smallest to biggest, to refer to when determining consequences. Don't decide consequences on the spot when you're angry or irritated. Tell the child they will be getting" a consequence" and fill them in on the details later after you've thought about it and they've calmed down.

10. Have a Strong Personal and Parenting Support Network

If you are happy, chances are your kids will be happy and easier to deal with. If you are married, make sure you have a date scheduled with your spouse regularly. Meet with friends regularly. Talk about your frustrations and celebrate your joys. Allow yourself time to relax and have fun. Get a long list of trusted babysitters and hire them. If a pattern is established early, your children will consider a babysitter a treat for them as well. Practice being grateful every day and share the stories with the people you care about. Avoid getting in the habit of complaining or always having a problem. Create a life that involves more than just being a good parent.

CHAPTER 11: PARENTING Q&A

Infant-Toddler Q&A

When my toddler tantrums, I get desperate and give him my smartphone to settle him down. Please tell me this is OK.

I'm not going to lie. I totally would have used screen devices as a distraction when my kids were little. The key is to think about brain and skill development at this age as you make your screen-use decisions. Remember the *use it or lose it* phenomenon of brain development described in Chapter One? During certain developmental periods, the brain is ripe to learn if stimulated appropriately. However, if this learning-receptive window closes without the appropriate experiential stimulation, learning that skill is much more difficult, and, in extreme cases, may be impossible.

Substitution risk: That means your toddler needs buckets of face-to-face interaction and three-dimensional play experiences to grow the neurological wiring necessary for skill mastery. Too much screen time takes the place of critical learning experiences. Also, there is no evidence that educational software is beneficial until your child is three years old. That does not mean there is no benefit; it means we have not seen sufficient evidence of it for significant research conclusions. Favor play in the nonvirtual world over screen time. There's a good reason tech developers like Steve Jobs and Bill Gates restricted screen use with their kids.

Conditioning/habit risk: Also, young kids quickly become accustomed to habit. If handed a screen every time they get bored, children will not learn how to soothe themselves. Too much screen time sets your family up for demanding tantrums. It's the classic case of a short-term fix that sets up a long-term problem. Kids learn to prefer screen distraction instead of caregiver- or self-soothing.

Content risk: Not all screen time is equal. Socially interactive screen time (like video conferencing with grandma and grandpa) is best, followed by edutainment content. Avoid frantic, frenetic activity and inappropriate content that can cause stress and burn out the autonomic nervous system (as in tantrums). Also, even young kids mimic behavior they see on screens, so keep it age-appropriate. Screens developed for kids is better than borrowing mom and dad's screens.

Considering substitution, habit, and content risks, I think occasionally using screens as a distraction is fine. Just keep it short, and don't cave too often. Our job as parents is to enrich our children's environment with variety of opportunities for learning for healthy neurological development and mastery. Rather than give in to your little one's frequent screen demands, provide a travel kit of non-screen activities like puzzles, stringing beads, and crayons. Let him explore your Tupperware cabinet or stir a bowl of water on the porch. Even better, let him follow you around as you verbally narrate your thoughts and activities, interspersed with face-to-face play, conversation, and hugs and kisses. If you are following these guidelines, release the guilt and spend the saved energy on self-nurturance. Parenting toddlers is a tough gig, but remember, this age is temporary. Soak in those squishy cheeks and yummy hugs while you can. As a mom of teens, I promise you will miss this one day.

My toddler tantrums and is inconsolable when I take her screen away. Why? What can I do about it?

In Chapter Eight, I discussed the risk of screen addiction and the processes of tolerance and withdrawal. Over time, it takes evermore screen time to get the same satisfaction. In addiction studies we call this *tolerance*. When the screen is taken away, the child experiences anxiety and irritability until it is back in her hands. For kids who do not use screens that often, the tantrum may be simply frustration with intent to provoke the parent to give it back. However, with kids who overuse screen devices, a tantrum may be an expression of *withdrawal* resulting from an overly aroused autonomic nervous system (fight-or-flight system) and an inability to self-soothe.

What goes up must come down. Trying to recalibrate back to emotional calm after intense arousal may strain a toddler's limited capacities. The excitement triggered by screen use is neurological stimulation from the dopamine rush to the pleasure center and a cortisol and adrenaline dump into the bloodstream. But recovery comes much more slowly as those hormones filter out, ultimately leaving the child irritable and fatigued. Clinicians call this dynamic *"rebound."* We often see rebound behaviors with kids taking psychostimulants for Attention-Deficit Hyperactivity Disorder (ADHD), for instance. And it is not just the kids that suffer; tired cranky babies leave parents strained as well.

To avoid baby and parent tantrums, limit screen time and don't allow overly arousing, frenetic screen content. Transition away from the screen slowly with calming emotional support. Kids synch to their parents' emotional state, so choose calm over unexpected grabs and hollering. If a tantrum has already begun, assess which type of tantrum you are dealing with. If your child is simply communicating what she wants in the most persuasive way possible, validating understanding and negotiating between two options may settle her down. Distraction also works, especially for younger kids. Even a firm request for what they can do instead of tantrum is in order ("Let's go wash hands" instead of "Stop crying right now"). If the tantrum is inconsolable possibly due to autonomic hyperarousal, allow your child time in a quiet space, a hot bath, or maybe rock her so she has the safe space to pull it together. Too much talking or further stimulation may escalate the problem rather than help. Reasonable expectations are key. If your child is often too hard to handle after screen time, maybe she's still too young for screen use.

What are your three best tips for infants and toddlers regarding safe screen use?

Be proactive and keep a positive attitude. Set a goal every morning to minimize screen use that day for you and your toddler. Plan fun activities proactively. If you are struggling, get together with friends rather than turning to Facebook or wine. Our mothers and grandmothers had more social support than we do, and I think they had it right. Mindfully soak in the present and filter in the yummy aspects of parenting rather than complaining by habit or zoning out with distractions.

Kids don't know what is good for them, so don't let them run the show. You must choose a healthy screen diet in the same way you don't let your kids eat cookies for breakfast, lunch, and dinner. Screen time is a dopamine hit much like an addictive drug. Main course should be calming, education content with game play for dessert.

Don't be a sucker for slick product marketing. Marketers are targeting infants and toddlers as the next lucrative customer population, but that does not mean it's justified outside of profit earnings. Research has thus far demonstrated no benefit for babies and toddlers, instead finding that screen use can cause developmental delay. Forming a strong attachment is critical for life-long cognitive and psychological health. Screen time does not strengthen parent-child attachment, eye contact and good old-fashioned one-to-one play does. Read a book aloud instead, as this has been proven to have distinct neurological advantages for kids. The synchronized dance between parent and baby is the best neurological and socioemotional enrichment with, by far, the most learning payoff. Don't let screens interfere.

Preschool Q&A

I can't take it! My preschooler pesters obsessively to play his computer. I only allow educational games, but how much is too much at this age? It seems he's learning a lot and, frankly, it gives me a much-needed break!

Chapter Two provides all you need to know about quality and quantity of screen use for preschoolers. Consider the psychology behind the "pestering" you describe. He's communicating that his brain craves the dopamine stimulated by the fun and problem solving from his video game. I may even go so far as to say he thinks he NEEDS this stimulation. Keep in mind that he will also try to convince you that he NEEDS marshmallows for breakfast. My point is, only you have the mature judgment to make sound decisions about when screen use is appropriate, how much is too much, and what type of content is best.

To keep pestering down, keep a consistent screen-use activity schedule that allows your child the convenience of knowing there is structured time set aside for fun and that pestering does not have a payoff. Do not reward pestering by giving in; that rewards the unwanted behavior. Instead, explain (just once) that it is not scheduled screen time and consequate further pestering with a 1-2-3 warning and then a time out. With no reward or payoff, your child will quickly learn that complying with your command to stop is the better option. Even better, he will learn the resiliency skills of self-soothing, managing his impulses, and sticking to a reasonable screen schedule.

Here's an example of the application of the 1-2-3 compliance technique:

"No, it is not our scheduled screen time, don't ask again."
"But MOM!"
"Don't ask again. One."
"But MOM!!"
"Two."
"I want screen time!"
"That's 3, time out."

Notice that mom only explained her reasoning once. She kept it short and simple, and she avoided further escalation by staying emotionally neutral. It does not take too many trials for kids to learn that a firm tone, a concise command, and a count means business and immediate compliance is the best option. If you maintain your authority and power, your child is forced to self soothe and comply. That makes for a mutual respect and a peaceful household. If you give in just one time, your child's pestering will likely escalate. Consistency and emotional neutrality is key.

Like I explained in Chapter Ten, any time you start a new intervention, expect an escalation at first. It may get worse before it gets better. Don't lose faith. When you try for the first time, make sure you have time for a prolonged battle. Also, before you implement 1-2-3, teach soothing skills so they know how to stop obsessing. The soothing tools described in Chapter Four, like *tummy breathing* with a six-second exhale, *can-do thinking,* and *distraction,* are three go-to emotional soothing skills that are useful for all ages, even parents.

My preschooler loves to use my smartphone, but I don't want to use the parental controls because it will restrict my use. Any suggestions?

Each device has different options; however, many have a setting that allows different levels of restricted use for different users on the same device. On an iPhone, you can enable *Restrictions* in *Settings* > *General.* You can turn restrictions on and off with a passcode. Be careful though. If you lose your passcode (or accidentally share it with your child), the only way to reset it is factory restarting your device. Computers typically have options to have multiple login users with different restriction settings as well. If you allow them their own child devices, make sure it's clear you own the device and will establish the rules.

What is your best tip for families with preschool age children regarding safe screen use?

STAGING your house for safe screen use is my best tip for preschool age kids. Kids are creatures of habit. Preschool age is an awesome time to set permanent expectations about screen limits and boundaries. If little ones learn it as a way of being, it will save you years of arguing and negotiating later. Young kids are grateful for their first screens, creating the perfect time to establish rules, expectation of monitoring, and reasonable controls. As they age, gradually allow more devices, more apps, and less filtering and monitoring. Too often parents do the opposite. They allow everything at once and then shave privileges as trouble crops up triggering anger and resentment from the kids. As detailed in Chapter Three, frame your allowance schedule like a funnel with the narrow part on the bottom (start heavily restrictive and add more gradually) rather than an upside-down funnel (adopt apps all at once and then shave them as trouble crops up).

My favorite staging tips for preschool age is to get them accustomed to limits by:

Establishing *GKIS Screen Free Zones,* like short car rides, the dinner table, the bedroom, the bathroom, or behind closed doors;

Setting up *GKIS Co-Work Stations* with body-friendly ergonomics in community areas optimizes parental supervision and sibling engagement. Add nonvirtual materials next to screens to encourage complimentary play like dress up, pretend play, and arts and crafts.

Creating *GKIS Family Docking Stations* for management and control.

Following *blackout days and times* using the parental controls on devices and with filtering and monitoring apps and software.

School Age Q&A

My kids play video games and independently select apps on their tablets and hand-held screen devices, what are the basics I should be aware of regarding safety and privacy?

That's a great question. I love that you have your mind set at being proactive instead of reactive. My first suggestion is to keep in mind that any Internet activity involves three windows of risk: posting, viewing, and mutual access to others. That means your kids need to know skills for each activity.

Posting: Self-Disclosure and Privacy, Netiquette, and Screen Smarts

Be aware that anything posted online can be used by those intent on harm. Therefore, the best approach to posting is to be conservative and avoid posting personal identifying information like your name, address, school, location, and birthdate or account numbers. Use nicknames for usernames and screen names and disable face recognition, tagging, and geotagging (location/GPS) features. Also, don't over-share about personal feelings and opinions. Sexual predators overwhelmingly report that they use information gleaned from social media sites to help snare and groom their victims (e.g., "My favorite dog is a pug. What? Yours is too? We totally "get" each other. Your parents don't really understand you, do they?").

Micro blogging sites like *Tumblr* and *YouTube* vlogging are virtual gold mines for predatory adults looking for vulnerable kids and teens, because they create an online culture of personal disclosure. Teach your kids to consider if they would mind having their posts, texts, or browsing history on a big screen at a school assembly for public viewing. Would teachers or grandparents be offended? How might these posts reflect on them in the future when they're older and trying to get into college or get a job? Remind them that you, other parents, teachers, and unkind peers may see their texts, posts, and browsing histories. NOTHING on their device is private. Also agree on a zero-tolerance policy about cyberbullying or sexy poses in photos or videos.

Viewing

Although most social media and gaming apps have parental controls and reporting features, they only work if people use them. Violent, sexual, and cruel images are often posted for hours or days before they are taken down. Before you allow your child a new screen activity, research these features and search by keywords to investigate accessible content (e.g., search terms like "self-harm," "suicide," "anorexia," "boobs"). Have frequent conversations with your kids about the fact that they will accidentally run into inappropriate content. Teach the difference between accidental exposure and purposeful browsing. Let them know that you expect this to happen, and they will not be punished when it does. If they feel safe sharing with you, your kids will come to you with feelings that may result from such exposure.

Mutual Access

The only screen activity a child needs to be personally exploited is instant messaging or texting. That means most handheld devices, gaming platforms, or smart phones have the potential to be a nuclear football to their safety and privacy. One conversation with somebody strategically dangerous to your child is all that is needed to earn enough trust for a meeting. More frequently I am seeing kids and teens victimized due to these kinds of contacts. Set parental controls on all devices and build your digital toolbox from the beginning to block unwanted access from hostile peers or strangers. Become familiar with their gaming activities by playing with them to get a feel for risk potentials. Teach netiquette and assertiveness skills while playing together. Teach your kids to trust their gut when contacted online. If it feels weird or creepy, it probably is and you should bail or seek consult.

Healthy kids will make lots of mistakes in their virtual and nonvirtual worlds before adulthood. Mistakes lead to learning and mastery. When your kids make them, do not freak out, ambush them, yank screen privileges, take over, or get defensive. Stay calm, help them generate solutions, and support them as they choose and implement those solutions like I demonstrated in Chapter Nine. It is fine if the first trial doesn't work very well, they need this process to learn to problem solve. Just as with the nonvirtual world, growing up in the virtual world means two steps forward one step back.

I worry my kids are becoming socially isolated, because they are constantly on their phones and gaming devices instead of playing outside or asking for play dates. Should I allow this, or is it unhealthy?

One of the reasons I launched GetKidsInternetSafe is because I have seen screen media change childhood profoundly in the last twenty years. No longer do kids run the town on bicycles and come home when the porch lights turn on. Now kids are sequestered behind closed doors to protect against stranger danger, bored and captive to limited availability of overtasked parents. Because parents cannot possibly supervise and entertain everybody all the time, play dates happen online. Kids are "connected" to the Internet and each other many hours a day in ways that are changing how they interact with the world and their peers and family. Screens provide enormous access to information in multiple formats that outsource abilities and literally change brain wiring. One can debate if this is good society or not, but most agree that both harm and benefit result from screen use. What must happen to keep relationships healthy are consistently teaching kids social skills, including empathy and boundary setting.

In my practice, I have seen kids become extremely intimate with other kids thousands of miles away, sometimes diving so deep into their opinions and feelings that the interaction becomes overly personal and dependent. They get into the habit of sharing every thought during every moment. Yes, it feels safer to tell your secrets to somebody far away, separate from your social circle. But these complex relationships can also spark impulsive disclosures, be shared among mutual friends, and feed dangerous plans. For instance, just yesterday a mother of a client contacted me to say she had intercepted her daughter's texts to an unknown peer expressing her wish to die and disappear off the planet. It was frightening for both of us as we planned to approach her with our concern. Are these disclosures truly suicidal in nature or is she simply sharing her thoughts in a constant stream of consciousness, like a free association journal? Several of my clients have posted video diaries (or *vlogs*) expressing suicidal and homicidal urges, resulting in fear for safety, suspension from school, and social isolation. Others have been radicalized by hate groups and cults after visiting forums intent on being persuasive and manipulative.

How can parents avoid these intense online entanglements? Awareness is the first step. Setting up filtering and monitoring and letting your kids know that it is in place not only sets a boundary for them to think about before they post or text, but it also gives parents a piece of mind about what their kids are up to. Use it heavily with young kids and back off appropriately as your child gets old enough to have sophisticated skill sets and deserves more privacy. Of course, kids primarily message through social media apps like Snapchat, because we can't monitor those. Therefore, keep that in mind before social media app adoption.

Set up rules and regulations. If your children are taking their devices into the bedrooms or bathrooms or staying up late engaging in screen activities, they may be destined for real trouble. Make sure you home is staged with the techniques detailed in Chapter 2. For instance, set up a *GKIS Family*

Docking Station to avoid late night texting that may become too intimate as eyes get sleepy and judgment wanes. Make sure the docking station is near supervising parents, otherwise kids WILL sneak. Sneaking and punishing will lead to a strained parent-child alliance.

Young kids also need *GKIS blackout days and time boundaries*. This requires kids to develop a variety of interests and skills, which results in confidence, skill development, and an overall well-balanced life. Ask questions and have conversation about what and who is important to them. Consistent, warm engagement is how you can track interests, activities, and entanglements online as well as offline.

We have set time parameters for screen use at our house, but they are almost impossible to enforce. My kids say they need their screens for homework and group projects; or if they stop abruptly when playing games, they will let down their team and lose progress. If I make them comply, they get angry and sneak screen use at every opportunity. How can I keep them compliant with screen limits?

I am fond of telling parents not to yank screen privileges as their go-to consequence for disobedience; otherwise their kids will become resentful around screen matters and refuse to disclose about their virtual lives. However, not following time and blackout parameters is the correct reason for taking away screen time. There is a clear and reasonable connection between learning to demonstrate reasonable control and pulling back screen time until self-control skills are mastered. Pulling screen time for overuse and sneaking is justifiable and reasonable.

However, learning does not stop at consequences. Parents must also teach kids how to walk away from that ever-compelling screen content. To keep your authority and credibility, it is important to maintain your emotional neutrality when giving consequences. Do not yell and take opposition personally. Your kids screen limit defiance and sneaking is not a personal attack nor is it a sign of immorality. Testing limits and craving screen time is expected. You must stay on top of it.

Kids have legitimate reasons why they struggle to comply with screen limits. Not only are their brains begging for that screen-triggered dopamine hit, but game and app developers are very aware of that screen-brain interface and exploit it for profit. Developers build in game characteristics that attract your child's obsessive want for MORE, MORE, MORE. Common strategies include offering incentives for lots of logged-in time like earned levels or prizes, scheduled events with other players that have severe response cost if the player comes late or leaves the challenge early, and social chat incentives for bonding with others and earning elite titles. Do your research before game purchases and keep an eye out of built-in compulsive use features.

GKIS Parenting Strategies to Increase Compliance:

Offer a *heads-up transition* (e.g., "I'm going to ask you to turn you're your computer in fifteen minutes. Make sure you wrap up when you get to a good spot.") Timer apps are a useful transitioning tool. Parental controls and special tech tools can also forcibly pause or time out screen access.

When stating your command, make sure you have your child's eye contact and attention. So often we make our request to a busy child lost in another task. Initial engagement and understanding is required to achieve compliance.

Give your one- or two-step command concisely. Preferably, use one short sentence.

Tell them what you want them to do rather than what you want them to stop doing (e.g., please turn off your computer and wash your hands" rather than "don't play too long"). The fewer the necessary steps to compliance, the better.

Eye till comply. Do not just give your command and walk away before your child responds. Keep your eye on him until he starts the follow-through. Many of my clients have marveled about how well this simple strategy works.

Praise compliance sincerely. We all love to be acknowledged for a job well done. Not only does this reward compliant behavior, but it also feeds that important parent-child connection.

If you notice that your child is struggling to pull away from his screen activity, be validating and empathetic and teach soothing skills. Virtual identity development is important to kids. Be understanding, calm, and kind when asserting parental authority. The parent-child connection is the most valuable tool you have for influence. Don't squander it on arguments of little worth (choose the hill you want to die on). Most of all, don't humiliate or shame them for being passionate about video games or social media use. To you it may seem like chasing meaningless lights around a screen, but for them it's their lifeline to friends.

Use positive reinforcement rather than withdrawal of privilege when possible. Reinforce what you want more often than punishing what you don't want. As we learned in Chapter Ten, this is the most powerful parenting tool available. It has the added benefit of making you the good guy that your kids will want to engage with. Charts also work well with young kids. For example, set up a *Bennett Box Challenge* from Chapter Ten for compliance, so they can earn recognition points for argument-free compliance. Acknowledgement and earned privilege is different than bribery. It's kindness, validation, and relationship building. Just as adults appreciate it from their friends and spouses, kids appreciate it from their parents.

Dr. Bennett, I lose sleep over the idea that a sexual predator could have influence over my child on- and off-line. What do you suggest to build my child's awareness and assertiveness skills?

Believe it or not, I would say my position on teaching empowerment and assertiveness are among my more controversial parenting strategies. Some parents believe that a more authoritarian style, which is characterized by being stern, strict, and unbendable, is more effective than being authoritative. The latter is characterized by being firm, but willing to empathize and negotiate. The psychological research supports that authoritative parenting makes for happier, healthier families. So, do I, based on over twenty-five years of academic, clinical, and personal experience.

I am a firm believer that the parent must maintain authority with respectful dominance and insistence on compliance. This parenting hierarchy is best established when the child is young and consistently enforced throughout the child's lifespan. However, as the child grows, it is important for parents to ease up and allow the child to participate in decision-making, problem-solving, and negotiated limits. Not only does this provide positive fuel for the parent-child connection, it also teaches critical life skills under the loving and watchful eyes of experienced parents.

Yelling at a child and demanding silent obedience cheats your child of important learning and emotional safety. Too often, kids who are silenced and cornered suffer from mood and anxiety problems and will either become helpless, hopeless, and depressed or angrily act out. Blindly obedient and naïve kids are easy targets. A good parent's obligation is to encourage independence and confidence. That means giving they room to negotiate and even mess up once is a while.

So back to the specifics of the question…if we raise our kids to analyze situations, think for themselves, and weigh in on the solution, they are far better equipped to recognize danger online and assert themselves for safety. In session I practice these skills with kids over card and board games. During problem solving and assertiveness practice, we discuss online risks like the grooming techniques of online predators. As kids build skills, they learn to trust their gut when it comes to safety. Even the feistiest kids love this mutually respectful, dynamic interaction, and the social skill development during cooperative play is extremely valuable. Plus, it just plain feels goods. The human need for connection and intimacy is more powerful than food or drink. Kids who are engaged with caring adults are more likely to seek consult if they run into something uncomfortable. If the parent doesn't instinctually adjust from being commanding to openly negotiating, tweens and teens will demand it. These changes are not always smooth or easy, but they are normal and healthy.

What is your best tip for families with school age kids regarding safe screen use?

Get in the habit of having *GKIS Family Meetings* with a teaching agenda that goes over important online issues your kids will face. During these low-key, fun conversations, cover current events like cyberbullying and violence desensitization. Encourage sharing of opinions and active problem solving. This provides opportunity for mutual education and skill building, and it also builds the alliance and a cooperative framework that will come in very handy during the upcoming teen years. For current-event content involving Internet safety, check out my blog page on ***GetKidsInternetSafe.com***.

Tween and Teenage Q&A

After reading Chapter Eight about the costs of multitasking, I am convinced that we need to revamp homework and study strategies now that my child has hit middle school. But he's going to be very upset and defiant. Any ideas to help?

Great question. In short, prepare, buckle in, and stay calm. With reason and consistency, you should be able to negotiate changes that may have big payoffs in regard to your tween's academic performance, mood, and overall cognitive energy. Here are some sensible guidelines for success:

Don't Ambush

Sprinkle in your intent and justification over time rather than in one aggressive attack. Intervention doesn't have to happen all at once (even though you may be anxious to get it over with). Introduce your ideas over time to give teens a chance to digest the information. Start with a discussion, then a meeting, then the implementation in doable steps. It's unlikely you'll ever get their full buy-in, but gradual tweaks will be accepted far better than a hostile takeover. Plus, you get cred for being reasonable.

Prepare for Push-Back

When I work with families, I often start with coping skills before I suggest parenting strategies. Listening, assertiveness, negotiation, and relaxation skills are key. It also helps if you are prepared. These push-back possibilities are offered so you won't be surprised when they arise and will stay calm and strategic and avoid getting pulled in and manipulated. If it gets too heated, walk away (eyes off the behavior you don't want) and return to the issue another time (eyes on the behavior you want). Most important, don't let them see you sweat. Maintain your credibility with calm authority.

Typical teen push-backs:

Act like they don't care with plans to sneak later

Justify, lie, or make excuses

"I didn't do it"

"Everybody does it"

"My teacher says I have to"

"You don't know what it's like now [I know everything about everything]"

Deflect and distract

By triggering you with real-time bad behavior, you may forget to follow through ("Look squirrel!"). I call this "throwing a fireball into the room."

While the parent is running around putting out fires, the issue at hand gets lost and the kid wins. Fireballs can be:

Eye-rolling

Talking back or cussing

Pulling out a list of grievances with absolutes ("You never let me" "This always happens")

Tantrum

Name calling ("You suck")

Self-deprecation ("I'm a terrible kid")

Emotional extortion: Threaten to hurt you or themselves

Physically aggress (throwing, slamming, hitting)

Defy you and do it anyway

Listen and Validate

It's healthy for teens to push back and manipulate. You want your kids to test things out on you, their safe person. Don't take oppositionality personally. Manipulative kids are simply smart, strategic kids. Your job isn't to squash their spirits, it's to manage it and coach them to success.

For kids to engage in a discussion, you'll need to listen as much as you talk. Lectures turn them off immediately. No engagement means you've lost any hope of influence. Once your child has responded and you've confirmed that you understand their position (whether you disagree with it or not, his position is legitimate), firmly state your intent to establish sensible rules. Remember that screen use is their lifeline to learning and socialization. Compulsive screen use happens because it has real meaning and benefit. If you tell them to "turn it off," they get anxious. Anxious kids are the most defiant, because they will endure almost anything to avoid the feelings from anxious rebound. Making a non-negotiable announcement will make for hard-going later and interfere with the opportunity for teens to take accountability for positive change. Modeling, mentorship, and teamwork are keys to success.

Negotiate the Rules

If the issue is that multitasking interferes with homework, help your kids plot when multitasking contributes to learning and when it interferes. Multitasking is beneficial when generating ideas, acculturating oneself to vocabulary and ideas around a particular topic, identifying experts and networking with community, enriching understanding using multimodal formats (reading, listening, viewing video), and when browsing for entertainment. Multitasking activities that have performance costs include screen activities that interrupt demanding cognitive learning tasks like reading, homework, or studying. Perhaps pulling back on bad habits rather than eradicating them entirely is a good start for now. For best success, outline goals, commit to honest learning objectives, and download time management and tracking apps. Let them try out their ideas, then swing around later to discuss outcome. Tweak, repeat.

There you have it, a plan! Remember to set an expectation for success and prepare for follow-through. If you capitulate to teen freak outs, it will be far harder next time because you've taught them you'll cave in the face of tantrums. If you follow through, they'll eventually respect your authority. Staying firm, consistent, and emotionally neutral is also important. You're empowered and so are they. Small consequences (one night when devices are docked early) are usually just as impactful as big ones (taking their phone for a week), and you are less likely to cave because it's doable. Don't forget to remind them that you will lighten up as they get close to graduating. High school seniors need more independence to build resilience prep them for success in college.

My middle schooler wants a social media app that is not rated for kids. Most of her friends are already on it. I'm worried that I'm interfering with her social success if I don't let her get it. Worse than that, she's getting really angry with me. I'm starting to cave against my better judgment. What do you suggest?

You are not alone. Parents often get railroaded into allowing screen activities they know little about, because it's too much work to research and they fear their children's resentment. After the first app adoption, more get downloaded all at once. Before you know it, parents are so in the dark they are immobilized. An example is allowing an Instagram profile that you monitor. Then your child creates a second secret, private profile for friends (unmonitored) and then an ultra-private profile for best, exclusively chosen friends (unmonitored). Within these ultra-private profiles, the most outrageous posts and comments happen including cyberbully comments reflecting exclusion and rejection.

Post: *"Janie friend requested AGAIN, as if. LMAO"*

Reply comment: *"Desperate."*

Second comment: *"Def."*

Third comment: *"Go kill yourself already."*

(all for Janie to see)

Slow and steady increases in screen activities are the way to go. Although most parents fear their kids will hate them for it, in my experience kids are generally tolerant of fair online limits and rules. The earlier you adopt these strategies, the more accepting they will be. The key ingredient is that you take into serious account what they want and go about your decisions with fairness, communication, and measured negotiation.

Keep in mind that it is developmentally appropriate for older kids and teens to stretch the limits and demand parents to progress to a more negotiative parenting strategy. Teens are in the process of developing an independent identity, which is necessary for a successful launch into the real world. This is sometimes a tough transition for parents from demanding strict obedience to less efficient, messier negotiations. Rather than take offense and blow up at their teens for mouthing off and pushing limits, parents do better when they maintain a sense of humor, firmly hold a reasonable line, and stay calm and sensible. As your kids grow, so must your parenting strategies.

Implement the easy and effective *GKIS Launch Techniques* offered in Chapter Three. Notice that the teen is increasingly expected to do the research, participate in implementation, and consistently take accountability for online choices. Everything is probationary and reversible. They will have successes and failures. Two steps forward and one step back is common course.

GKIS privacy protection tips for Facebook and Twitter:

Facebook:

- Even on the strictest privacy settings, assume anybody can see what you post and share.

- Mobile downloads, timeline photos, profile pictures, and cover photos can only be deleted one at a time. Consider keeping them up for a day or two then deleting from your timeline to avoid a large accumulation of images.
- Face recognition technology allows identification from any face shot, even profile. If you don't want to be automatically tagged, select photos at a distance or where faces are concealed. Use an animated image for your profile picture. (These and the cover photo are always public).
- Photos from your smartphone may be geotagged. Ensure settings disable location or strip metadata from photos before posting with third party software.
- Monitor your browsing history to track all access points.
- Use the Privacy tab to limit who sees your posts. Select "only me" or "friends only."
- The Limit Past Posts tab allows you to retroactively change all "public" posts to a "friends-only" audience.
- Prevent FB from using your data by selecting "no one" in the Ads tag settings "third-party sites" and "Ads and friends."
- Do not enter personal information in the "About" section.
- To hide friends, select "Only Me" under "Friends" > "Manage" > "Edit Privacy."
- FB tracks and builds a history of your location and may share with friends unless you disable those features in the "Activity Log" and "Location History" in "Nearby Friends" and "Nearby Places."
- Use the "View Activity Log" to edit individual posts that appear on your timeline.
- Use "Settings" > "Download a Copy of your Facebook Data" > "And More". "Start My Archive" to view a FB report of data collected on you.

Twitter

- Even on the strictest privacy settings, assume anybody can see what you post and share.
- Use a nickname as your username/Twitter handle and change it often to limit exposure of your profile.
- Only enter country as your location.

- Recognize that hashtags highlight keywords, so they are searchable within the Twitter search engine and mentions (@username) tag users so the link to the private profile becomes visible to the public.
- Do not share links to personal photos or other online profiles.
- Do not allow Twitter to use your location on mobile devices.
- Under privacy, do not allow others to tag you in photos.
- Protect your Tweets to make them private.
- Do not add locations to your tweets.
- Do not allow Twitter to use third-party data for promotion or personalization.

I'm devastated to find out that my son and his girlfriend have been sexting. To make matters worse, I read his texts after assuring him he had privacy. Not only did I read things I'm very upset about (like sexual behaviors beyond what we think is reasonable at his age), but I don't know how to tell him I know without revealing that I spied and broke our agreement. He needs his phone so taking it away is not reasonable nor will he comply with a request to break up with his girlfriend. What should I do?

I have treated MANY parents in the same boat, and I personally have made many parenting choices where hindsight was 20/20. I believe parents should tell their kids they are monitoring and filtering screen activities. I think it provides practice for thinking before posting, demonstrates that other parents and adults will be viewing texts and posts, and reveals a willingness to work together about online choices. But security and parenting experts have disagreed with me, saying that if a parent reveals intent they will miss out on secret plans and sneaky behaviors. The controversy is real.

Let's move to solutions for your current situation. First, I believe that the trust between you and your son has been breached, and if not handled delicately, it could damage your relationship. For that reason, I suggest you put your ego at the door and get out your knife and fork because you are going to have to eat crow and apologize. Where is it written that parents can't make mistakes? Let's face it. We are new at parenting teens just as kids are new at being teens. This adds up to a rocky road of successes, failures, stops, and starts.

Schedule a time to have a private discussion with your son when you will not be interrupted. Tell him the truth. Admit that you were concerned and you screwed up; that in hindsight you realize you should have had more safety parameters in place and told him that his screen use would be monitored. Express your concerns while validating that his loving and sexual feelings towards his girlfriend are normal and natural (assuming there were no safety or legal violations here). Explain your philosophy about what you think is appropriate regarding intimacy and relationships at his age. Assure him that you will keep his confidence. Don't go telling grandma and Aunt Linda about the intimate details you uncovered. Let him know that these are his facts to share if he chooses to, not yours.

Second, ask him what suggestions he has to resolve the very real conflict of privacy versus safety. Actively negotiate screen safety parameters. Some of my GKIS Staging Tips apply, such as no screens in bedrooms, bathrooms, or behind closed doors and GKIS blackout times to optimize judgment and supervision. Also, consider if monitoring and filtering programs and apps apply in this situation. Keep in mind it is best not to tell him which specific programs you will be implementing. If your son is a young teen, then monitor more closely. If he is older, you may just want to set a lighter monitoring option. Most importantly, let him know what you plan and why. And absolutely consider his input. By the time he's an adult, he should be mostly on his own off-screen and on.

Finally, plan relationship-building opportunities with your son to repair the damage done. Perhaps this means getting to know his girlfriend better, so they understand that he has a family to take into consideration when it comes to friendship and love. Of course, they deserve privacy, but you may choose to set stricter limits for now. Keep in mind that not every mistake requires traditional discipline, like taking screens away. The humiliation of you reading his texts and the face-to-face conversation about it is probably consequence enough. The truth is, his best resource for keeping intimate relationships healthy is the support and competition for his time from his friends. He needs his friends right now.

My teen appears to be desperate for online attention from her peers and even strangers. How do I teach her the social skills necessary to be socially successful in the brutal online world of adolescents?

Parents often ask me if screens have introduced more drama among teens. In my clinical experience, I would have to say, "Yes it has." It used to be that kids only maneuvered in big groups during school hours and much of that time was supervised by teachers and administrators. After school, they went home to hang out with chosen friends and family members. Time with peers was limited and supervised. Now kids stumble around online in huge groups of anonymous members for many hours a day, every day. That means little supervision and poor accountability. It also means online disinhibition, or an "everything goes" mentality.

Much of my clinical time is spent mentoring teens in the digital world. The social skills I teach include how to develop an online reputation that will not come back to bite them, to think before they post, and to be aware of their vulnerability online, especially as relationships change. Teens have very strict, unspoken online rules that, when broken, is punished publicly and severely. For example, one must never ask to be friended on somebody's ultra-private profile unless invited. A public profile is fair game for anybody, but private and ultra-private profiles are invitation-only. These profiles are public postings for who is "in" and who is "out." Submitting a request without invitation opens you to a humiliating public comments and cyberbullying.

Another favorite cyberbully tactic detailed in Chapter Seven is phishing and outing, or eliciting private information from an unsuspecting victim, and then sharing it with others to humiliate them or drive a wedge between friends. Simple screen shots can be used as evidence for trash talk, even when it was enticed and manipulated through devious means. Teach your teen that ANYTHING they post or text can be used against them, even by seemingly BFFs.

If you feel ill equipped to teach these impossibly complicated teen skills, bring in an older mentor, like a cousin or friend, for consult over pizza. Specific bullet points of do's and don'ts may be necessary for teens who are unusually kind, optimistic, or naïve to the brutal virtual battleground that is teen social media.

When you worry there are too many friends on a social media buddy list, consider the concept of *Dunbar's number*, which is 150, or the number of people we are close enough with to be real "friends." The inner core of friendships is typically five intimate friends, the next outer circle is made up of ten best friends, the next thirty-five are good friends, and final 100 are acquaintances. It is hypothesized that 150 friends are all our brain has slots for. Even in the age of social media, that number has remained steady. That means we all need our 150 friends to share resources, to help us see fact from fiction, and to help us feel important and loved. Maintain empathy and understanding as you set limits. For younger teens, you may choose to ask for a buddy list limit until they have developed better impulse control.

If you do not have skin thick enough to see the vulgar language and cruel behavior that is typical online among teens, seek support yourself. You must be in tiptop shape to provide the frequent love and validation teens need as they walk the virtual gauntlet. It is mostly an arena for fun, excitement, and humor, but few escape adolescence online without being targeted for online humiliating experiences here and there. Remind them that difficult online situations are usually temporary. One day the spotlight is on one kid, and the next day everything changes. No matter what, you want them to know that you will always provide a soft place to fall where they are admired, loved, and cherished. Screen-free weekends can also be rejuvenating to parents and kids. Take the heat and stage a tech detox and go on vacation.

I'm horrified to say I just found online porn on my son's browser. What should I do?

We covered the risks of online pornography viewing in Chapter Six. The key take-away here is that the parent-child alliance is the highest priority. Mutual respect, compassion, and understanding will optimize the chance that your son will accept your influence. Focus on staying calm, honest, and be your normal self so this is a learning opportunity rather than a shaming lecture that could damage your relationship. Try to keep your sense of humor without being silly. Here are steps to deal with your recent discovery:

Have a matter-of-fact, emotionally neutral discussion with your son about your beliefs and family rules around online pornography viewing. Keep in mind that sexual curiosity is healthy, and most kids will access pornography if given the chance. Frankly, almost all of them will be given the chance. This is not anybody's fault. It is now part of growing up.

Ask how he came across the sites. Did it happen unintentionally, did somebody introduce it to him, or did he seek out information? Of course, he will be embarrassed, but this question will determine if you need to talk to the school, a sibling, or friend's parent. If he came across a site due to the browser history of an adult in your home, study up on using private browsing, create different log-ins on the family computer, and frequently delete browser history.

Revisit your parental controls on devices (keep password protected), browser and device safe search modes, and an age-appropriate filtering and monitoring tech toolkit. You may need to install more filtering software at the router level.

Revisit your *GKIS Connected Family Screen Agreement* and reestablish rules like location parameters, *GKIS Family Docking Stations,* and a W-Fi curfew.

Establish an open dialogue free of shame and blame about sexuality. The sex education tips in Chapter Seven are a great start. Remember, this represents opportunity, not failure.

Our family is out of control with our screen use. We need help. We are not willing to give them up, but something has to give. Any suggestions?

I thought you'd never ask. ☺ Here are some immediately doable measures to slow you down between tech vacations. The trick is to break the compulsive use habits by making your screens less attention-grabbing and interrupt the mind-mesmerizing techniques that Silicon Valley has captured us with. Beyond the suggestions offered throughout the book, here are some innovative quick-fixes:

Cut your buddy lists to 150. Remember Dunbar's number? You'll only keep your bffs and cut out those you are only distantly acquainted with. That translates to lots of time saved.

Dull the mind-piercing colors and go grayscale. On your iPhone, you have the option to toggle between colors and grayscale by going to Settings>General>Accessibility>Display Accommodations. Turn on the Accessibility Shortcut to triple tap colors on and off.

Turn off autoplay. Autoplay can keep you passively consuming endless content dished up without specific selection. YouTube, Facebook, Hulu, and Amazon Prime allow you to turn it off in settings and preferences.

Hide apps with eye-catching notifications on your second phone screen. That way you will have to sideways swipe to see them and can batch check them when it's convenient rather than exhaust yourself by frequently fracturing your attention.

Rotate your social media apps. Rather than juggle many social media platforms at once, keep only one active at a time. Better yet, retire some forever.

Opt for communications that resemble best communication practices without ads and news. For instance, Whatsapp, FB Messenger, Marco Polo, and audio notes rely exclusively on people-to-people communications, which is why we're on social media apps in the first place.

Adopt helper apps. There are so many to choose from, including those that help you track time spent, block specific websites and apps, turn off flashy features, and eradicate or blur newsfeeds, sidebars, and notifications. Three great ones are Forest, Freedom, and Moment.

Most importantly, make a deal to accept each other's bids for attention and put the screens away, preferably in a different room altogether!

CONCLUSION

With virtual reality, our busy lives have become even more complicated. As protectors of our little people, we have our eyes open and our hands full. But no matter how well we filter and how gently we tuck them in, the risks of unwanted elements of the world leak into our homes through screens. The genie is out of the bottle. We cannot impede progress. The world moves forward, sometimes faster than we can keep up. With the recent advent of mobile technology, our iGen kids are technology natives, the first generation to learn code as a second language. They are adapting to being cyborgs in ways we barely understand and can scarcely keep up with.

In my work as a psychologist working with families every day, one thing holds most true for me. WE ARE ALL CONNECTED. Whether it is the miracle of watching a baby come into the world, the first day of preschool, watching our teen graduate, or feeling spiritual rapture in church or while watching a vibrant sunset, we all know that love is why we exist on Earth. Parents are the hub for teaching connection and love.

We are a truly global community now. In a single day I may be on a conference call at my kitchen table with screen safety experts from all over the planet in the morning and skyping an author from London into my California classroom in the afternoon. Seamlessly our voices carry through the stratosphere in seconds. It reminds me of the paradigm-shifting work of scientist, Dr. Suzanne Simard. Dr. Simard discovered that we are not the only communities that are connected in miraculous ways on Earth.

Amazingly, forest trees communicate with each other through their root networks in more complex ways than we ever imagined. They are able to identify threat and need in their neighbors and share nutrients amongst each other, even across species. Neighboring trees keep the struggling stump alive and old couple trees nurture each other throughout decades. And like us, the most powerful *supercooperators*, called "Mother Trees," nurture their saplings and the saplings of others so expertly, they will even sacrifice their own health to do it. The more diverse the ecosystem with the largest, oldest, and strongest Mother Trees, the more resilient the forest. These tree communities even have a collective memory that helps defend against threat. Like our human communities, they feed and heal each other. They are strong as single beings, but more powerful as one community.

The world wide web has become our connecting root system. Alone we are weak, but together we are strong. In the debate about whether I am a tech optimist or a tech pessimist, the verdict is I am a tech optimist with a caveat. If we use tech to share with each other, form stronger connections, and learn how vibrantly diverse we are; if it helps us recognize how we each contribute to the whole and that we must nurture each other, then we will thrive with our technology. If we use technology to compete, spread hate, or distract us from ourselves, we will collapse.

Screen Time in the Mean Time was written to inspire us to better connect with our kids and the communities that surround us throughout the world. Like the supercooperators of the forest, I challenge you to reach out and connect with other parents. Warmly share your knowledge, strategies, and time to preserve the sense of community our parents and the parents before them thrived in. Do not let this overtasked digital culture rob you of your most precious resource – the love you have for your family and the powerful personal connections that await you. Enjoy your parenting journey.

ABOUT THE AUTHOR

Dr. Tracy Bennett is the Founder and CEO of GetKidsInternetSafe.com and frequently appears on radio, podcasts, and television as a Screen Safety Expert. She is a licensed clinical psychologist and adjunct faculty at California State University Channel Islands (teaching addiction studies, parenting, clinical psychology, and directed studies). She has maintained a successful private practice for over twenty years working with families, kids, teens, and adults and has worked with thousands of individuals with screen-related challenges. Dr. Bennett consults with corporate and nonprofit organizations and is a keynote speaker for employers, parents, and teens from schools, communities, PTAs, religious groups, and corporate and nonprofit organizations. She is the mother of three, a grown daughter and two teenagers. Dr. Bennett lives with her family in Southern California.

Visit her websites at

http://getkidsinternetsafe.com

https://www.drtracybennett.com

REFERENCES

Chapter 1

[1] https://kaiserfamilyfoundation.files.wordpress.com/2013/04/8010.pdf

[2] Kabali, H., Irigoyen, M., Nunez-Davis, R., Budacki, J., Mohanty, S., Leister, K., & Bonner, R. (2015). "Exposure and Use of Mobile Media Devices by Young Children." *Pediatrics* 136.6: 1044-050. Web.

[3] Kabali, H., Irigoyen, M., Nunez-Davis, R., Budacki, J., Mohanty, S., Leister, K., & Bonner, R. (2015). "Exposure and Use of Mobile Media Devices by Young Children." *Pediatrics* 136.6: 1044-050. Web.

[4] Prensky, M. (2001). *Digital Natives, Digital Immigrants*. Place of Publication Not Identified: Marc Prensky. Print.

[5] Lauricella, A., Cingel, D., Beaudoin-Ryan, L., Robb, M., Saphir, M., & Wartella, E. (2016). *The Common Sense census: Plugged-in parents of tweens and teens*. San Francisco, CA: Common Sense Media.

[6] Https://mottpoll.org

[7] "American Academy of Pediatrics Announces New Recommendations for Children's Media Use." 10/21/2016. https://www.aap.org/en-us/about-the-aap/aap-press-room/pages/american-academy-of-pediatrics-announces-new-recommendations-for-childrens-media-use.aspx

[8]https://www.commonsensemedia.org/about-us/news/press-releases/common-sense-media-research-documents-media-use-among-infants-toddlers

[9] Zimmerman, F., Christakis, D., & Meltzoff, A. (2007). Television and DVD/video viewing in children younger than 2 years. *Arch Pediatr Adolesc Med*.;161(5):473-479.

[10] Hirsh-Pasek, K., Zosh, J., Golinkoff, R., Gray, J., Robb, M., & Kaufman, J. (2015). Putting education in "educational" apps: lessons from the science of learning. *Psychological Science in the Public Interest*, 3-34. doi:10.1177/1529100615569721

[11] Chonchaiya, Weerasak, & Chandhita P. (2008). "Television Viewing Associates with Delayed Language Development." *Acta Paediatrica* 97.7: 977-82. Web.

[12] "American Academy of Pediatrics Announces New Recommendations for Children's Media Use." 10/21/2016. https://www.aap.org/en-us/about-the-aap/aap-press-room/pages/american-academy-of-pediatrics-announces-new-recommendations-for-childrens-media-use.aspx

[13] American Academy of Pediatrics. "Handheld screen time linked with speech delays in young children: New research being presented at the 2017 Pediatric Academic Societies Meeting suggests the more time children under 2 years old spend playing with smartphones, tablets and other handheld screens, the more likely they are to begin talking later." ScienceDaily, 4 May 2017. <www.sciencedaily.com/releases/2017/05/170504083141.htm>.

[14] "American Academy of Pediatrics Announces New Recommendations for Children's Media Use." 10/21/2016. https://www.aap.org/en-us/about-the-aap/aap-press-room/pages/american-academy-of-pediatrics-announces-new-recommendations-for-childrens-media-use.aspx

[15] Christakis, D. (2013). "Infant Video Viewing and Salivary Cortisol Responses: a Randomized Experiment." *The Journal of Pediatrics.*, U.S. National Library of Medicine, www.ncbi.nlm.nih.gov/pubmed/23164310/.

[16] Christakis, D., Zimmerman, F., DiGuiseppe, D., & McCarty, C. (2004). Early television exposure and subsequent attentional problems in children. *Pediatrics*, 113(4), 708-713.

[17] Zimmerman, F., Christakis, D., & Meltzoff, A. (2007). Television and DVD/video viewing in children younger than 2 years. *Arch Pediatr Adolesc Med.*;161(5):473-479.

[18] Lillard, A. & Peterson, J. (2011). "The Immediate Impact of Different Types of Television on Young Children's Executive Function." *Pediatrics*, vol. 128, no. 4, pp. 644–649. doi:10.1542/peds.2010-1919.

[19] Christakis, D., Zimmerman, F., DiGuiseppe, D., & McCarty, C. (2004). Early television exposure and subsequent attentional problems in children. *Pediatrics*, 113(4), 708-713.

[20] Christakis, D., Zimmerman, F., DiGuiseppe, D., & McCarty, C. (2004). Early television exposure and subsequent attentional problems in children. *Pediatrics*, 113(4), 708-713.

[21] Zimmerman, F., Christakis, D., & Meltzoff, A. (2007). Television and DVD/video viewing in children younger than 2 years. *Arch Pediatr Adolesc Med.*;161(5):473-479.

[22] Lapierre, M., Valla, S., & Linebarger, D. (2011). Influence of licensed spokescharacters and health cues of children's ratings of cereal taste. *Archives of Pediatric & Adolescent Medicine, 165,* 229-234. doi:10.1001/archpediatrics.2010.300

[23] Calvert, S., & Richards, M. (2014). "Chapter 12. Children's Parasocial Relationships." *Media and the Well-Being of Children & Adolescents.* S. l.: Oxford UP. 187-200. Print.

[24] Lauricella, A., Gola, A., & Calvert, S. (2011). Toddler's learning from socially meaningful video characters. *Media Psychology,* 14, 216-232. DOI:10.1080/15213269.2011.573465

[25] Christakis, D. (2014). Interactive media use at younger than the age of 2 years: Time to rethink the American Academy of Pediatrics guideline. *Jama Pediatrics.* Doi:10.1001/jampediatrics.2013.5081.

[26] Parish-Morris, J., Neha Mahajan, K., Hirsh-Pasek, R., Golinkoff, M., & Collins, M. (2103). "Once Upon a Time: Parent-Child Dialogue and Storybook Reading in the Electronic Era." *Mind, Brain, and Education* 7.3: 200-11. Web.

[27] Goswami, U. (2015). Children's Cognitive Development and Learning. *Research Reports: CPRT Research Survey 3 (new Series).* http://cprtrust.org.uk/wpcontent/uploads/2015/02/COMPLETE-REPORT-Goswami-Childrens-Cognitive-Development-and-Learning.pdf

[28] Brown, T. & Jernigan, T. (2012). "Brain Development During the Preschool Years." *Neuropsychology Review* 22.4: 313-33. Web.

[29] Bartzokis, G. (2005). Brain Myelination in Prevalent Neuropsychiatric

Developmental Disorders: Primary & Comorbid Addiction. *Adolescent Psychiatry, 29,* 55-96.

[30] Brown, T. & Jernigan, T. (2012). "Brain Development During the Preschool Years." *Neuropsychology Review* 22.4: 313-33. Web.

[31] Mumme, D., & Fernald, A. (2003). 12-month olds avoid and react negatively to an object that elicited a fearful reaction of an adult on TV. *Child Development, 74*(1), 221-237.

[32] Bowlby, J. (1982). *Attachment and Loss.* New York: Basic, Print.

[33] Christakis, D., Zimmerman, F., DiGuiseppe, D., & McCarty, C. (2004). Early television exposure and subsequent attentional problems in children. *Pediatrics*, 113(4), 708-713. Web.

[34] Sigman, A. (2012). "Time for a View on Screen Time." *Archives of Disease in Childhood* 97.11 (2012): 935-42. Web.

[35] Wartella, E., Rideout, V., Lauricella, A., & Connell, S. (2013). "Parenting in the Age of Digital Technology: A National Survey." Center on Media and Human Development, School of Communication, Northwestern University, http://vjrconsulting.com/storage/ PARENTING_IN_THE_AGE_OF_DIGITAL_TECHNOLOGY.pdf, pp. 1– 30.

Chapter 2

[36] Christakis, D., Zimmerman, F., DiGuiseppe, D., & McCarty, C. (2004). Early television exposure and subsequent attentional problems in children. *Pediatrics*, 113(4), 708-713. Print.

[37] Schmidt, M., Haines, J., O'Brien, A., McDonald, J., Price, S., Sherry, B., & Taveras, E. (2012). "Systematic Review of Effective Strategies for Reducing Screen Time Among Young Children." *Obesity.* Web/

[38] Robinson, T. (1999). "Reducing Children's Television Viewing to Prevent Obesity: A Randomized Controlled." *JAMA* 282: 1561-567. Web.

[39] Swing, E., Gentile, D., Anderson, C., & Walsh, D. (2010) "Television and Video Game Exposure and the Development of Attention Problems." *Pediatrics* 126.2: 214-21. Web.

[40] Lenroot, R. & Giedd, J.(2006). "Brain Development in Children and Adolescents: Insights from Anatomical Magnetic Resonance

Imaging." *Neuroscience & Biobehavioral Reviews*, vol. 30, no. 6, 2006, pp. 718–729., doi:10.1016/j.neubiorev.2006.06.001.

[41] Brown, T. & Jernigan, T. (2012). "Brain Development During the Preschool Years." *Neuropsychology Review* 22.4: 313-33. Web.

[42] Christakis, D., Zimmerman, F., DiGuiseppe, D., & McCarty, C. (2004). Early television exposure and subsequent attentional problems in children. *Pediatrics*, 113(4), 708-713. Print.

[43] Lenroot, R. & Giedd, J. (2006). "Brain Development in Children and Adolescents: Insights from Anatomical Magnetic Resonance Imaging." *Neuroscience & Biobehavioral Reviews*, vol. 30, no. 6, 2006, pp. 718–729., doi:10.1016/j.neubiorev.2006.06.001.

[44] Hong, S. (2013). "Reduced Orbitofrontal Cortical Thickness in Male Adolescents with Internet Addiction." 9.11. Print.

[45] Piaget, J. (1952). *The child's conception of number*. London: Routledge & Kegan Paul.

[46] Shelov, S., Altmann T., Hannermann R. (2014). *American Academy of Pediatrics: Caring for Your Baby & Young Child: Birth to Age 5*. (6th ed). New York. Bantam Books.

[47] Chonchaiya, Weerasak, & Chandhita P. (2008). "Television Viewing Associates with Delayed Language Development." *Acta Paediatrica* 97.7: 977-82. Web.

[48] Freud, S. (1940). "An Outline of Psychoanalysis." *The Standard Edition of the Complete Psychological Works of Sigmund Freud*. London: Hogarth. Vol 23. Print.

[49] Erikson, E. (1964). *Childhood & Society*. New York: Norton. Print.

[50] Shaffer, D. *Developmental Psychology: Childhood & Adolescence*. (1989). Pages 512-513. 9th ed. Pacific Grove, CA: Brooks/Cole. Print

[51] Newton, E., & Jenvey, V. (2011). "Play & Theory of Mind: Associations with Social Competence in Young Children." *Early Child Development & Care* 181.6: 761-73. Web.

[52] Cole, M., & Cole, S. (1993). *The Development of Children*. New York, NY: Scientific American. Print.

[53] Cole, M., & Cole, S. (1993). *The Development of Children*. New York, NY: Scientific American. Print.

[54] Kohlberg, L. (1984). *The Psychology of Moral Development: The Nature & Validity of Moral Stages*. San Francisco: Harper & Row. Print.

[55] Piaget, J. (1952). *The child's conception of number*. London: Routledge & Kegan Paul. Print.

Chapter 3

[56] FOSI. (2014). "Who Needs Parental Controls? A Survey of Awareness, Attitudes, & Use of Online Parental Controls." http://www.fosi.org/images/stories/research/fosi_hart_survey-report.pdf

[57] Takahashi, D. (2016). Worldwide Game Industry Hits $91 Billion in Revenues in 2016, with Mobile the Clear Leader. http://venturebeat.com/2016/12/21/worldwide-game-industry-hits-91-billion-in-revenues-in-2016-with-mobile-the-clear-leader/

[58] Ravitz, J. (2016). Varsity Gamers Making History & Dumbfounding Parents http://www.cnn.com/interactive/2015/07/us/varsity-gamers-american-story/

[59] "FTC Undercover Shopper Survey on Enforcement of Entertainment Ratings Finds Compliance Worst for Retailers of Music CDs & the Highest Among Video Game Sellers". Federal Trade Commission. 2011-04-20. Retrieved 2017-10-04

[60] Samuel, A. "Parents: Reject Technology Shame," Atlantic, November 4, 2015, accessed February 3, 2017, http:// www.theatlantic.com/ technology/ archive/ 2015/ 11/ whyparentsshouldnt-feel-technology-shame/ 414163/.

[61] Shaffer, D. (1989). *Developmental Psychology: Childhood & Adolescence*. 9th ed. Pacific Grove, CA: Brooks/Cole. Print.

[62] Walker, L., Hennig, K., & Krettenauer, T. (2000). "Parent & Peer Contexts for Children's Moral Reasoning Development." *Child Development* 71.4: 1033-048. Web.

[63] Lenroot, R. & Giedd, J. (2006). "Brain Development in Children and Adolescents: Insights from Anatomical Magnetic Resonance

Imaging." *Neuroscience & Biobehavioral Reviews*, vol. 30, no. 6, 2006, pp. 718–729., doi:10.1016/j.neubiorev.2006.06.001.

64 Brown, T. & Jernigan, T. (2012). "Brain Development During the Preschool Years." *Neuropsychology Review* 22.4: 313-33. Web.

65 Lenroot, R. & Giedd, J. (2006). "Brain Development in Children and Adolescents: Insights from Anatomical Magnetic Resonance Imaging." *Neuroscience & Biobehavioral Reviews*, vol. 30, no. 6, 2006, pp. 718–729., doi:10.1016/j.neubiorev.2006.06.001.

66 Lenroot, R. & Giedd, J. (2006). "Brain Development in Children and Adolescents: Insights from Anatomical Magnetic Resonance Imaging." *Neuroscience & Biobehavioral* Reviews, vol. 30, no. 6, 2006, pp. 718–729., doi:10.1016/j.neubiorev.2006.06.001.

67 Berlucchi, G. (1981). Interhemispheric asymmetries in visual discrimination: a neurophysiological hypothesis. *Documenta Ophthalmologica Proceedings Series*, 30, pp. 87-93.

68 Zaidel, D., & Sperry, R. (1974). Memory impairment after commissurotomy in man. *Brain*, pp. 263-272.

69 Levy, J. (1985). Interhemispheric collaboration: single mindedness in the asymmetric brain.C.T. Best (Ed.), Hemisphere Function and Collaboration in the Child, Academic Press, New York, pp. 11-32.

70 Cook, N. (1986). The Brain Code. Mechanisms of Information Transfer and the Role of the Corpus Callosum. Methuen, London.

71 Lenroot, R. & Giedd, J. (2006). "Brain Development in Children and Adolescents: Insights from Anatomical Magnetic Resonance Imaging." *Neuroscience & Biobehavioral Reviews*, vol. 30, no. 6, 2006, pp. 718–729., doi:10.1016/j.neubiorev.2006.06.001.

72 https://www.cdc.gov/growthcharts/clinical_charts.htm#Set1

73 Piaget, J. (1952). *The child's conception of number*. London: Routledge & Kegan Paul. Print.

74 Erikson, E. (1964). *Childhood & Society*. New York: Norton. Print.

[75] Cole, M., & Cole, S. (1993). *The Development of Children*. New York, NY: Scientific American. Print.

[76] Maccoby, E. (1984). "Middle Childhood in the Context of Family." *Development during Middle Childhood: The Years from Six to Twelve*. Washington D.C.: National Academy. Print.

[77] Freud, S. (1940). "An Outline of Psychoanalysis." *The Standard Edition of the Complete Psychological Works of Sigmund Freud*. London: Hogarth. Vol 23. Print.

[78] Piaget, J. (1952). *The child's conception of number*. London: Routledge & Kegan Paul. Print.

[79] Shaffer, D. (1989). *Developmental Psychology: Childhood & Adolescence*. 9th ed. Pacific Grove, CA: Brooks/Cole. Print.

[80] Cole, M., & Cole, S. (1993). *The Development of Children*. New York, NY: Scientific American. Print.

Chapter 4

[81] National Center for Education Statistics, https://nces.ed.gov

[82] Giedd, J., Blumenthal, J., Jeffries, N., Castellanos, F., Liu, H., Zijdenbos, A., Paus, T., Evans, A., and Rapoport J. (1999). *Brain development during childhood & adolescence: a longitudinal MRI study*. Nat Neurosci; 2(10):861-3.

[83] Chechik, G., Meilijson, I., & Ruppin, E. (1999). "Neuronal Regulation: A Mechanism for Synaptic Pruning During Brain Maturation." *Neural Computation* 11.8: 2061-080. Web.

[84] Brown, T. & Jernigan, T. (2012). "Brain Development During the Preschool Years." *Neuropsychology Review* 22.4: 313-33.

[85] D'Souza, Cyril, D., Pittman, B., Perry, E., & Simen, A. (2009). "Preliminary Evidence of Cannabinoid Effects on Brain-derived Neurotrophic Factor (BDNF) Levels in Humans." *Psychopharmacology* 202.4: 569-78. Web.

[86] Zammit, S. (2002). "Self-Reported Cannabis Use as a Risk Factor for Schizophrenia in Swedish Conscripts of 1969: Historical Cohort Study." Bmj 325.7374: 1199. Web. http://dx.doi.org/10.1136/bmj.

[87] Andréasson, S., Engström, A., Allebeck, P. & Rydberg, U. (1987). "Cannabis and Schizophrenia. A Longitudinal Study of Swedish Conscripts." *The Lancet* 330.8574: 1483-486. Web.

[88] Stefanis, N., Dragovic, M. Power, B., Jablensky, A. Castle, D., & Morgan, V. (2013). "Age at Initiation of Cannabis Use Predicts Age at Onset of Psychosis: The 7- to 8-Year Trend." Schizophrenia Bulletin 39.2: 251-54. Web. http://schizophreniabulletin.oxfordjournals.org/content/early/2013/01/1 0/schbul.sbs188.abstra ct

[89] https://www.cdc.gov/growthcharts/clinical_charts.htm#Set1

[90] Mead, M. (1928). Coming of Age in Samoa. William Morrow Paperbacks. pp. 59–122. ISBN 978-0688050337. Retrieved 22 March 2017.

[91] Freud, S. (1940). "An Outline of Psychoanalysis." *The Standard Edition of the Complete Psychological Works of Sigmund Freud.* London: Hogarth. Vol 23. Print.

[92] Choudhury, S., Blakemore, S., & Charman, T. (2006). "Social Cognitive Development during Adolescence." *Social Cognitive & Affective Neuroscience* 1.3: 165-74. Web.

[93] Piaget, J. (1952). *The child's conception of number.* London: Routledge & Kegan Paul. Print.

[94] Erikson, E. (1964). *Childhood & Society.* New York: Norton. Print.

[95] Adler, P., & Adler, P. (1998). Peer power: Preadolescent culture & identity. New Brunswick, NJ: Rutgers University Press.

[96] Adler, P., & Adler, P. (1998). Peer power: Preadolescent culture & identity. New Brunswick, NJ: Rutgers University Press.

[97] Shaffer, D. (1989). *Developmental Psychology: Childhood & Adolescence.* 9th ed. Pacific Grove, CA: Brooks/Colem, p 579. Print.

Chapter 5

[98] Howe, N., & Strauss, W. (2000). Millenials rising. The next generation. New York: Vintage Books.

[99] Twenge, J. (2014). *Generation Me: Why Today's Young Americans Are More Confident, Assertive, Entitled--and More Miserable than Ever Before.* Atria Paperback.

[100] Rushkoff, D. (1997). Ecstasy club. San Francisco: Harper San Francisco.

[101] Prensky, M. (2001). Digital natives, digital immigrants, part II: do they really think differently? On the Horizon, 9(6), 1e9.

[102] Oblinger, D., & Oblinger, J. (2005). Educating the net generation. Online e-book. Educause.

[103] Kuipers, G. (2006). The social construction of digital danger: debating, defusing & inflating the moral dangers of online humor & pornography in the Netherlands & the United States. *New Media & Society*, 8,379e400.

[104] Twenge, J. (2014). *Generation Me: Why Today's Young Americans Are More Confident, Assertive, Entitled--and More Miserable than Ever Before.* Atria Paperback.

[105] Libert, B. (2014). "What Airbnb, Uber, and Alibaba Have in Common." *Harvard Business Review*, 20 Nov. 2014, hbr.org/2014/11/what-airbnb-uber-and-alibaba-have-in-common.

[106] Anderson, D., Huston, A., Schmitt, K., Linebarger, D., & Wright, J. (2001). "Early childhood television viewing & adolescent behavior". *Monographs of the Society for Research in Child Development* 66 (1, Serial No. 264). Web.

[107] Fish, A., Li, X., McCarrick, K., Butler, S., Stanton, B., Brumitt, G., et al. (2008). Early childhood computer experience & cognitive development among urban low-income preschoolers. *Journal of Educational Computing Research*, 38, 97-113.

[108] Wright, J., Huston, A., Murphy, K., St. Peters, M., Pinon, M. Scantlin, R., & Kotler, J. (2001). "The relations of early television viewing to school readiness & vocabulary of children from low-income families: The early window project." *Child Development* 72 (5): 1347–1366. Web.

[109] Jackson, L., Von Eye, A., Biocca, F., Barbatsis, G., Zhao, Y., & Fitzgerald, H. (2006). Does home Internet use Influence the academic performance of low income children? *Developmental Psychology*, 42, 429-435.

[110] Tankersley, J. (2015). Study: Kids can learn as much from 'Sesame Street' as from preschool. Retrieved from https://www.washingtonpost.com/business/economy/sesame-street-and-its-surprisingly-powerful-effects-on-how-children-learn/2015/06/07/59c73fe4-095c-11e5-9e39-0db921c47b93_story.html

[111] Blacker, K., Curby, K., Klobusicky, E., & Chein, J. (2014). Effects of action video game training on visual working memory. *Journal of Experimental Psychology: Human Perception & Performance, 40*(5), 1992-2004. doi:10.1037/a0037556

[112] DeBell, M., & Chapman, C. (2006). Computer & Internet use by students in 2003. National Center for Educational Statistics. U.S. Department of Education, Washington, DC. Retrieved February 22, 2009, from http://nces.ed.gov/pubs2006/2006065.pdf.

[113] Van Deventer, S., & White, J. (2002). Expert behavior in children's video game playing. *Simulation & Games*, 33, 28-48.

[114] Maclin, E., Mathewson, K., Low, K., Boot, W., Kramer, A., Fabiani, M., & Gratton, G. (2011). Learning to multitask: Effects of video game practice on electrophysiological indices of attention & resource allocation. *Psychophysiology, 48*(9), 1173-1183. doi:10.1111/j.1469-8986.2011.01189.x

[115] Burton, L. (2015). Media benefits for children & teenagers. Retrieved from http://raisingchildren.net.au/articles/media_benefits.html

[116] Higgin, T. (2014). Inventive Games That Teach Kids About Empathy & Social Skills. Retrieved from https://ww2.kqed.org/mindshift/2014/04/18/inventive-games-that-teach-kids-about-empathy-and-social-skills/

[117] Mahood, C., & Hanus, M. (2017). Role-playing video games & emotion: How transportation into the narrative mediates the relationship between immoral actions & feelings of guilt. *Psychology of Popular Media Culture, 6*(1), 61-73. doi:10.1037/ppm0000084

[118]Reinecke, L. (2009). Games & recovery: The use of video & computer games to recuperate from stress & strain. *Journal of Media Psychology: Theories, Methods, & Applications, 21*(3), 126-142. doi:10.1027/1864-1105.21.3.126

[119] O'Connor, E., Longman, H., White, K., & Obst, P. (2015). Sense of

community, social identity & social support among players of massively multiplayer online games (MMOGs): A qualitative analysis. *Journal of Community & Applied Social Psychology, 25*(6), 459-473. doi:10.1002/casp.2224

[120] Calvert, Sandra L., & Jennifer A. Kotler. (2003). "Lessons from Children's Television: The Impact of the Children's Television Act on Children's Learning." *Journal of Applied Developmental Psychology* 24.3: 275-335. Web.

[121] Ferguson, C., & Donnellan, M. (2014). Is the association between children's baby video viewing & poor language development robust? A reanalysis of Zimmerman, Christakis, & Meltzoff (2007). *Developmental Psychology, 50*(1), 129-137. doi:10.1037/a0033628

[122] Kirkorian, H., Wartella, E., & Anderson, D. (2008). Media & Young Children's Learning. Retrieved from http://www.futureofchildren.org/publications/journals/

[123] Radesky, J., Silverstein, M., Zuckerman, B., & Christakis, D. (2014). Infant Self-Regulation & Early Childhood Media Exposure. *Pediatrics, 133*(5), e1172–e1178. http://doi.org/10.1542/peds.2013-2367

[124] Hanley, S. (2016). Major Milestones in the Biological Development of Children. Retrieved from http://oureverydaylife.com/major-milestones-biological-development-children-1883.html

[125] Kirkorian, H., Wartella, E., & Anderson, D. (2008). Media & Young Children's Learning. Retrieved from http://www.futureofchildren.org/publications/journals/

[126] Lee, S., & Chae, Y. (2007). Children's Internet use in a family context: Influence on family relationships & parental mediation. *CyberPsychology & Behavior*, 10, 640-644.

[127] Johnson, G. (2010). Internet Use & Child Development: Validation of the Ecological Techno-Subsystem. *Educational Technology & Society*, 13 (1), 176–185.

[128] Li, X., & Atkins, M. (2004). Early childhood computer experience & cognitive & motor development. *Pediatrics*, 113, 1715-1722.

[129] Facer, K., Furlong, J., Furlong, R., & Sutherland, R. (2003). *Screen play: Children & computing in the home.* London: Routledge Falmer.

130 Wartella, E., Rideout, V., Lauricella, A., & Connell, S. (2013). "Parenting in the Age of Digital Technology: A National Survey." Center on Media and Human Development, School of Communication, Northwestern University, http://vjrconsulting.com/storage/ PARENTING_IN_THE_AGE_OF_DIGITAL_TECHNOLOGY.pdf, pp. 1– 30.

131 "Kids & The Connected Home: Privacy in the Age of Connected Dolls, Talking Dinosaurs, & Battling Robots." *Future of Privacy Forum*. Future of Privacy Forum & Family Online Safety Institute, 09 Jan. 2017. Web. 11 Apr. 2017.

Chapter 6

132 Lieber, M., & Blumberg, A. (2017). "Is Facebook Spying on You." Reply All, episode 109, 2 Nov. 2017.

133 "FTC Undercover Shopper Survey on Enforcement of Entertainment Ratings Finds Compliance Worst for Retailers of Music CDs & the Highest Among Video Game Sellers". Federal Trade Commission. 2011-04-20. Retrieved 2017-10-04

134 Walrave, M., Lenaerts, S., & De Moor, S. (2008). Cyberteens @ risk: Tieners verknocht aan het Internet, maar ook waakzaam voor 'risico's? [Cyberteens @ risk: Teenagers addicted to the Internet, but aware of the risks?] Antwerp: Antwerp University, TIRO Teens & ICT: Risks & Opportunities.

135 Bridle, James. "Something Is Wrong on the Internet." Medium, 6 Nov. 2017.

136 Henke, L., & Fontenot, G. (2007). Children & Internet use: perceptions of advertising, privacy, & functional displacement. *Journal of Business & Economics Research*, 5(11), 59–65.

137 Wilcox, B. "Report of the APA Task Force on Advertising & Children." *PsycEXTRA Dataset* (n.d.): n. pag. *Report of the APA Task Force on Advertising & Children*. American Psychological Association, 20 Feb. 2004. Web. 13 Apr. 2017.

138 https://www.privacyrights.org/blog/bill-breakdown-ab-1580-child-id-theft

[139] Huston, A., Donnerstein, E., Fairchild, H., Feshbach, N., Katz, P., Murray, J., Rubinstein, E., Wilcox, B. & Zuckerman, D. (1992). Big World, Small Screen: The Role of Television in American Society. Lincoln, NE: University of Nebraska Press.

[140] National Institute of Mental Health - NIMH (1982). Television & Behavior: Ten Years of Scientific Progress & Implications for the Eighties, Vol. 1. Rockville, MD: U.S. Department of Health & Human Services.

[141] Murray, J. P. (1973). Television & violence: Implications of the Surgeon General's research program. *American Psychologist*, Vol. 28, pp. 472-478.

[142] Krahe, B., Moller, I., Kirwil, L., Huesmann, L., Felber, J., & Berger, A. (2011). Desensitization to Media Violence: Links with Habitual Media Violence Exposure, Aggressive Cognitions, & Aggressive Behavior. *Journal of Personality & Social Psychology*, Vol. 100, No. 4.

[143] Calvert, S. & Kotler, J. (2003). "Lessons from Children's Television: The Impact of the Children's Television Act on Children's Learning." *Journal of Applied Developmental Psychology* 24.3: 275-335. Web.

[144] Calvert, S. & Kotler, J. (2003). "Lessons from Children's Television: The Impact of the Children's Television Act on Children's Learning." Journal of Applied Developmental Psychology 24.3: 275-335. Web.

[145] Taylor, J. (2012, December 4). How Technology is Changing the Way Children Think & Focus. Retrieved October 18, 2012, from http://wwpsychologytoday.com/glog/the-power-prime/201212/how-technology-is-changing-the-say-children-think-and-focus

[146] Holfeld, B., Cicha, J. & Ferraro, F. (2014). "Executive Function & Action Gaming among College Students." *Current Psychology Curr Psychol* 34.2: 376-88. Web.

[147] Brown, S., Liebermann, D., Gemeny, B., Fan, Y., Wilson, D., & Pasta, D.

(2009). Educational video game for juvenile diabetes: Results of a controlled trial. Vol. 22 (Issue 1), p. 77-89. Doi:10.3109/14639239709089835

[148] NPD Group (2011). Kids & gaming, 2011. Port Washington, NY: The NPD Group, Inc.

[149] Ferguson, C. (2011). Video Games & Youth Violence: A Prospective

Analysis in Adolescents. *Journal of Youth & Adolescence*, Vol. 40, No. 4.

150 Anderson, C., Ihori, Nobuko, Bushman, B., Rothstein, H., Shibuya, A., Swing, E., Sakamoto, A., & Saleem, M. (2010). Violent Video Game Effects on Aggression, Empathy, & Prosocial Behavior in Eastern & Western Countries: A Meta-Analytic Review. *Psychological Bulletin*, Vo. 126, No. 2.

151 Norcia, M. (2014, June 1). The Impact of Video Games. Retrieved October 26, 2014, from http://www.pamf.org/parenting-teens/general/media-web/videogames.html

152 Weger, U., & Loughnan, S. (2014). Virtually numbed: Immersive video gaming alters real-life experience. *Psychonomic Bulletin & Review*, 21(2), 562-565. Doi:10.3758/s13423-013-0512-2

153 http://www.forbes.com/sites/julieruvolo/2011/09/07/how-much-of-the-internet-is-actually-for-porn/#434a4de761f7

154 https://www.pornhub.com/insights/2018-year-in-review#us

155 Brown, J., & L'Engle, K. (2009). "X-Rated: Sexual Attitudes & Behaviors Associated with U.S. Early Adolescents' Exposure to Sexually Explicit Media." *Communication Research* 36, 129, 133.

156 Kierkegaard, S. (2008). Cybering, online grooming & age-play. *Computer Law & Security Report*, 24(1), 41–55.

157 Kanuga, M. & Rosenfeld, W. (2004). "Adolescent Sexuality & the Internet: The Good, the Bad, & the URL." *Journal of Pediatrics & Adolescent Gynecology* 17, 117, 120

158 Peter, J., & Valkenburg, P. (2016): Adolescents & Pornography: A Review of 20 Years of Research, *The Journal of Sex Research*, DOI: 10.1080/00224499.2016.1143441

159 Sabina, Chiara, et al. "The Nature and Dynamics of Internet Pornography Exposure for Youth." *CyberPsychology & Behavior*, vol. 11, no. 6, 2008, pp. 691–693., doi:10.1089/cpb.2007.0179.

160 Rich, M. (2005). "Sex Screen: The Dilemma of Media Exposure & Sexual Behavior." *Pediatrics* 116, 329, 330.

161 Zillmann, D. (2000). "Influence of Unrestrained Access to Erotica on

Adolescents' & Young Adults' Dispositions Towards Sexuality." *Journal of Adolescent Health* 27, 41, 42.

[162] Peter, J. & Valkenburg, P. (2016): Adolescents & Pornography: A Review of 20 Years of Research, *The Journal of Sex Research,* DOI: 10.1080/00224499.2016.1143441

[163] Sabina, Chiara, et al. "The Nature and Dynamics of Internet Pornography Exposure for Youth." *CyberPsychology & Behavior,* vol. 11, no. 6, 2008, pp. 691–693., doi:10.1089/cpb.2007.0179.

[164] https://www.pornhub.com/insights/2018-year-in-review#us

[165] Wolak, J., Mitchell, K., & Finkelhor. D. (2007). "Unwanted & Wanted Exposure to Online Pornography in a National Sample of Youth Internet Users." *Pediatrics* 119.2: 247-57. Web.

[166] Ybarra, M., et al. (2011). "X-Rated Material & Perpetration of Sexually Aggressive Behavior Among Children & Adolescents: Is There a Link?" *Aggressive Behavior* 37, 1, 3, 7.

[167] Zillmann, D. (2000). "Influence of Unrestrained Access to Erotica on Adolescents' & Young Adults' Dispositions Towards Sexuality." *Journal of Adolescent Health* 27, 41, 42.

[168] Peter, J. & Valkenburg, P. (2016): Adolescents & Pornography: A Review of 20 Years of Research, The Journal of Sex Research, DOI: 10.1080/00224499.2016.1143441

[169] Zillmann, D. (2000). "Influence of Unrestrained Access to Erotica on Adolescents' & Young Adults' Dispositions Towards Sexuality." *Journal of Adolescent Health* 27, 41, 42.
[170] Hald, Gert, Martin, et al. (2009). "Pornography & Attitudes Supporting Violence Against Women: Revisiting the Relationship in Nonexperimental Studies." *Aggressive Behavior* 35, 1, 3, 5.

[171] Peter, J., Valkenburg, P., & Schouten, A. (2006). Characteristics & motives of adolescents talking with strangers on the Internet. *Cyberpsychology & Behavior,* 9, 526–530.

[172] Peter, J. & Valkenburg, P. (2016): Adolescents & Pornography: A Review of 20 Years of Research, *The Journal of Sex Research,* DOI: 10.1080/00224499.2016.1143441

[173] Zillmann, D. (2000). "Influence of Unrestrained Access to Erotica on Adolescents' & Young Adults' Dispositions Towards Sexuality." *Journal of Adolescent Health* 27, 41, 42.

[174] Peter, J. & Valkenburg, P. (2016): Adolescents & Pornography: A Review of 20 Years of Research, *The Journal of Sex Research*, DOI: 10.1080/00224499.2016.1143441

[175] Zillmann, D. (2000). "Influence of Unrestrained Access to Erotica on Adolescents' & Young Adults' Dispositions Towards Sexuality." *Journal of Adolescent Health* 27, 41, 42.

[176] Peter, J. & Valkenburg, P. (2016): Adolescents & Pornography: A Review of 20 Years of Research, *The Journal of Sex Research*, DOI: 10.1080/00224499.2016.1143441

[177] Peter, J. & Valkenburg, P. (2016): Adolescents & Pornography: A Review of 20 Years of Research, *The Journal of Sex Research*, DOI: 10.1080/00224499.2016.1143441

[178] Ybarra, M., et al. (2011). "X-Rated Material & Perpetration of Sexually Aggressive Behavior Among Children & Adolescents: Is There a Link?" *Aggressive Behavior* 37, 1, 3, 7.

[179] Ybarra, M., et al. (2011). "X-Rated Material & Perpetration of Sexually Aggressive Behavior Among Children & Adolescents: Is There a Link?" *Aggressive Behavior* 37, 1, 3, 7.

[180] Villani, S. (2001). "Impact of Media on Children & Adolescents: A 10-Year Review of the Research." *Journal of the American Academy of Child & Adolescent Psychiatry* 40, 392, 399.

[181] Bartlett, J. (2014). The Dark Net. Random House USA.

Chapter 7

[182] https://www.justice.gov/criminal-ceos/child-pornography

[183] Thornberg, R. (2007). "A Classmate in Distress: Schoolchildren as Bystanders & Their Reasons for How They Act." *Social Psychology of Education* 10.1: 5-28. Web.

[184] Bartlett, J. (2014). The Dark Net. Random House USA.

Chapter 8

[185] https://www.youtube.com/watch?v=h3nhM9UlJjc
[186] https://www.youtube.com/watch?v=fGoWLWS4-kU

[187] https://www.cdc.gov/healthyyouth/sexualbehaviors/

[188] Madigan, S. (2018). Prevalence of Multiple Forms of Sexting Behavior Among Youth. *JAMA Pediatrics, 172*(4), 327-335.

[189] Przybylski, A., & Weinstein, N. (2012). "Can You Connect with Me Now? How the Presence of Mobile Communication Technology Influences Face-to-Face Conversation Quality." *Journal of Social & Personal Relationships*, vol. 30, no. 3, pp. 237–246., doi:10.1177/0265407512453827.

[190] Baron-Cohen, S. (2011). The Science of Evil (pp. 17-18). Philadelphia: Basic Books.

[191] Levy-Warren, M. (2012). Press Pause Before Send: A Case in Point. *Journal of Clinical Psychology J. Clin. Psychol.* 68.11: 1164-174. Web.

[192] Suler, J. (2004). The Online Disinhibition Effect. *CyberPsychology & Behavior* 7.3: 321-26. Web.

[193] Sung, Y., Lee, J., Kim, E. , & Choi, S. (2016). Why we post selfies: Understanding motivations
[194] https://en.oxforddictionaries.com/word-of-the-year/word-of-the-year-2013

[195] https://www.pixability.com/industry-insights/beauty-youtube-2015/

[196] Sykes, S. (2014). "Making Sense of Beauty Vlogging." Theses. Paper 75.

[197] Boon, S. & Lomore, C. (2001). Admirer-celebrity relationships among young adults. *Human Communication Research*, 27: 432–465.

[198] Cosmetic & Beauty Products manufacturing in the U.S: Market Research Report. (2016, September). Retrieved December 07, 2016, from http://www.ibisworld.com/industry/default.aspx?indid=499

[199] Press Association Newswire (2014). 'Very High Rates of Anxiety &

Depression for Young Women. Newsquest Media Group.

200 Press Association Newswire (2014). 'Very High Rates of Anxiety & Depression for Young Women. Newsquest Media Group.

201 Wade, T., Keski -Rahkonen A., & Hudson J. (2011). Epidemiology of eating disorders. In M. Tsuang and M. Tohen (Eds.), Textbook in Psychiatric Epidemiology (3rd ed.) (pp. 343 - 360). New York: Wiley.

202 Smolak, L. (2011). Body image development in childhood. In T. Cash & L. Smolak (Eds.), Body Image: A Handbook of Science, Practice, and Prevention (2nd ed.). New York: Guilford.

203 Leit, R. (2002). "The Media's Representation of the Ideal Male Body: A Cause for Muscle Dysmorphia?" *International Journal of Eating Disorders*, vol. 31, no. 3, pp. 334–338., doi:10.1002/eat.10019.

204 Aslund, C., Starrin, B., Leppert, J., & Nilsson, K. (2009). "Social Status and Shaming Experiences Related to Adolescent Overt Aggression at School." *Aggressive Behavior* 35.1: 1-13. Web.

205 Rajanala, S., Maymone, M., Vashi, N. (2018). 'Selfies—Living in the Era of Filtered Photographs'. *JAMA Facial Plast Surg,* 20(6):443–444. doi:10.1001/jamafacial.2018.0486

206 https://www.cbsnews.com/news/transgender-gender-identity-terms-glossary/

207 Xie, L., Kang, H., Xu, Q., Chen, M., Liao, Y., Thiyagarajan, M., O'Donnell, J., Christensen, D., Nicholson, C., Iliff, J., Takano, T., Deane, R., &

Nedergaard, M. (2013). *Sleep Drives Metabolite Clearance from the Adult Brain. Science* 342.6156: 373-77. Web.

208 Goel, N., Rao, H., Durmer, J., & Dinges, D. (2009). Neurocognitive Consequences of Sleep Deprivation. *Seminars in Neurology* 29.04: 320-39. Web.

209 Dewald-Kaufmann, J., Oort, F., Bogels, S., & Meijer, A. (2013). "Why Sleep Matters: Differences in Daytime Functioning Between Adolescents with Low & High Chronic Sleep Reduction & Short & Long Sleep

Durations." *Journal of Cognitive & Behavioral Psychotherapies*, 13, 171-182.

[210] Garrison, M. & Christakis, D. (2012). The impact of a healthy media use intervention on sleep in preschool children. *Pediatrics*, 2011-3153; DOI: 10.1542/peds.2011-3153

[211] Chang, A., Aeschbach, D, Duffy, J., & Czeisler, C. (2014). Evening Use of Light-emitting EReaders Negatively Affects Sleep, Circadian Timing, & Next-morning Alertness. Proceedings of the National Academy of Sciences 112.4: 1232-237. Web.

[212] Killgore, W., Kamimori, G., & Balkin, T. Caffeine Protects Against Increased Risk-taking Propensity During Severe Sleep Deprivation. *Journal of Sleep Research* 20.3 (2010): 395-403. Web.

[213] Elgar, F., Napoletano, A., Saul, G., Dirks, M., Craig, M., Poteat, V., Holt, M., & Koenig, B. (2014). "Cyberbullying Victimization and Mental Health in Adolescents and the Moderating Role of Family Dinners." *JAMA Pediatrics168*.11: 1015. Web.

[214] Lindsey, E., & Colwell, M. (2013). Pretend & physical play: Links to preschoolers' affective competence. *Merrill-Palmer Quarterly*, 59 (3), 330-360.

[215] LaFreniere, P. (2013). Children's play as a context for managing psychological arousal & learning emotional regulations. *Psiholojiske Teme*, 22 (2), 183-204.

[216] Lindsey, E., & Colwell, M. (2013). Pretend & physical play: Links to preschoolers' affective competence. *Merrill-Palmer Quarterly*, 59 (3), 330-360.

[217] Milteer, R., Ginsburg, K., & Mulligan, D. (2012). The importance of play & promoting healthy child development & maintaining strong parent-child bond: Focuses on children & poverty. *American Academy of Pediatrics*, 129 (1). 204-213.

[218] Madlen D. (2015) Average person now spends more time on their phone & laptop than sleeping, study claims http://www.dailymail.co.uk/health/article-2989952/How-technology-taking-lives-spend-time-phones-laptops-SLEEPING.html

[219] Matthew, H. (2017) The Indian government is spending $62 billion on Wi-Fi hotspots http://www.businessinsider.com/the-indian-government-is-spending-62-billion-on-wi-fi-hotspots-2017-1

[220] What is Wi-Fi & How Does it Work? (Sept. 2017) CCM.

http://ccm.net/faq/298-what-is-wifi-and-how-does-it-work

221 Markham H. (2016) You Asked: Should I Worry About Wi-Fi Radiation? http://time.com/4508432/what-is-wifi-radiation-cancer/

222 http://www.saferemr.com

223 Yüksel M, Nazıroğlu M, Özkaya M. (2015). Long-term exposure to electromagnetic radiation from mobile phones & Wi-Fi devices decreases plasma prolactin, progesterone, & estrogen levels but increases uterine oxidative stress in pregnant rats & their offspring. Endocrine.

224 Markham H. (2016) You Asked: Should I Worry About Wi-Fi Radiation? http://time.com/4508432/what-is-wifi-radiation-cancer/

225 Jung, S. I., Lee, N. K., Kang, K. W., Kim, K., & Lee, D. Y. (2016). The effect of smartphone usage time on posture and respiratory function. *Journal of Physical Therapy Science, 28*(1), 186–189. http://doi.org/10.1589/jpts.28.186

226 https://www.cdc.gov/safechild/child_injury_data.html

227 https://www.nhtsa.gov/risky-driving/distracted-driving

228 AT&T, https://www.itcanwait.com/pledge

229 DMV. https://www.dmv.org/distracted-driving/texting-and-driving.php

230 Rideout, V., Foehr, U., & Roberts, D. (2010). *Generation M2: Media in the Lives of 8- to 18- Year-Olds.* Menlo Park, CA: Henry J. Kaiser Family Foundation.

231 Alzahabi, R., & Becker., M., (2013). "The Association between Media

Multitasking, Task-switching, and Dual-task Performance." *Journal of Experimental Psychology: Human Perception and Performance* 39.5:1485-495. Web.

232 Conard, M., & Marsh, R., (2013). "Interest Level Improves Learning but

Does Not Moderate the Effects of Interruptions: An Experiment Using Simultaneous Multitasking." *Learning and Individual Differences*: n. pag. Web.

233 Ie, A., Haller, C., Langer, E., & Courvoisier, D. (2012). "Mindful Multitasking: The Relationship between Mindful Flexibility and Media

Multitasking." *Computers in Human Behavior* 28.4: 1526-532. Web.

[234] Finley, J., Benjamin, A., & McCarley, J., (2014). "Metacognition of Multitasking: How Well Do We Predict the Costs of Divided Attention?" *Journal of Experimental Psychology: Applied,* 20.2: 158-65. Web.

[235] Wagner, D., & Ward, A. (2013). "The Internet Has Become the External Hard Drive for Our Memories." Scientific American, 1 Dec. 2013, www.scientificamerican.com/article/the-internet-has-become-the-external-hard-drive-for-our-memories/.

[236] Ward, A., Duke, K., Gneezy, A., & Bos, M. (2017). "Brain Drain: The Mere Presence of Oneâs Own Smartphone Reduces Available Cognitive Capacity." *Journal of the Association for Consumer Research* 2.2: 140-54. Web.

[237] Clayton, R. (2015). "The Extended ISelf: The Impact of IPhone Separation on Cognition, Emotion, & Physiology." *Journal of Computer-Mediated Communication,* vol. 20(2), pp. 119–135., doi:10.1111/jcc4.12109.

[238] Ward, A., Duke, K., Gneezy, A., & Bos, M. (2017). "Brain Drain: The Mere Presence of Oneâs Own Smartphone Reduces Available Cognitive Capacity." *Journal of the Association for Consumer Research* 2.2: 140-54. Web.

[239] Sano, A. (20160. "Neurotics Can't Focus: An in Situ Study of Online Multitasking in the Workplace – MIT Media Lab." MIT Media Lab, www.media.mit.edu/publications/neurotics-cant-focus-an-in-situ-study-of-online-multitasking-in-the-workplace/.

[240] Sparrow, B., et al. (2011). "Google Effects on Memory: Cognitive Consequences of Having Information at Our Fingertips." *Science,* vol. 333, no. 6043, pp. 776–778., doi:10.1126/science.1207745.

[241] Conard, M., & Marsh, R., (2013). "Interest Level Improves Learning but Does Not Moderate the Effects of Interruptions: An Experiment Using Simultaneous Multitasking." *Learning and Individual Differences:* n. pag. Web.

[242] Wood, E., Zivcakova, L., Gentile, P., Archer, K., De Pasquale, D., & Nosko, A. (2012). "Examining the Impact of Off-task Multi-tasking with Technology on Real-time Classroom Learning." *Computers & Education* 58.1: 365-74. Web.

[243] Conard, M., & Marsh, R., (2013). "Interest Level Improves Learning but Does Not Moderate the Effects of Interruptions: An Experiment Using Simultaneous Multitasking." *Learning and Individual Differences*: n. pag. Web.

[244] Fein, S., Jones, S., & Gerow, J. (2013). "When It Comes to Facebook There May Be More to Bad Memory than Just Multitasking." *Computers in Human Behavior* 29.6: 2179-2182. Web.

[245] Fox, A., Rosen, J., & Crawford, M. (2009). "Distractions, Distractions: Does Instant Messaging Affect College Students' Performance on a Concurrent Reading Comprehension Task?" *CyberPsychology & Behavior*, 12(1): 51-53.https://doi.org/10.1089/cpb.2008.0107

[246] Ophir, E., Nass, C., & Wagner, A. (2009). "From the Cover: Cognitive Control in Media Multitaskers." *Proceedings of the National Academy of Sciences* 106.37: 15583-5587. Web.

[247] Gregoire, C. (2016). "The American Workplace Is Broken. Here's How We Can Start Fixing It." The Huffington Post, TheHuffingtonPost.com, 22 Nov. 2016, www.huffingtonpost.com/entry/american-workplace-broken-stress_us_566b3152e4b011b83a6b42bd.

[248] Sano, A. (2016). "Email Duration Batching and Self-Interruption: Patterns of Email Use on Productivity and Stress – MIT Media Lab." MIT Media Lab, 17 May 2016, www.media.mit.edu/publications/email-duration-batching-and-self-interruption-patterns-of-email-use-on-productivity-and-stress/.

[249] Sridharan, D., et al. (2008). "A Critical Role for the Right Fronto-Insular Cortex in Switching between Central-Executive and Default-Mode Networks." Proceedings of the National Academy of Sciences, vol. 105, no. 34, pp. 12569–12574., doi:10.1073/pnas.0800005105.

[250] Sano, A. (20160. "Neurotics Can't Focus: An in Situ Study of Online Multitasking in the Workplace – MIT Media Lab." MIT Media Lab, www.media.mit.edu/publications/neurotics-cant-focus-an-in-situ-study-of-online-multitasking-in-the-workplace/.

[251] Becker, M., Alzahabi, R., & Hopwood, C., (2013). "Media Multitasking Is Associated with Symptoms of Depression and Social Anxiety." *Cyberpsychology, Behavior, and Social Networking* 16.2: 132-35. Web.

[252] Lin, L., Robertson, T., & Lee, J. (2009). "Reading Performances Between Novices and Experts in Different Media Multitasking Environments."

Computers in the Schools 26.3: 169-86. Web.

253 Armstrong, G. Blake, & Chung, L. (2000). "Background Television and Reading Memory in Context: Assessing TV Interference and Facilitative Context Effects on Encoding Versus Retrieval Processes." *Communication Research* 27: 327–352.

254 Zhang, W., Jeong, S., & Fishbein, M. (2010). "Situational Factors Competing For Attention: The Interaction Effect of Multitasking and Sexually Explicit Content on TV Recognition." *Journal of Media Psychology* 22: 2–13. Web.

255 Furnham, A., & Bradley, A. (1997). "Music While You Work: The Differential Distraction of Background Music on the Cognitive Test Performance of Introverts and Extraverts." *Applied Cognitive Psychology* 11.5: 445-55. Web.

256 Perham, N., & Vizard, J. (2011), Can preference for background music mediate the irrelevant sound effect? *Appl. Cognit. Psychol.*, 25: 625–631. doi:10.1002/acp.1731

257 Hembrooke, H., & Gay, G. (2003). "The Laptop and the Lecture: The Effects of Multitasking in Learning Environments." *Journal of Computing in Higher Education* 15.1: 46-64. Web.

258 Wood, E., Zivcakova, L, Gentile, P., Archer, K., De Pasquale, D., & Nosko, A. (2012). "Examining the Impact of Off-task Multi-tasking with Technology on Real-time Classroom Learning." *Computers & Education* 58.1: 365-74. Web.

259 Sana, F., Weston, T., & Cepeda, N. (2013). "Laptop Multitasking Hinders Classroom Learning for Both Users and Nearby Peers." *Computers & Education* 62: 24-31. Web.

260 Watson, J., & Strayer, D. (2010). "Supertaskers: Profiles in Extraordinary Multitasking Ability." *Psychonomic Bulletin & Review* 17.4: 479-85. Web.

261 Holland, K., & Riley, K. (2014). ADHD by the Numbers: Facts, Statistics, & You. For: Healthline. Retrieved April 4th, 2017 from: http://www.healthline.com/health/adhd/facts-statistics-infographic

262 Faraone, S., Sergeant, J., Gillberg, C., & Biederman, J. (2003). The worldwide prevalence of ADHD: is it an American condition? *World Psychiatry*, 2(2), 104–113.

263 Christakis, D., Zimmerman, F., DiGuiseppe, D., & McCarty, C. (2004). Early television exposure and subsequent attentional problems in children. *Pediatrics*, 113(4), 708-713.

264 Andreassen, C, Billieux, J., Griffiths, M., Kuss, D., Demetrovics, Z., Mazzoni, E., & Pallesen, S. (2016), The Relationship between Addictive Use of Social Media & Video Games & Symptoms of Psychiatric Disorders: A Large-scale Cross-sectional Study. *Psychology of Addictive Behaviors* 30.2: 252-62. Web.

265 Kiss, J. (2015). ADHD & the relentless internet – is there a connection? For: the guardian, retrieved May 7th, 2017 from: https://www.theguardian.com/technology/2015/mar/16/adhd-internet-is-there-a-connection-sxsw

266 Dovis, S., Van der Oord, S., Huizenga, H., Wiers, R., & Prins, P. (2014). Prevalence & diagnostic validity of motivational impairments & deficits in visuospatial short-term memory & working memory in ADHD subtypes. *Eur Child Adolescence Psychiatry* 24, 575–590.

267 King, D., Delfabbro, P., Griffiths, M., & Gradisar, M. (2012). Cognitive-Behavioral Approaches to Outpatient Treatment of Internet Addiction in Children & Adolescents. *Journal of Clinical Psychology* 68.11: 1185-195. Web.

268 Bajarin, B. (2016). "Apple's Penchant for Consumer Security." Tech.pinions, 18 Apr. 2016, techpinions.com/apples-penchant-for-consumer-security/45122.

269 Amanda L. (2015) Teens, Social Media & Technology Overview 2015 http://www.pewInternet.org/2015/04/09/teens-social-media-technology-2015/

270 Common Sense (2015). The Common Sense Census: Media Use by Teens &Tweens.www.commonsensemedia.org/sites/default/files/uploads/research/census_executivesummary.pdf

271 Petry, N., & O'Brien, C. (2013). Internet Gaming Disorder & the DSM-5. *Addiction* 108.7: 1186-187. Web.

272 Petry, N., Rehbein, F., Gentile, D., et al. (2014). An International Consensus for Assessing Internet Gaming Disorder Using the New DSM-5 Approach. *Addiction* 109.9: 1399-406. Web.

273 Kuss, D., Griffiths, M., Karila, L., & Billieux, J. (2014). Internet addiction: A systematic review of epidemiological research for the last decade. *Current Pharmaceutical Design*, 20, 4026–4052. 10.2174/13816128113199990617

274 Strittmatter, E., Parzer, P., & Brunner, R. (2016). "A 2-year longitudinal study of prospective predictors of pathological Internet use in adolescents." *Eur Child Adolesc Psychiatry* 25(7): 725.

275 Kuss, D., Griffiths, M., Karila, L., & Billieux, J. (2014). Internet addiction: A systematic review of epidemiological research for the last decade. *Current Pharmaceutical Design*, 20, 4026–4052. 10.2174/13816128113199990617

276 Andreassen, C., Griffiths, M., Gjertsen, S., Krossbakken, E., Kvam, S., & Pallesen, S. (2013). The relationships between behavioral addictions & the five-factor model of personality. *Journal of Behavioral Addictions*, 2, 90–99. 10.1556/JBA.2.2013.003

277 Ferguson, C., Coulson, M., & Barnett, J. (2011). A meta-analysis of pathological gaming prevalence & comorbidity with mental health, academic & social problems. *Journal of Psychiatric Research*, 45, 1573–1578. 10.1016/j.jpsychires.2011.09.005

278 Chiu, S.-I., Hong, F.-Y., & Chiu, S.-L. (2013). An analysis on the correlation & gender difference between college students' Internet addiction & mobile phone addiction in Taiwan. ISRN *Addiction*, 2013, 360607. 10.1155/2013/360607

279 Davenport, K., Houston, J., & Griffiths, M. (2012). Excessive eating & compulsive buying behaviours in women: An empirical pilot study examining reward sensitivity, anxiety, impulsivity, self-esteem & social desirability. *International Journal of Mental Health & Addiction*, 10, 474–489. 10.1007/s11469-011-9332-7

280 van Deursen, A., Bolle, C., Hegner, S., & Kommers, P. (2015). Modeling habitual & addictive smartphone behavior: The role of smartphone usage types, emotional intelligence, social stress, self-regulation, age, & gender. *Computers in Human Behavior*, 45, 411–420. 10.1016/j.chb.2014.12.039

[281] Maraz, A., Eisinger, A., Hende, B., Urbán, R., Paksi, B., Kun, B., Demetrovics, Z. (2015). Measuring compulsive buying behaviour: Psychometric validity of three different scales & prevalence in the general population & in shopping centres. *Psychiatry Research*, 225, 326–334. 10.1016/j.psychres.2014.11.080

[282] Black, D., Belsare, G., & Schlosser, S. (1999). Clinical features, psychiatric comorbidity, & health-related quality of life in persons reporting compulsive computer use behavior. *J Clin Psychiatry* 60(12):839–844.

[283] Ha, J., Yoo, H., Cho, I., Chin, B., Shin, D., & Kim, J. (2006). Psychiatric comorbidity assessed in Korean children & adolescents who screen positive for Internet addiction. *J Clin Psychiatry* 67(5):821–826.

[284] Kaess, M., Durkee, T., Brunner, R., Carli, V., Parzer, P., & Wasserman, C. (2014). Pathological Internet use among European adolescents: psychopathology & self-destructive behaviours. *Eur Child Adolesc Psychiatry* 23(11):1093–1102.

[285] Ko, C., Yen, J., Chen, C., Yeh, Y., & Yen, C. (2009). Predictive values of psychiatric symptoms for internet addiction in adolescents: a 2-year prospective study. *Arch Pediatr Adolesc Med* 163(10): 937–943.

[286] Lin, I., Ko, C., Chang, Y., Liu, T., Wang, P., & Lin, H. (2014). The association between suicidality & Internet addiction & activities in Taiwanese adolescents. *Compr Psychiatry* 55(3): 504–510.

[287] Liu, M., Ming, Q., Yi, J., Wang, X., Yao, S. (2016). Screen time on school days & risks for psychiatric symptoms & self-harm in mainland Chinese adolescents. Frontiers In Psychology [serial online]. April 25, 2016;7Available from: PsycINFO, Ipswich, MA. Accessed June 11, 2017.

[288] Mehroof, M. & Griffiths, M.D. (2010). Online gaming addiction: the role

of sensation seeking, self-control, neuroticism, aggression, state anxiety, & trait anxiety. *Cyberpsychol Behav Soc Netw* 13(3): 313–316.

[289] Shapira, N., Goldsmith, T., Keck, P., Khosla, U., & McElroy, S. (2000). Psychiatric features of individuals with problematic internet use. *J Affect Disord* 57(1–3): 267–272.

[290] Durkee, T., Kaess, M., Carli, V., Parzer, P., Wasserman, C., Floderus, B., Wasserman, D. (2012). Prevalence of pathological internet use among

adolescents in Europe: Demographic & social factors. *Addiction*, 107, 2210–2222. 10.1111/j.1360-0443.2012.03946.x

291 Strittmatter, E., Parzer, P., & Brunner, R. (2016). "A 2-year longitudinal study of prospective predictors of pathological Internet use in adolescents." *Eur Child Adolesc Psychiatry* 25(7): 725.

292 Fauth-Buhler, M., & Mann, K. (2017). Neurobiological Correlates of Internet Gaming Disorder: Similarities to Pathological Gambling. Addictive Behaviors, vol. 64, 349–356.

293 Yuan, K., Qin, W., Wang, G., Zeng, F., Zhao, L., & Yang, X. (2011). Microstructure Abnormalities in Adolescents with Internet Addiction Disorder. PLoS ONE 6(6): e20708.

294 Kim, S., Baik, S., Park, C., Kim, S., Choi, S. & Kim, S. (2011). Reduced Striatal Dopamine D2 Receptors in People with Internet Addiction. *NeuroReport* 22.8: 407-11. Web.

295 Koepp, M., Gunn, R., Lawrence, A., Cunningham, V., Dagher, A., Jones, T., Brooks, D., Bench, C., & Grasby, P. (1998). Evidence for striatal dopamine release during a video game. *Nature* 393: 266-268.

296 Kühn, S., Romanowski, A., Schilling, C., Lorenz, R., Mörsen, C., Seiferth, N., & Banaschewski, T. (2011). The Neural Basis of Video Gaming. Translational Psychiatry 1: e53.

297 Dong, G. Hu, Y., & Lin, X. (2013). Reward/punishment sensitivities among internet addicts: Implications for their addictive behaviors. *Progress in Neuro-Psychopharmacology & Biological Psychiatry*, 46, 139–145.

298https://www.cbsnews.com/news/groundbreaking-study-examines-effects-of-screen-time-on-kids-60-minutes/

299 Weng, Chuan-Bo et al. (2013) Gray matter & white matter abnormalities in online game addiction *European Journal of Radiology, Volume 82 , Issue 8 , 1308 – 1312*

300 Lin, X., Zhou, H., Dong, G., & Du, X. (2015). Impaired risk evaluation in people with internet gaming disorder: fMRI evidence from a probability discounting task. *Progress in Neuro-Psychopharmacology & Biological Psychiatry*, 56, 142–148.

[301] Ding, W., Sun, J., Sun, Y-W., Chen, X., Zhou, Y., Zhuang, Z., & Du, Y. (2014). Trait impulsivity & impaired prefrontal impulse inhibition function in adolescents with internet gaming addiction revealed by a Go/No-Go fMRI study *Behavioral & Brain Functions*: BBF, 10, 20.

[302] Zhou, Z., Yuan, G., & Yao, J. (2012). Cognitive biases toward internet game-related pictures & executive deficits in individuals with an internet game addiction. *PloS One*, 7 (11), Article e48961.

[303] Chen, C., Huang, M., Yen, J., Chen, C., Liu, G., Yen, C., 7 Ko, C. (2015). Brain correlates of response inhibition in internet gaming disorder. *Psychiatry & Clinical Neurosciences*, 69 (4), 201–209.

[304] Dong, G. Hu, Y., & Lin, X. (2013). Reward/punishment sensitivities among internet addicts: Implications for their addictive behaviors. *Progress in Neuro-Psychopharmacology & Biological Psychiatry*, 46, 139–145.

[305] Yuan, K., Qin, W., Wang, G., Zeng, F., Zhao, L., & Yang, X. (2011). Microstructure Abnormalities in Adolescents with Internet Addiction Disorder. *PLoS ONE* 6(6): e20708.

Chapter 9

[306] Yuan, K., Qin, W., Wang, G., Zeng, F., Zhao, L., & Yang, X. (2011). Microstructure Abnormalities in Adolescents with Internet Addiction Disorder. *PLoS ONE* 6(6): e20708.

[307] Piaget, J. (1952). *The Child's Conception of Number*. London: Routledge & Kegan Paul. Print.

[308] Pellegrino, G., Di, L., Fadiga, L., Fogassi, V., Gallese, & Rizzolatti, G., (1992). "Understanding Motor Events: A Neurophysiological Study." Exp Brain Res Experimental Brain Research 91.1: 176-80. Web.

[309] Falck-Ytter, T., Gredebäck, G. & Von Hofsten, C. (2006). "Infants Predict Other People's Action Goals." Nature Neuroscience Nat Neurosci 9.7: 878-79. Web.

[310] Rizzolatti, G., Fogassi, L., & Gallese, V. "Mirrors in the Mind." Scientific American 295(5) (2006): 54-61 SPECIAL SECTION: NEUROSCIENCE

[311] Feldman, R., Gordon, I., & Zagoory-Sharon, O. (2010). "Maternal & Paternal Plasma, Salivary, & Urinary Oxytocin & Parent-infant Synchrony:

Considering Stress & Affiliation Components of Human Bonding." *Developmental Science* 14.4: 752-61. Web.

312 Moore, S., et al. (2017), "Epigenetic Correlates of Neonatal Contact in Humans." *Development and Psychopathology*, vol. 29, no. 05, pp. 1517–1538., doi:10.1017/s0954579417001213.

47385160R00149

Made in the USA
Middletown, DE
06 June 2019